Metaphysics in Midwestern America

metaphysics in midwestern america

MELINDA BOLLAR WAGNER

Ohio State University Press : Columbus

Library of Congress Cataloging in Publication Data

Wagner, Melinda Bollar, 1948–
  Metaphysics in midwestern America.

  Bibliography: p.
  Includes index.
  1. Spiritual Frontiers Fellowship. I. Title.
BP605.S66W33   1983   299′.93   83-2158
ISBN 0-8142-0346-9

This book is dedicated to my mother, Jean McDowell Bollar, who has
been a constant source of uncritical aid and encouragement,
not only for this book but for everything I have ever undertaken.
The respect she taught me for other peoples, other cultures, and
especially for other religions, gave me an anthropological
perspective long before I studied anthropology.

This book is dedicated also to Everett F. Wagner and
Dorothy M. Wagner, my parents-in-law, whose good influence
on me and my work came later in my life, when these sensitive
world travelers often shared their insights with me.

contents

Contents

Preface

One purpose of anthropology is to make the concepts that make up one culture understandable to readers in another. As anthropology "moves into" the American scene, perhaps this function can be extended to promoting understanding among the various factions of our own diverse culture. I hope the description and analysis contained in this book will add to the understanding of a portion of the "nonmainstream" religious movements existing in the United States today.

The reader should bear in mind that the accuracy of a description is "time-bound"; a description is a snapshot of how one group "looks" at one particular time, in this case, Spiritual Frontiers Fellowship in 1975 and 1976. Some things about Spiritual Frontiers Fellowship have changed in the ensuing years —its "vital statistics," for example, and a few elements of policy and practice. SFF's *Principles, Purposes, and Program* (now *Principles, Purposes, Guidelines*) was revised in 1982. In the revision, references to "man" are broadened to "human beings," and ties with the established churches, traditionally desired by SFF leaders, are perhaps loosened a bit by changing "the Church" to "the Christian community" in some passages. But most things discussed here have not changed, such as the underlying philosophy of SFF. Thus, the overall picture is, I think, an accurate one.

The time and efforts of many people contributed to this work, and they deserve my thanks. An anthropologist always owes his greatest debt of gratitude to the people who allowed themselves to be the object of his study. The people I studied were more than generous with their time and kindness. They chauffeured me, introduced me, and explained to me tirelessly. I was allowed to participate in all the group's activities, and to tape record many of them.

I have chosen to treat the group members and locations anonymously in this book, not because their activities are in any way covert, but to protect them from anyone who may overlook the positive aspects of groups like these. I especially wish to thank the group leaders I have named Jenny, Joe, and Barbara. Although I have given them common names, they were uncommon people. I hope I will always count people of their character among my friends. The research for this study could not have been accomplished without their aid. Thanks are due also to the chairpersons of Spiritual Frontiers Fellowship's "Metro Area" for 1974 through 1976 and to numerous leaders at the national level. Since anthropologists are rarely "commissioned" to conduct their studies, there are few sanctions on their activities. If anthropologists were hired by groups on a contractual basis, I hope my behavior in the group I studied was such that they could recommend me to other groups.

Several professors in the University of Michigan's Departments of Anthropology and Sociology have my gratitude for the aid they gave with the research and with the analysis of the results. Many hours of illuminating conversation with Dr. Roy A. Rappaport were instrumental to my understanding and conceptualization of what I had observed in the field. His responses to my embryonic ideas, his abstraction of my concrete examples, pervade this book; and I am indebted to him for sharing his knowledge and intellect with me. Dr. Gertrude Enders Huntington was extremely helpful in the field work stage, and in directing me to relevant literature. Sharing field experiences with her helped me maintain the balance of participation and observation necessary to this endeavor. Dr. Horace M. Miner worked to establish and maintain focus and organization in the writing. Dr. Max A. Heirich helped place the study in the context of broader social developments.

I would also like to express my thanks to the professionals who reviewed an earlier version of the manuscript for the Ohio State University Press, including Dr. Vivian Garrison and other anonymous reviewers. I hope they will feel that their insightful comments have borne fruit in an improved publication.

While these professors and reviewers were very generous with their ideas, any misrepresentation or misapplication of these ideas, or the ideas of others cited in the book, must rest upon my own shoulders.

The Ohio State University Press, personified by Weldon A. Kefauver, director, and Robert S. Demorest, senior editor, has handled this manuscript and its author in a thoroughly professional and kind manner, and I thank them very much for that.

The giant mechanical burden of preparing the manuscript was relieved by the expert typing skills of Drema Thomas.

My husband, Stephen Everett Wagner, deserves many years of thanks for giving support of every possible variety to this project, from the very beginning.

Metaphysics in Midwestern America

1

"New Religions" in Modern Society

The bulk of the literature on "nonmainstream" contemporary religious groups leaves the impression that these groups are new, exist mainly in California, and attract disaffected youth. The function most often ascribed to these groups is that they provide their youthful adherents with a sense of "community," which they find otherwise missing in their lives. Some recent unfortunate incidents, such as the mass suicide at Jonestown and the publicity accompanying Scientology's conflict with the federal government, have added a new dimension to the popular vision of non-Establishment religious groups. Now religious movements or "cults" are viewed as dangerous mind-benders. Television talk show hosts interview "deprogrammers" who can help parents wrest their children from the clutches of cults.

These impressions have indeed been empirically verified for a proportion of the "new religions," but there is another type of religious group that has gone largely unaccounted for in the literature. This is a study of one of these groups, and it paints a quite different picture. The study describes a religious movement that is not so new, exists mainly in the midwestern United States,

3

and attracts middle-class, middle-aged people. It will be argued that this movement does not provide a sense of "community" for its followers, but that it is adaptive in another way. The study posits that this group offers its members a flexible "meaning" in a flexible and changing world.

The focus of study here is Spiritual Frontiers Fellowship (SFF). This group, along with Spiritualism, Theosophy, Christian Science, the Unity School of Christianity, Astara, the Association for Research and Enlightenment, several New Thought groups that are loosely organized into the International New Thought Alliance, and others have been labeled the "American metaphysical movement" (Judah 1967).[1]

The groups in the American metaphysical movement are not affiliated in any organizational way, but they share a definition of metaphysics and certain characteristics. All subscribe to the view that metaphysics is a "practical religious philosophy," and all are interested in relating spiritual and psychic phenomena to every-day life. According to metaphysical students, metaphysics

> stands for the deeper realities of the universe, the things which are external—which stand above and beyond the outer phenomenal realm. . . . It especially concerns itself with the practical application of the absolute Truth of Being in all the affairs of daily and hourly living. (Judah 1967:11)

> Metaphysics means a practical idealism, which emphasizes spiritual sensation and the accessibility of spiritual mind power, acting in accord with law and available to all people. (Braden 1951:138)

Among the characteristics shared by the metaphysical groups is a monistic view of God as "all and in-all." (This is opposed to the traditional Judeo-Christian dualism, which sets humanity apart from God.) A central belief of the metaphysical groups is that the inner, or real, self of man is divine; each person has a spark of divinity. Salvation is equated with the discovery of this divine inner self.

Some metaphysical groups consider themselves to be

Christian; others do not. But all make a place for Jesus as a way-shower, one who was more aware of his divine nature than others. However, these groups have revolted against the traditional Christian view that man is a sinner, standing under God's judgment and in need of repentance and forgiveness. Rather, the metaphysical groups are highly optimistic. Since God is in-all, and is all good, evil is only an error of our minds, or it is caused by man's ignorance of his true nature. Man's state depends upon understanding his real (divine) nature and upon the proper use of spiritual laws. It is thought that God gives pleasant things freely to all who realize their unity with Him.

The metaphysical groups consider themselves to be scientific as well as religious. They are pragmatic, and ask practitioners to test their principles rather than rely on faith. Most of the groups believe in the power of mind, as expressed in words and thoughts, to change things. All make healing through the mind or spirit a part of their mission. Some also have an interest in psychic development (Judah 1967:12–19).

The metaphysical groups in America were formed beginning in the late nineteenth century and continuing into the 1970s (53 percent were founded from 1950 to 1970 [Melton 1977]). The history of the ideas they now espouse is much longer, however. The roots of their monistic thought may be traced back to the Platonic sense of the "whole of being" (Ellwood 1973) and to the Gnostics, the heretics who existed side-by-side with early Christians. The Gnostics believed the soul of the individual contained a spark of the divine.

The philosophy that in the mind lies the power to correct earthly situations has as its source the idea of "correspondences": what "is" in spirit is reflected in matter; spiritual causes (and thought) affect material things. This idea was popularized by the Swedish Emmanuel Swedenborg (1688–1772), whose ideas were spread in America by John Chapman (Johnny Appleseed) when he left Swedenborgian tracts along with apple trees on the American frontier. The Austrian Franz Antoine Mesmer (1733–

5

1815) also advanced the cause of the power of the mind to heal and to preconceive.

The New England transcendentalists Emerson, Thoreau, Whitman, Alcott, and others were purveyors of the idea of the divine in all persons, the philosophy of the "sovereignty of mind," and the principle of correspondences among all parts of the universe. The transcendentalists favored intuition over reason, as do the metaphysicians today (Albanese 1977; Ellwood 1973; Judah 1967).

Theosophy, founded by Madame Helena Petrovna Blavatsky and Colonel Henry Steele Olcott in 1875, introduced into this mix ideas from the East: the theory of reincarnation, and communication with spiritual masters. More recently other Eastern ideas have reached the metaphysical groups through popular literature such as the *Autobiography of a Yogi*, by Paramahansa Yogananda, the founder of the Self-Realization Fellowship.

When the long history of the ideas now espoused by the metaphysical movement is traced, it becomes clear that Ellwood (1973) is right when he suggests that "new religions" is something of a misnomer when applied to them (see Ahlstrom 1978; Ellwood 1973, 1979; Judah 1967 for more information on the antecedents of the metaphysical movements).

It must be understood, however, that though the ideological genealogy of the metaphysical concepts has been explored by scholars, the antecedents are not widely recognized within the rank and file of the groups themselves. A kinship of ideas (as well as some points of contention) are recognized among the various American metaphysical movement groups, but few metaphysicians would discuss Plato, Emerson, or even Swedenborg as intellectual ancestors. Indeed, Judah (1967) states that neither Phineas P. Quimby nor Andrew Jackson Davis, both progenitors of New Thought, which holds mind or thought to be fundamental and causative, had read Swedenborg, though they were familiar with his ideas through Spiritualism. In the same way today, a variety of philosophies are "out there" in the cultic milieu; their origins are of little concern to the practitioners.

6

The metaphysical group that is the focus of this study, Spiritual Frontiers Fellowship, was founded in Evanston, Illinois, in 1956 by about seventy-five religious leaders and laymen, mostly from Protestant denominations. In 1975 membership had reached almost eight thousand.[2] The data for this study of SFF were collected during sixteen months of participant observation in SFF's local, regional, and national organizational levels.[3]

The primary goal of metaphysical groups is to promote individual spiritual growth,[4] which is perceived as a process of becoming more aware of one's divine inner self. The questions "Why do people join?" "What is gained by this 'growth of the spirit'?" were asked for me one evening by the leader of the small local study group whose weekly meetings I attended for one year. "What has spiritual growth meant to you?" asked our moderator. Sara, a thirty-three-year-old housewife and mother of one, answered this way:

> What spiritual growth has meant to me is a change in attitude, a change in life. It's knowing truth, knowing life. It's being honest with myself, and knowing myself—learning about my inner self. In me there's been an evolutionary change—a complete change from ten years ago to the present. For a long time I was not honest with myself. I spent too much time trying to prove myself to others. Those were troubled times then. When people I knew in high school used to see me on the street, I would deny who I was. I'd say, "No, I'm not her, I'm from California." Now people stop me on the street and say, "You look good, and happy." People have said I'm different—people I've known for 20 years.
>
> The past is gone. It's like a new life. I feel so different. If I find myself in any kind of trouble with myself, any kind of problem or anything, I turn myself to God, just tune myself into God. And I just vibrate from my feet right up to the top of my head. (Study Group 6/18/75; 1/8/75)

Grace, a widow in her fifties who was preparing to retire from her job as a stenographer, gave this response:

> In 1955, I had a tragedy in my family. At that time, I decided there had to be something more to life. I had sort of gotten into just eating,

sleeping, and working. I began searching. We started a healing class at church, where we read all the parts of the Bible having to do with healing. Then, I went into Silva Mind Control, Transcendental Meditation, and other classes. Never until now did I feel that I'd found it. (Study Group 6/18/75)

The feelings expressed by the group members are concrete examples of the abstract phenomenon social scientists discuss as "meaninglessness" or "lack of identity."[5] Meaning is attained by identifying with something "beyond oneself." Thus, meaning is a referent used for establishing identity. It is the set of reference points that enables a person to know, and to tell others, who he is. Meaning integrates a person's life (Klapp 1969). The "it" Grace has found, and the "new life" that allows Sara to accept herself, are examples of renewed and improved "identity." In these cases the identifying reference point is an "inner self." Through discovery of this particular (divine) self, these women have found their "something more," their "meaning."

Individuals in complex societies seem especially troubled by meaninglessness, and have devised all sorts of ways of combating it. Social scientists have developed various theories to account for modern humanity's attempts to counteract "meaninglessness." The theories are variations on the theme that the "conditions of modern life" (e.g., rapid social change [Nelson 1969]; conflicts, brought on by rapid industrializaton, between science and religion, intellect and emotion, pragmatism and spirituality [Baum 1970, Goldfarb 1971, Greeley 1974, Macklin 1974, Mandic 1970]; the churches' overemphasis on social activism and rational understanding of liturgy [to the detriment of personal transcendental experience] [Bach 1946, Bateson 1974, Eliade 1976, Judah 1967, 1974]) have rendered it quite different from earlier evolutionary stages and have made the "identity search" a major American pastime (see Robbins, Anthony, and Richardson 1978 for a review of theoretical explanations for the new religions).

Evolution in general, whether biological or cultural, is a move from less to more differentiated. Modern society has become increasingly differentiated due to the functional specialization of societal institutions (different institutions to serve different functions) that was made possible by the discovery of agriculture. Agriculture produced the "farmer" who could produce a surplus, and all sorts of "nonfarmers" who could now, for the first time, devote full time to tasks other than food-getting. Institutional specialization has been accelerated by industrialization. Following on the heels of institutional differentiation (different institutions for different functions) came institutional diversification (many different institutions to handle the same function, for example, "multiple means of fulfilling family functions" [Wuthnow 1976:197]).

A comparison between two polar extremes on the evolutionary scale, the hunting-and-gathering society and the industrialized society, brings the differences into sharp focus. In primitive society there is no special apparatus for government, religion, education, or economy. All these processes are carried out by the multifunctional kinship structure. The family is a social group, a ritual group, the unit of production, and the means of education.

In the hunting-and-gathering society, then, roles are very few. There is an "unmarried woman's role" and a "married woman's role," an "uninitiated (subadult) man's role" and an "initiated man's role." All the able-bodied adult men play the same role in the society, and thus do the same things. The same is true for all adult women.

Contrasted with this is the myriad of unifunctional institutions that characterize industrialized society. Unifunctional institutions create a diversity of roles. In industrialized societies, an adult man, and increasingly an adult woman, can choose from a host of roles.

What is true for roles is also true for life-styles in general. In primitive societies there is one life-style, one god (or set of gods), one belief system. In industrial societies life-styles have burgeoned, as have gods and beliefs that give lives meaning.

This trend toward variety may, of course, be viewed as an

opportunity rather than a problem. Diversity is freeing, as has been recognized since the beginning of sociological studies of cities ("Stadt Luft macht frei"). The early Chicago and German schools of urban scholars noted that it is in the cities, the prime example of diversity in our time, that we are free to deviate (Park 1915) and to express our own natures (Simmel 1950). Diversity offers persons in modern society the "freedom to be."

Yet, diversity can be problematic, too. The negative aspects of diversity have come to be called under the rubric "fragmentation." Society is "fragmented" by diversity; it tears asunder "consensus." In America the core of shared values is shrinking (Gruen 1966). Individual lives can also feel "fragmented." Each of us plays a variety of roles. A woman may be mother, wife, lawyer, recreation leader, school board chairperson, all in one day. Our constant turnover in "hats" makes our lives less "all of a piece" than that of the primitive man, who is preacher, teacher, ruler, all by virtue of being the elder kinsman in a multifunctional kinship structure.

There are other "conditions" of modern society that add to fragmentation of individual lives. For Marx the key to alienation is the separation of the laborer from the fruits of his labor. A man's separation from his productive activity lays the foundation for competitive relationships that separate the producer from both the seller and the user of his product. By extension, men are alienated from one another in general. According to Marx this condition—essentially a conflict between man and society—is not conducive to the realization of human potential (Ollman 1971). I do not take the separation of man from his product to be the source of all "fragmentation." Rather, fragmentation is a concomitant of the highly differentiated nature of modern society in general. The separation of man from his product does contribute to the sense of fragmentation, but so do other conditions, such as mobility and "modernism," which are indicative of sweeping and fast-paced change. Because of mobility, the job, the friends and neighbors that serve as identity-giving reference points keep changing.[6] "Modernism" suggests that any edifice or scene old enough to have accumulated sentimental attachments is likely to be razed to make way for something new (Klapp 1969:23–38).

One effect diversity-produced fragmentation has that exacerbates meaninglessness is that it generates a feeling of separation among people. We no longer have so much in common with our fellows, and thus may feel "separated" from them. This is exacerbated by the kind of roles we play vis-à-vis one another. The *Gemeinschaft/Gesellschaft* dichotomy described by Tönnies (1887) and extended by Durkheim (1893), Cooley (1909), Redfield (1947), Weber (1947), and Parsons (1951), contrasts the roles played in a small, premodern *Gemeinschaft* ("community" in German) with those played in a large modern *Gesellschaft* ("society"). In *Gemeinschaft*, relations among persons are determined by tradition, consensus, and kinship, and are characterized by intimacy and informality. In *Gesellschaft*, relationships are more often specialized and functional, and therefore tend to be formal, contractual, and impersonal. Most of the roles in premodern societies are "expressive," in Parsons' (1937, 1951) terms. They involve the "total" person, are ends in themselves, and are affective in tone. In contrast, in industrialized society most areas of life are characterized by specialized "instrumental" roles that need only a "partial" involvement of the players, are means to ends, and are affectively neutral (Parsons 1937). In modern society a person is most often known by a specialized unifunctional role, and not by a generalized multifunctional role that would provide a variety of interconnections among people. Although members of modern society are dependent upon *more people* than their predecessors, they are "less dependent upon *particular persons*, and their dependence upon others is confined to a highly fractionalized aspect of the other's round of activity" (Wirth 1964:71, emphasis mine).

The greatest effect institutional differentiation and its concomitant diversity have, however, is that they lead to the necessity to make a choice about meaning. A sense of individual autonomy

11

arises from institutional segmentation, which leaves "wide areas in the life of the individual unstructured" (Luckmann 1967:97). In primitive society life was structured, and a "one possibility thing" (Bellah 1970:40). In modern society a relativity has been accorded life-styles and roles, as well as values, ideals, myths, and traditions, which were not questioned in primitive societies (Cox 1965). "From the interstices of the social structure that resulted from institutional segmentation emerged what may be called a 'private sphere'" (Luckmann 1967:97). Meaning in modern society is a matter for the private sphere. In modern society there is no monopoly on meaning. Life in modern society is an "infinite possibility thing" (Bellah 1970:40).[7]

Modern man thus feels he is free to choose from a variety of identity-givers. In America there is a myriad of life-integrating principles and styles available from which to choose. So many, in fact, that we may suffer from "overchoice"—"the point at which the advantages of diversification and individualization are canceled by the complexity of the consumer's decision-making process" (Toffler 1970:239). Yet, "as the number of potential reference points has multiplied, the ability to refer oneself to these points has declined" (Klapp 1969:21). An explanation for this can be found in a second "condition" of modern society.

In modern American culture, there is an emphasis on rational messages and modes of communication. Our culture emphasizes information, facts, numbers. Each of these is understood with rational, analytical, logical reasoning. This emphasis has tended to crowd out nonrational, nonlogical concerns such as sentiments like love, loyalty, and faith, which are understood by intuitive, expressive, emotional means. Our cultural storehouse of symbols and ways of knowing favors fact over metaphor, history over myth, knowledge over experience, and technique over ritual (Klapp 1969:324).

The overly rational nature of our culture has exacerbated "identity problems" because it is the nonrational symbols and ways of knowing that are best suited to serve as means for establishing identity.

12

The most meaningful (in the sense of meaning that identifies) statements are likely to be devoid of information (facts). For example, statements that make implicit or explicit reference to some idea, doctrine, or supernatural entity, such as "Hear O Israel, the Lord Our God, the Lord is One" and "Jesus Christ is the Son of God," have no material terms. The terms of these propositions cannot be seen, heard, tasted, or touched. They are not empirical. "They are not amenable to verification, but neither are they vulnerable to falsification" (Rappaport 1971:29). Facts and information can change daily without affecting the "unquestionable truthfulness" imparted to a "reality which cannot be verified empirically" (van Baal 1971:3).

The best meaning-givers, then, are nonmaterial and nonfactual —such things as ideals and supernatural entities. Their "truthfulness" cannot be negated by changing reality. This contrasts with facts, which are empirical and can be falsified. The "truth" of facts does change, at a rapid pace, as the modern information explosion continues. As an illustration, if a person builds his meaning around the existence of God, he cannot prove that God does exist, but neither can anyone else prove God does not exist. The "truth" of God is unchanging because it does not lend itself to experimentation. If a person builds his meaning around the Newtonian principle of physics, on the other hand, and Einstein disproves that principle, the principle, and the meaning associated with it, are negated.

Just as facts do not make good identity referents, logical reasoning does not lend itself to the sense of union by which a person can come to identify with something "beyond himself." Thinking about something separates the thinker from the object of his thought. Conscious, rational reasoning perpetuates a sense of separation from the universe and from other persons. It endorses the individual's feeling of autonomy that arises from institutional differentiation (Rappaport 1976a). It is a characteristic of religious experience, in fact, that it overcomes this separation and makes a person feel "one with" the universe, and with all that lives (Bellah 1970; Greeley and McCready 1974; James 1958).

13

These "fragmenting" conditions of modern society, then—autonomy of choice, separation from our fellows, and an emphasis on rational symbols and modes of communication—have made us a nation of seekers after "meaning."

The search for meaning in American society takes many forms, not all of which are "religious." The women's liberation movement, the cooperative movement, or conservation groups like the Sierra Club may provide identity. Natural foods, art, travel, surfing, or motorcycle clubs can be used as referents for establishing identity. Athletics can be a "medium of self-realization and self-recognition" (Kortzfleish 1970).

But it cannot be denied that interest in things spiritual and "occult"[8] is high; the extent of this interest has been well-documented. Measures such as the number of books in print dealing with occult topics (which increased by five times from 1968 to 1969), the number of astrologers in the United States (10,000 full-time and 175,000 part-time), and the sale of Ouija boards (2,000 sold in 1967, after forty years of collecting dust on store shelves) demonstrate the extent of the interest over the last fifteen years (Galbreath 1971; Scott 1976; Truzzi 1972).

The *Directory of Religious Bodies in the United States* (Melton 1977) reports that fewer than 80 religious organizations (both Establishment and non-Establishment groups) were formed in each five-year period from 1805 to 1955. But in the three five-year periods from 1955 to 1970, 128, 150, and 123 new groups were formed, respectively. Rowley (1971) estimates that the membership in 20 religious groups in America (such as Spiritualism, the Association for Research and Enlightenment, Scientology, Maharishi's Transcendental Meditation, Hare Krishna, Meher Baba, and Nichiren Shoshu) grew from less than 100,000 in 1960 to 1,700,000 in 1970.

The interest in the occult, or "spiritual realms of the universe and the mind" (Scott 1976:29), is a broad-based one. A survey of households in the San Francisco Bay area of California (Wuthnow 1978) showed that more than 70 percent of the respondents

14

professed some degree of belief in astrology's claim that "the stars, the planets, and our birthdays have a lot to do with our destiny in life." Eighty-six percent of the younger respondents (ages 16–30), and 76 percent of their elders (ages 31 and over) believed in the existence of extrasensory perception (ESP). All but 12 percent of the sample had had at least one religious or mystical "peak experience" in which they reported experiencing "the beauty of nature in a deeply moving way," feeling "in harmony with the universe," or being "in close contact with something holy or sacred" (Wuthnow 1978:100–101).

The widespread interest in the psychic and mystical is by no means confined to California. A study undertaken by Melton (1976) "has concluded that there is a larger psychic/metaphysical/mystical community functioning in Chicago than in either Los Angeles or San Francisco" (Melton 1977:14). A nationwide survey undertaken by the National Opinion Research Center (McCready 1976:132–33) showed that nearly three-fifths of the sample reported having some sort of mystical or psychical experience (such as déjà vu, precognition, communication with a dead person, or feeling close to a powerful spiritual force) at least once. These experiences were widespread at all age levels, from the teens through the seventies. Nearly one-fifth of the sample had psychic or mystical experiences *frequently*.

Interest in the psychic is becoming quite respectable. The Parapsychology Association gained membership in the American Association for the Advancement of Science in 1969. In England a poll of the readers of the *New Scientist*, a magazine read mainly by scientists and technicians, indicated that nearly 70 percent of the respondents believed in the possibility of extrasensory perception. The San Francisco Bay area survey (Wuthnow 1978) showed that more people believed in the existence of ESP than expressed a belief in God (54% of the younger people and 75% of the older people). Courses in parapsychology, meditation, and astrology are gaining popularity at community colleges and in adult education programs (Galbreath 1971:630; field notes).

15

Some police departments "now call on recognized mediums to help them locate lost property, missing persons, and bodies, and suggest suspects in a crime" (Scott 1976:232–33; field notes). Miss America 1980 testified that she had undergone a miraculous spiritual healing that cured her of a physiological defect and changed her life.

It is important to note that not all persons who are interested in the occult build their meaning around it. Truzzi (1972:36) posits that most Americans play with the occult, rather than using its beliefs and principles in a "serious search for new sacred elements." He draws a distinction between persons who have a relatively superficial connection with the occult and the "small but significant minority" of serious students. For these highly committed persons, the occult is filling a meaning-giving function.

This "small but significant minority" uses occult ideas and practices in a way that can be defined as religious in Geertz's (1966) terms. For Geertz religion is "a system of symbols which acts to establish powerful, pervasive, and long-lasting moods and motivations in men, by formulating conceptions of a general order of existence, and clothing those conceptions with such an aura of factuality that the moods and motivations seem uniquely realistic." That is, religion—whatever ideas and symbols a person uses as "religion"—provides answers to the questions posed by the existence of life and death and "good" and "evil." The answers, of course, are varied. They are sometimes tentative, sometimes dogmatic; but the fact that there *are* answers provides the human with the comforting assumption that his place in the universe is interpretable.

The new groups that are "religious" in these terms are themselves quite varied. There have been many attempts to categorize these religious groups along various dimensions (e.g., Bird 1978; Ellwood 1973; Hargrove 1978; Melton 1977; Robbins, Anthony, and Richardson 1978; Richardson 1976; Tipton 1978; Wallis 1974; Wuthnow 1978). Others have determined that traditional classification schemes offer little enlightenment when

16

applied to the new religious groups (Zaretsky and Leone 1974). Classifying the various groups would serve to show, however, that seemingly contradictory findings (Are the groups youthful or are they gray-haired? Are they communal or individualistic? Are they dangerous or benign?) are the result of studying very different phenomena.

At the risk of vastly oversimplifying, a simple dichotomy among groups will serve to make a distinction important to this study. This discrimination is often missed by more complex taxonomies using finer distinctions. Martin Marty (1970) labeled the two forms of new religious groups the Occult Underground (perhaps Occult Counterculture would be better, since not even Satanists can be said to be "underground" today) and the Occult Establishment.

The "occult counterculture" category consists of recently founded groups that appeal to the young. These groups are often based on principles transferred from the East or are syncretistic religions, blending Christian and Eastern philosophies. Generally, these groups are both countercultural and communitarian in orientation. Thus, these groups counter the "problems" of modern life in a very direct way. To the problems of autonomy and "overchoice," they offer an authoritarian leader or set of principles that shows "the way" to salvation, however salvation may be defined. To the problem of separation from others, these groups offer live-in communities, some of which are structured in nearly every detail. They worship a numinous symbol or principle of the type that cannot be negated by logical thought. Religious experience that affords a sense of oneness with this symbol is a part of the ritual of these groups. A brief description of just one such group, Hare Krishna (International Society for Krishna Consciousness), may help illustrate the kind of meaning found within them.

The solution Hare Krishna provides to "confusing questions of morality and belief," is to provide an external (to oneself) and absolute authority in the person of the guru. The promise of

17

transcendental religious experience, missing in institutionalized religion, is a primary reason for joining Hare Krishna. Judah (1974) pinpoints five other values of Hare Krishna that have "particular relevance to many of our youth." Hare Krishna emphasizes (1) happiness, (2) anti-intellectualism, (3) non-violence, (4) the spiritual, as opposed to the material, and (5) chanting and dancing (which Judah says provide an outlet for emotional expression).

Hare Krishna devotees live together in a community and practice a life style that includes dietary and sexual restrictions. The daily schedule of the adherents is:

A.M.

3:45	Rise, shower, and dress
4:30	Chant
5:45	Read about Krishna
8:30	Communal (vegetarian) breakfast
9:00	Temple cleaning
10:00	Work (some to street chanting; some to work in group-owned incense factory; others to outside jobs)

P.M.

2:00	Afternoon (vegetarian) meal
3:00	Afternoon work
6:00	Shower
7:00	Evening worship ceremony (chanting, dancing, offering)
10:00	A cup of warm milk before retiring

Sources of income for the group include the assets of those joining, profits of group-owned enterprises, and wages earned by members who work at outside jobs (Ellwood 1973).

Hare Krishna, then, offers a communitarian and authoritarian response to the problem of finding meaning. Admittedly, Hare Krishna is an extreme example of the structured community.

Other imported groups, Meher Baba (Anthony and Robbins 1974; Robbins 1969) and Nichiren Shoshu (Ellwood 1973), for example, have certain strict rules for living that their adherents must follow, but are not as fully structured as Hare Krishna. Melton (1977:271) categorizes such groups as Hare Krishna, Nichiren Shoshu, the Divine Light Mission, and Sai Baba together, and says that in each of these the "guru, the teacher of religious wisdom, is a key to the structure. . . . He possesses the mystic truth and teaches the techniques—yoga, dancing, meditation, study, and community—which lead to the truth." He says, too, that these groups have "expanded in the counterculture community across the nation."

The occult counterculture groups, then, respond to society's fragmentation and rationality by emphasizing the opposite. These groups respond to "overchoice" by removing themselves from society (to varying degrees), and forming small communities where life is structured and authority for "truth" (i.e., meaning) rests with a leader figure. They concentrate on the emotional, the expressive, and the spiritual sides of life, to offset the materialistic emphases that have been troubling to them in modern society. These communities are reminiscent of the Gemeinschaft in the totalness of their structure and their fostering of expressive relationships.

Thus, to the "unstructured" autonomous rational miasma that is modern life, the occult counterculture groups offer a structured existence centered around a nonrational symbol. For these groups the "powerful, pervasive, and long-lasting moods and motivations" established by the symbol system is of the type Geertz (1966) originally had in mind. Geertz, like Radcliffe-Brown, sees these moods as both "expressing the world's (qua community's) climate and shaping it." The *community's* goals are expressed and formulated in the liturgy and rituals of these religions.

It will be argued here that Spiritual Frontiers Fellowship and the American metaphysical groups, which Marty (1970) would

19

dub the "Occult Establishment," offer a quite different response to the same "conditions" of society. The American metaphysical groups make their appeal to "what is now called 'middle America,' or the 'silent majority' " (Marty 1970:216). These groups attract middle-aged, middle-class people, and are not counter-cultural or communitarian. Adherents of these groups are often well-established in terms of the criteria American society applies: they have mostly white-collar jobs and middle-class incomes; some have advanced educational degrees. Yet they still seek the "something more" that they find missing in their lives.

It will be argued that, in the metaphysical groups, the search for "something more" is pursued in an individualistic manner. Those who have studied the youthful manifestations of religious experimentation posit a decline in individualism in our culture (Bellah 1976; Wuthnow 1976). But individualism is alive and well in metaphysics. American metaphysics cannot be analyzed as a religion whose ritual expresses and maintains the goals of a collectivity. Rather, its rituals create and maintain individual identity.

Metaphysics is decidedly noncommunitarian. Members of Spiritual Frontiers Fellowship, for example, do not form small live-in communities. Members are joined by a "mail-order fellowship" in that they receive correspondence from the national organization. Members may meet at week-long national retreats, held annually. They may also participate in the activities of SFF's 73 regional organizations (called "areas") located in 35 states, but these usually consist of lectures, presented monthly or less frequently. Some SFF members join together into small "study groups" of eight to twelve people that meet weekly for short periods of time. There were 330 such groups in existence in 1975.

Through the rituals of meditation and prayer, SFF members focus on a God who dwells within the souls of men. The authority for truth does not rest with a leader figure, but within oneself. "Truth" is validated only by one's own experience.

20

The American metaphysical movement groups share with the occult counterculture groups an epistemology that emphasizes intuitive and emotional ways of knowing, and a focus on the spiritual, as opposed to the material, side of life. These elements provide a corrective to the American cultural emphasis on the rational. But in contrast to the occult counterculture groups, the American metaphysical movement groups are not countercultural in other ways. The people in the metaphysics groups abide by the traditional American values of hard work, achievement, democracy, and individualism. The metaphysical organizations do not form structured communities reminiscent of the Gemeinschaft. The short-term groupings they do form do not remove their members from mainstream American society. Rather, these groups help them deal with problems encountered in their everyday lives. These groups use their rituals, not only to focus on an integrating spiritual symbol (the God within), but also to solve pragmatic problems.

The premise to be developed here is that Spiritual Frontiers Fellowship's response to meaninglessness serves to maintain the societal status quo, yet provides individuals with the means to establish personal identity. It will be argued that SFF's beliefs, ritual, and structure epitomize and legitimate the individual autonomy that results from societal fragmentation. Rather than turning back toward structured Gemeinschaft, the metaphysical groups bring Gesellschaft's lack of structure and freedom of choice into the religious realm. At the same time, the nonrational explanations and spiritual symbols provided by SFF enable the individual to achieve personal identity.

In this chapter several conditions of modern society have been discussed—autonomy in the process of finding meaning and a plethora of choice, separation among people, an overly rational system of symbols—all of which were posited to make finding meaning problematic for Americans. The chapters to follow will analyze Spiritual Frontiers Fellowship's response to these various "problems." The description in chapter 2 will supply themes and events for analysis in succeeding chapters; chapters 3 and 4 discuss Spiritual Frontiers' expression of autonomy; chapter 5 describes the type of identity found in SFF; chapter 6 describes the tenuous fellowship that is a response to separation; and chapter 7 describes SFF's response to the rational emphases in American culture. It will be posited that SFF's individualistic and flexible responses are adaptive in a flexible and changing world.

1. Throughout this discussion the term "American metaphysical movement" will be used to label the kinds of groups (Spiritual Frontiers Fellowship, Spiritualism, New Thought, Theosophy, etc.) that J. Stillson Judah discussed in his book *The History and Philosophy of the Metaphysical Movements in America* (1967). Other authors have used the term "American metaphysical movement" to refer to contemporary religious movements in general (cf. Prince 1974; Zaretesky and Leone 1974b). I have restricted it to include only organizations that share the characteristics of the groups discussed by Judah (1967) (see Leone 1974 for this usage of "American metaphysical movement"). These groups include Spiritualism, Theosophy, the Arcane School, Astara, New Thought, the Divine Science Church, the Church of Religious Science, the Unity School of Christianity, Christian Science, and Spiritual Frontiers Fellowship, among others. The *Directory of Religious Bodies in the United States* (Melton 1977) lists 264 groups under the "New Thought" and "Psychic" categories that would be, in our terms "metaphysical." These groups represent 21% of all the religious bodies currently functioning in the United States.

The American metaphysical groups (with the exception of Spiritualism) have been largely ignored by journalists and social scientists alike. Bach (1946), Braden (1951), and Ellwood (1973, 1979) have written descriptive works on many of these groups. Braden notes that most earlier writings pertaining to the groups were not objective (see Van Baalen [1956] for an example of a negative evaluation written by a Sunday school teacher). Judah's book is the best in this field.

By contrast, non-Christian communal groups, groups based on imported philosophies (Islamic, Hindu, Buddhist, Shinto, etc.), and magical groups (witchcraft, Satanism, etc.), have received much media and academic attention. These groups constitute 1%, 14%, and 6% of the religious bodies extant in the United States, respectively (Melton 1977).

2. This number is based on the official figure of 7,835 released by SFF (SFF 1975d). This number has been questioned on the possibility that it may have been inflated by possible failure to purge some membership "defaults" from the files. (A default refers to the death or resignation of a member, or failure to renew after three renewal letters have been sent.) The *SFF Membership Report*

and Publications Inventory, compiled as of 15 May 1975, presents data on renewal letters sent, defaults, renewals, and new members for 1973, 1974, and January–March 1975, shows members in each category of dues payment, and arrives at a total membership figure of 7,835. The amount of dues reported collected for the twelve months ending 30 April 1975, in a letter to members from the Finance Committee, is consistent with the membership data presented in the *Membership Report*. In December 1980 membership was reported at 4,432 (*SFF Newsletter* 15(4):5).

3. For a discussion of methodology, see Appendix A.

4. Spiritual Frontiers Fellowship is unique among metaphysical groups because, besides encouraging individual spiritual growth, SFF also wishes to interest orthodox churches in psychic phenomena and spiritual healing.

5. Problems in identity can manifest themselves in dissatisfaction with: (1) what a person thinks about himself introspectively; (2) his "reputation," how he believes others see him; (3) his feelings (lack of fullness of sentiments); or any combination of these three factors (Klapp 1969:39).

6. High rates of job turnover and unemployment make it increasingly difficult to identify with one's work role. Klapp (1969:18) expects that in societies where automation is pervasive "there will be a surge of discontent and restless mass groping for new kinds of significance." The physiological toll that unemployment, changing jobs, and simply moving from one place to another can take has been well documented (see, for example, Aldrich and Mendkoff 1963; Cobb 1974; and Rowland 1977). Surely it must affect one's identity structure as well.

7. This is, of course, an exaggeration. As Luckmann (1967:97) notes, "the sense of autonomy which characterizes the typical person in modern society" is "somewhat illusory." Modern man is freer than primitives, who have fewer choices. But he is not infinitely free because he is still a part of larger systems. Everything he is "free" to do may not be adaptive for his own survival. "Although men are metabolically separate from one another, and although consciousness is individual, men are not self-sufficient and their autonomy is relative and slight. Men are parts of larger systems upon which their continued existence is contingent" (Rappaport 1976a:33).

8. Scott (1976:30) has developed a definition of "occult" from an extensive study of occult literature and historical and sociological accounts of the occult. She says "to describe the occult as occultists view it, it is a specific body of beliefs and practices dealing with the hidden realms of existence and latent powers of the mind, dating from the days of the ancient mystery schools." The occult is not "hidden" because it is hidden from the view of the public (although in some periods of history it has been), but because it "deals with the hidden or spiritual realms of the universe and the mind" (i.e., the nonphysical realms) (Scott 1976:29).

2

A Spiritual Frontiers Fellowship Study Group

RECRUITMENT: METAPHYSICS CLASSES

I entered the metaphysical network by attending adult education classes in metaphysics sponsored by the Carroll County[1] Community Education Program. I had determined that I wanted to study an occult group. My past research had shown that many occultists believe everyone possesses latent psychic abilities. I wanted to study a group that was developing these abilities—to discover how the psychic talents were developed, and toward what end.

I reconnoitered the various manifestations of the occult in the area, which I learned about by scanning bulletin boards in metaphysical bookstores and by word-of-mouth. I sampled several of these groups, taking trips to Spiritualist church services and to séances, and attending classes in astrology. I discovered the Carroll County adult education classes in "metaphysics" in the same way as did every other resident of Carroll County—through a brochure addressed to "Boxholder." The announcement listed the course offerings—from "belly dancing," through "Christmas

24

crafts," to "college psychology," and including "Metaphysics I."
In the fall of 1974, I enrolled in "Metaphysics I—Introduction to
Metaphysics," and in the winter of 1975 took "Metaphysics II,"
which focused on death and life after death. The metaphysics
classes met one night a week for fifteen weeks, and cost
$15.00.

These classes serve as a means of recruitment into the Spiritual
Frontiers Fellowship organization. SFF, as noted earlier, has a
national office and 73 "area" or regional organizations in 35
states. One of these is in the nearby city of Metro, and the monthly Metro Area meetings are announced in the metaphysics classes. SFF's smaller, local "study groups" meet more frequently.
The formation of study groups in the Carroll County area is also
announced in the classes.

The metaphysics teacher, Joe, began leading these classes in
1971. When "Metaphysics I" began in 1974, Joe had recently been
laid off from his job as a skilled craftsman. He welcomed the lay-
off because it gave him an opportunity to expand his study and
teaching of metaphysics. Joe also has an office where he serves
paying clients as hypnotist, psychic counselor, and healer.

Joe was brought up as a Methodist, but metaphysics was not
foreign to his family. His grandmother and great-grandmother
were spiritual healers, and his parents are members of the Unity
School of Christianity, although they joined this metaphysical
group when Joe was away from home, in the military. Joe was for
a time Pentecostal, but he does not now attend church. He has
"Spiritualist minister papers," so he is entitled to the designation
"Reverend." He has been a Mason, and has received Astara's
correspondence lessons for several years. Joe is a member of
Spiritual Frontiers Fellowship, and is active in the SFF Metro
Area chapter, which serves a large city and its surrounds.

Joe, who is thirty-six, has five young children. His wife,
Barbara, shares his interest in metaphysics, and has followed him
into the various stages of his study. She is a willing cocounselor to
the people who seek Joe out for help.

Joe's typical week includes a Monday night adult education meditation class, a Tuesday night class in advanced metaphysics at his house, a Wednesday night adult education beginning metaphysics class, and once each month, a Thursday night SFF Metro Area meeting.

The setting for the adult education metaphysics classes was a classroom in a fairly new high school building. The classroom had barren cream-colored concrete block walls, and green plastic "student's desks" with built-in writing surfaces. Each evening Joe rearranged the straight rows of chairs into a semicircle.

The 20–30 people who came to the classes practically filled the room. Most of the class members were women (24 of 29 in Metaphysics I; 14 of 19 in Metaphysics II), and ranged in age from 22 to 55. All, including Joe, were dressed casually, in slacks and shirts or sweaters, but none had the look of a student (denim jeans and jogging shoes or hiking boots). Hairstyles were neat and trim. None of the men had beards.

Before each class session began, there was considerable chatter among the class members, several of whom were friends. As Joe, a very large man, took his usual position—standing at the front of the room beside the teacher's desk—the attention of the class became riveted on him. Several people took notes during class. A few of us brought tape recorders.

Although the classes had no standard schedule, they usually contained a lecture by Joe and questions from class members. Joe gave instruction in how to meditate in the second lesson, and subsequently time was usually set aside for the class to meditate. Sometimes the class did psychic experiments, such as trying to perform psychometry (receiving impressions about a person by holding an object that belongs to him); scanning (receiving impressions by looking into a person's eyes); seeing auras (the aura is a colored light that surrounds the body; the color gives clues to character and mood); and laying-on-of-hands healing. The classes always ended with a "healing circle" or "prayer circle" during which the class members stood in a circle and held hands.

26

Names of people who needed spiritual, mental, or physical help were then recited by everyone simultaneously.

Joe was serious, sometimes even somber, in his approach to teaching. Joe asked many rhetorical questions, and class members were encouraged to take part in discussion, yet Joe was seen as the expert in metaphysical matters.

Although the Community Education brochure listed the class time as 7:00–10:00 P.M., it often continued much longer. A small group followed Joe to a local restaurant after the classes to discuss metaphysics further, to report their individual psychic efforts, and to obtain interpretation of dreams or impressions they had received.

In his classes Joe explains that "metaphysics" is concerned with anything that is not physical. Metaphysics is, he asserts, a scientific religious philosophy. He draws a distinction between the "supernatural," which is forever scientifically inexplicable, and the "supernormal," which is amenable to eventual scientific explanation, though it is not yet fully understood by science.[2] Metaphysics' realm is the *supernormal* because there are physiological and neurological explanations for psychic phenomena.

> The vibrations we talk about are actually atoms vibrating. . . . In metaphysics you'll learn that everything is comprised of a vibrational frequency. . . .
> Everything has an aura, an electromagnetic force field around the body. . . . Thoughts are things. Thinking produces a millivolt of electricity. . . . Everything is based on electromagnetism. (Metaphysics I:9/16/74)

Nothing God does, and nothing Jesus did while he lived on earth, is supernatural. Their works proceed by the rules of spiritual laws, not all of which have been discovered by man.[3]

Joe teaches that the basic spiritual law is the Law of Cause and Effect, or the Law of Physics. This is the principle that for every action there is an opposite and equal reaction, or "What ye sow, so shall ye reap." Joe sometimes conceptualizes this law as the

27

Law of Love: "You give love, you receive love." There is a law that supersedes the Law of Cause and Effect called the Law of Grace, or the Law of Complete Forgiveness and Release. If a person truly forgives himself for wrongful past actions, his guilt will be released, and he will no longer be troubled by it. Joe also teaches that "prayer changes things."

Joe's method is to teach his philosophy of spiritual and psychic awareness ("what you are doing and why") before the class experiments with psychic abilities. Joe teaches that we all have a spark of divinity. God dwells within us, and the inner self of man is divine.[4]

> The organized churches have put God way up there, have showed God way out there, away from humanity. Actually, God is in here [touching his heart], within us. The organized churches have said that only men of God, that is the Prophets in the Bible, could do these things, perform miracles, etc. Actually we are all men of God, and all of us can do these things. God is within. We don't believe in a God "out there." (Metaphysics II:4/28/75)

Joe teaches that Jesus Christ, Buddha, and other great spiritual leaders had the same modicum of divinity that each individual has, but they were more *aware* of their divinity than most.[5]

Becoming increasingly aware of the divine inner self is "spiritual growth," and should be the goal of anyone who embarks on the study of metaphysics. In order to grow spiritually, a person must develop his ability to communicate with his divine inner self. Communication is through prayer, which is "talking to God," and meditation, "listening to God."

Joe teaches that there is no single correct way to achieve spiritual growth. The road to spiritual maturity has no guideposts to be followed universally. One class member, small dark-haired Lisa, in her twenties and the mother of two small boys, asked:

Lisa: Do you mean, then, that you might be able to do this, and this, and this, and never be able to do something else?

Joe: Right.

Lisa: There is no one set scheme. There is no this you do first, then this, then this?

Joe: No. No there's no particular steps. . . .

Lisa: So there is no starting place.

Joe: No. There isn't. There isn't a starting place, like you'll develop clairvoyance ["clear seeing"] first and clairaudience ["clear hearing"] second, and this third, and this fourth. That's why I say, when you go through these different experiences in meditation in class, each of you will pick up different things. Some of you may hear things. Some of you may see things. Some of you may have just an inner knowing. So that's why I say, it's up to each individual, how it works with you. (Metaphysics I:11/11/74)

Each person must find his own path to truth. Interspersed among Joe's views on the spiritual, the psychic, and life after death are admonitions that we are not to believe what he says until we experience its truth ourselves. A person's own experience is the only valid criterion for establishing his truth. Knowledge gained from reading or by listening to a teacher is not to be accepted until the person has experienced it himself.[6] For example, the phenomenon of clairvoyance is not to be believed until a person sees something clairvoyantly himself. The theory of reincarnation is not to be accepted until a person, usually during meditation, sees himself in a prior life, and so forth.

Each person's enlightenment must be done by themselves. I can teach you metaphysics, I can teach you these things, but I can't prove them to you. I cannot prove clairvoyance. I cannot prove telepathy. I cannot prove any phenomenon, except you experience it. And I'll tell this class the same as I tell all my beginners in metaphysics, don't believe a word that I'm teaching you until you experience it. (Metaphysics II:2/10/75)

Joe says, "Knowledge is gained by reading. Wisdom is gained by meditating and letting God show you" (Metaphysics II:5/12/75).

29

A person who is on the path to spiritual growth should attempt to gain *wisdom*.

Joe draws a distinction between "spiritual" and "psychic," and he values the spiritual above the psychic. The psychic consists of "the phenomena": manifestations of extrasensory perception (ESP), such as clairvoyance, clairaudience, clairsentience (literally, clear seeing, hearing, and knowing, meaning seeing, hearing, and knowing without the aid of the physical senses); telepathy (perceiving the thoughts of another person); and out-of-the-body experiences. The spiritual consists of attempting to become more aware of the divine inner self, and becoming a better person thereby. To attain spiritual growth is a higher, purer goal than concern only with "the phenomena," although psychic development can be a by-product of spiritual growth. This distinction between the spiritual and the psychic is, I found, a common and important one among metaphysicians.

The metaphysics classes serve as a means of acquainting people with Spiritual Frontiers Fellowship. Joe announces the monthly Metro Area SFF meetings, held in a nearby city, and the formation of SFF study groups. The area meetings provide an opportunity to hear a lecture,[7] to meet others with similar interests, and to obtain a healing or advice from a psychic, but the local study groups are the "vital heart of SFF" (SFF 1973b:4).

THE STUDY GROUP

Study groups have eight to twelve members, and usually meet weekly for a specified length of time, though some study groups continue as long as interest warrants. Study groups convene to study a particular topic such as spiritual development, prayer, healing, meditation, or the Bible.

Most of the study groups in Carroll County are taught by Jenny, who shares the psychic/spiritual leadership of the region with Joe. Jenny is fifty and survives her second husband, who was an engineer. Her first marriage ended in divorce. Her widow's pension allows her to live comfortably and "not to worry about the material side of life."

Jenny is a lively and cheerful woman, with twinkling, almost black eyes and blonde curly hair. She likes people, is quick to laugh out loud, and flirts jokingly with the men in the metaphysical network. Her three children, now grown with children of their own, would introduce her at high school functions as their "weird little mom," alluding to her interest in the psychic and her size.

Jenny has always been interested in "the spiritual side of life." She began teaching Sunday school when she was twenty, and maintains an active interest in her Presbyterian church, where she serves as an elder; but her interest in religion has expanded beyond the traditional. Five years ago, after the death of her husband, Jenny began to actively pursue her interest in the psychic. Until then she had refrained from doing so because she felt it would not be consistent with the image of a "corporate wife." She joined SFF, and is now a member of the governing board of the Metro Area SFF chapter. She belongs to the Association for Research and Enlightenment (ARE) (an organization based on Edgar Cayce's teachings and writings), attends Spiritualist churches, and sometimes lectures there. She is asked to give psychic readings at national SFF conferences, and to lead workshops (on out-of-the-body travel, for example) at Metro Area retreats.

Although Jenny's life had relatively humble beginnings, she has now attained stature within the metaphysical realm. Jenny was the first in her family to finish high school. Her grandfather immigrated to this country from England, and her father took a job after leaving school in eighth grade. When she was young, Jenny thought she would be "just a housewife" (although she reports having a recurrent dream about her less prosaic purpose in life). Now Jenny has little time for housework. A typical day in her life includes three hours of healing sessions or psychic consultations with a retinue of paying clients, perhaps a consultation with the police about a baffling murder case or a robbery, three or four hours of leading study groups, one or two hours of socializing with study group members, and numerous phone calls from clients and study group members. Jenny is acquainted with people all over the country. She knows learned people—people with academic credentials, psychiatrists, executives, stockbrokers —professionals of all sorts. What is more, these people turn to her for advice and counsel.

This counsel Jenny gives in a warm and homey style, which can, however, become disarmingly omniscient in tone. For example, when a group member told Jenny of a relative who had lain paralyzed and comatose for years, Jenny pronounced, "Someday she'll walk."

Jenny skillfully adapts her explanations and solutions for problems to her client's needs and preconceptions. She says if a person thinks he is possessed, then to help him, you have to first give him some way to deal with possession, whether you think he is possessed or not.

Zaretsky and Leone (1974) suggest that the profession of spiritual leader may be a kind of last frontier for entrepreneurship in the human services. Since the social service professions have been closed to persons without diplomas and certification, religion is the only "helping" field left open. It is relatively easy to acquire certification as a spiritual leader (ministerial papers from a Spiritualist church, for example). This field is particularly attractive to the middle-aged person (particularly a woman) who has had little opportunity to obtain the kind of certification required by other "helping" professions. This may be true for Jenny, and for Joe as well. In any case, Jenny has gained a degree of notoriety in the metaphysical network, and she is certainly not "just a housewife."

Jenny and Joe are complementary leaders; Joe emphasizes the philosophy and explanation of spiritual growth, Jenny the more practical considerations of how-to-do-it, and how-to-use-it in your life. Joe is serious; Jenny is lively and joking. Under Jenny's leadership, study group members joked and bantered, often provoked to "tears in the eyes" laughter.

The study groups Jenny leads use a book recommended by

SFF entitled *Know Yourself* (Hayes 1971), which contains enough weekly lessons for one year. SFF leader Patricia Hayes wrote the book from lesson plans used in her own study groups. Each lesson is three or four pages long, and contains an "inspirational reading" (most lessons leave the content of the reading to the leader's discretion), an "introduction" during which the group is to "share any spiritual or psychic experiences that the group members had during the week," a "discussion" topic, a "meditation," and a "healing circle." Most lessons do not require study outside class, though a few do have "homework."

The purpose of the lessons is to encourage spiritual growth, perceived as the increased awareness of the God within (or the divine inner self). Some lessons deal with spiritual or psychic concerns, such as "Heaven and Hell," "Love of God," "Communication with the Dead vs. Mental Telepathy," and "Psychic Experience or Psychological Hallucination." Others concern improvement in oneself or in relationships with others, such as "Selfishness and Selflessness," "What Kind of a Person Are You," "Have You Taken Your Experiences into Your Outside World," "The Art of Relating," "Self-Doubt," and "Depression."

The study group I observed met nearly every Wednesday evening from January 1975 through January 1976. The description of one of its meetings to be presented here is actually a montage of several meetings. The words of the study group members are direct quotes taken from field notes, or tape recordings (on 8 and 15 January 1975), of meetings. Their words are interrupted from time to time by explanatory comments. The goal here is to give the reader a snapshot look at the proceedings of an SFF meeting. Themes that emerge in this description will be analyzed in the succeeding chapters.

A MEETING OF THE WEDNESDAY EVENING STUDY GROUP

The study group met in Jenny's home. The first to arrive at the meeting this Wednesday evening are John, his wife Beverly, and Laura. They travel twenty miles from the end of Carroll County to attend Jenny's class.

John, age forty-three, looks as though he has come straight from his job as a plant manager, for he is wearing plaid pants, a sport shirt, and a tie. He has a tatoo on his arm, acquired in the navy when he was sixteen. Beverly, age thirty-eight, has also just come from work as a clerk in a variety store. As they go inside the house, Jenny comments that Beverly "looks nice in her red polyester pantsuit." Beverly, who is tall and thin, thanks her, but replies, "It's really too big. All my clothes are too big." "I wish being too thin was my problem," says Jenny, who is not really overweight herself.

John was introduced to metaphysics and to Jenny in Joe's Metaphysics I class, and there lamented that his wife and two teen-aged stepdaughters were not interested in metaphysics. In fact, he said, the girls laughed at him. But now, Beverly has joined John in the study group, and is earnest in her efforts to learn to meditate and perform psychic feats.

Although he is a relative newcomer to metaphysics, John is not new to religion. While growing up in the Midwest, John tried several Protestant religions: Nazarene, Southern Baptist, United Brethren, and Church of God. He says he converted to Catholicism when he was twenty-one because he decided he needed a "religion with rules." He "excommunicated himself" from the Catholic church, however, when he married Beverly, a Protestant, six years ago. He had been married previously, and has one grown child, whom he sees infrequently, from that marriage. Beverly had also been married before, at a young age. She divorced her husband, then remarried him, thinking it was best for their two small daughters, but eventually divorced him again. John has adopted Beverly's girls.

John and Beverly joined the Methodist church, with which Beverly was familiar, a few months ago, but do not really feel "at home" there.

John met Laura in Joe's Metaphysics I class. She and Beverly now have become friends also. Laura, age thirty, is married to an engineer who has been married before. She and her husband have a two-year-old son, and Laura is expecting another child. Laura was brought up as a Catholic and attended parochial schools. She left the Catholic church, and marriage to a divorced person complicated any thoughts she had of rejoining it. Laura says her mother was psychic, and Laura has been interested in the psychic for several years. She receives the literature of the Unity School of Christianity.

Laura is an intelligent and active person, who has pursued a career as a professional photographer. She has taken adult education classes at various times in crafts, yoga, and "effective listening." But she also enjoys the more domestic activities of decorating her house and looking after her two-year-old son. It is sometimes frustrating to her that her family is moved frequently because of her husband's employment. She has become used to moving, and likes some of the places they have lived better than others; but the moves always disrupt her dream-plan to buy some land, to live on a farm again, like the one where she had grown up.

Attending classes like the study group was a way in which Laura could occupy her active mind and still pursue the mundane chores that, after all, also gave her pleasure.

David and Grace come to the meeting together in David's car from Allen County, twenty-five miles away. David is acquainted with Jenny because she sometimes preaches in the Allen County Spiritualist Church, which David attends. David is the only black person in the group and, at sixty-six, its oldest member. His neat and trim appearance belies his age.

David was brought up as a Baptist, but he rebelled against its "fire and brimstone" preaching some time ago. Besides currently holding an office on the governing board of the Allen County Spiritualist Church, David has been a member of ARE.

David is retired from jobs as a musician "where there was no time for being alone" and a night watchman "where there was

35

much solitude." David's past, as he reports it, seems a 180 degree turn from the present. He had problems with alcoholism when he was younger, and obtained help from Alcoholics Anonymous. He is determined now to help others who have the same problem. He has taken adult education classes at the community college in "alcoholic counseling" and "speech" to help him in his work.

David quit drinking twenty years ago, when his third and last child was born. David reports that his wife "can't quite forgive him" for the problems his alcoholism caused when their three children were small, and now will not go along with his religious leanings.

David has introduced Grace, who also attends the Allen County Spiritualist Church, to the study group. Grace, age fifty-eight, is a widow with a grown son and grandchildren. She has a Protestant religious background and has taken Silva Mind Control and Transcendental Meditation classes. She is a court reporter, and hopes to retire soon. She is expanding her activities in anticipation of retirement; she is taking crafts classes, and she enjoys sailing in the boat she and her son own. Grace describes herself as "always on the go or fast asleep," yet she is a quiet and reserved person.

Louise, her husband, Dan, and their neighbor Sara also drive together from Allen County. Louise and Dan met Jenny at the Allen County Spiritualist Church.

Louise, forty-seven, is casually dressed, in slacks, but she is still wearing the make-up and earrings she wore to her job in the personnel department of a large store. She has recently been promoted to that position from cashier. Her earrings sport pictures of her grandson. Besides a married daughter, Louise has four children at home. Her children are from a previous marriage.

Louise was "brought up Southern Baptist," but she also rebelled against what she perceived as "fire and brimstone" preaching. Louise is enthusiastic and quick to say "I love you," yet there is sincerity in her words.

Louise and Dan, age fifty-three, were married ten years ago. Dan has also been married before. He works as a skilled craftsman. Dan has been interested in the psychic for a long time, and says his mother is "psychic."

Louise and Dan have "recruited" their neighbor, Sara, into the study group. Sara, thirty-three and stockily built, dresses casually and plainly. Tonight she has dressed up her brown short-sleeved knit top with some shiny gold jewelry. She explains to Jenny that the jewelry belonged to her husband's mother, and that it has been "refurbished by a friend in the jewelry business." Sara's husband drives for a government agency, and she baby-sits with a small child on weekdays. They have a daughter in grade school.

Sara's religious background is Protestant. She has, in the past, been a member of an ARE study group, but left because of incompatibilities with the group leader.

I come from the outskirts of the town where Jenny lives. I met Jenny, John, and Laura in Joe's metaphysics class, where the formation of this study group was announced. I am a student and a research assistant at the university, married with no children. At twenty-seven, I am younger than the other group members.

By now I have been in the local metaphysical network for several months, and have explained to Joe and Jenny that I wish to study the Spiritual Frontiers Fellowship, and to write a report about its activities. In this way my status as a *student* of the group, and not just a *member* of the group, has become known to the people in the metaphysical network.

My status as a student of the group is signified visually by my note-taking. Other members of the metaphysics classes and the study group took notes, too, but mine were by far the most voluminous. Still, there were times when it seemed that while I was viewing my role as a member of the group *because* I was studying it, the group was viewing me as a member who was *also* studying it. At these times I walked the tightrope between the two poles of explaining my researcher status in strident tones, which made the group uncomfortable, and explaining my status softly, meekly, which made me uncomfortable. I was, of course, by this time explaining my status to people who had ceased to be merely "informants," and who were now friends, as well. (See Appendix A for a discussion of methodology.)

The small parking lot behind Jenny's house is full now. The cars are large late-model American-made cars, except for John's mid-size and my Volkswagen. As members arrive, they go inside and talk. Sara sinks into the brown upholstered rocker in Jenny's living room, her "favorite chair."

A look at this scene would show you a group of neat, casually dressed people. Some, who have come from work, are more "dressed up" than the rest. Jeans are conspicuously absent. You would see stylish short or medium-length hair; the longest hair is my own. There are no symbols of the student or the "hippie" here.

The group members talk together, discussing their jobs, their bosses, their families, and their homes. The pre-meeting conversations leave no doubt that the class members are middle-class people, most with white-collar jobs.

The group members have in common the desire to find themselves or to improve themselves through spiritual development. Only Beverly is a metaphysical novice. The others have been to Spiritualist churches, have received literature from the Unity School of Christianity, have been members of ARE, or have attended Joe's metaphysics classes. Although their search for self-improvement has been in a religious direction, none but Jenny attends an orthodox church regularly.

David, John, Beverly, and Melinda joined Spiritual Frontiers Fellowship after the study group began. Jenny has been a member of SFF for five years. SFF membership is not a study group requirement. Jenny simply has membership applications and copies of the *Principles, Purposes, and Program*[8] available on a table at the fourth meeting. The membership application explains that to be a member of SFF it is necessary to pay annual dues to the national organization.[9] SFF members receive a monthly newsletter and a quarterly journal, and have the opportunity to use a mail-order lending library and bookstore. Members may vote at the national conference held each spring, and attend three week-long national retreats held around the country during the summer months. The SFF organization is rarely discussed in the study group beyond "Are you going to the area meeting tomorrow night?" Exceptions to this occur around the times of Metro Area retreats and national conferences, events that spark peak interest in SFF.

The *Principles, Purposes, and Program* of Spiritual Frontiers Fellowship explains that SFF's three main concerns are prayer, healing, and immortality. Spiritual Frontiers Fellowship was founded in 1956 "to sponsor, explore, and interpret the growing interest in psychic phenomena and mystical experience to the traditional churches and others, and relate these experiences to effective prayer, spiritual healing, personal survival (i.e., life after death) and spiritual fulfillment" (SFF 1974).

SFF believes the early Christian Church recognized and valued psychic and mystical experiences and spiritual healing. SFF wants to revive interest in these phenomena in modern-day orthodox Christian churches. This endeavor is salient for SFF's national leaders, many of whom are ministers. It holds less interest for the membership, who are more concerned with personal spiritual growth. Accordingly, the goal of most SFF activities is "the development of spiritual growth in the individual" (SFF 1977a:7) and the application of spiritual and psychic experiences to present-day living.[10]

There are ten of us assembled in Jenny's living room.[11] The room reflects Jenny's interest in all facets of the "spiritual side of life." On one wall are two pictures of Christ, one with a peaceful expression, the other pained, bearing a crown of thorns and drops of blood. Beside a bookcase full of religious and psychic literature is a large string-picture of the four-armed Hindu god Shiva. Very small round pictures of the Roman Catholic stigmatics Padre Pio and Sister Rosa Ferron, who were said to have borne the marks of the Crucifixion on their bodies and to have the ability to heal others, hang on the side of the bookcase. A table between two chairs has the shape of an elephant with an Indian howdah on its back. A gold-colored cobra statue coils on top of the television. In the corner stands a three-foot-high black Buddha, holding a candle in one outstretched hand. Behind the candle Jenny has stuffed bits of paper listing people who want to have healing prayers said for them. On one wall Jenny has hung portraits she has painted herself. One pictures a nun, meant to represent Jenny in a prior life. Another is a portrait of a psychic colleague. Arranged on the fireplace mantle are candles, a Confucius figurine, a bronze bust of an American Indian, a figure of a tree, a madonna, and a crystal ball. Only photographs of Jenny's children and grandchildren, hanging on one wall, break the spell of an eclectic shrine woven by the decor of the room.

The furniture is arranged in a semicircle, with an opening where the living and dining rooms meet. Jenny sits at the end of the circle on a hassock. After a few meetings, some members have claimed their "favorite chair" or a preferred place on a couch.

Jenny begins the meeting at 7:00 P.M. with an inspirational reading. These readings are taken from such sources as the Bible, or Kahlil Gibran's *The Prophet*, Jeane Dixon's *Prayers to Live By*, *Springs of Living Water*, by Carl Shutzer, and the *Blue Water Bulletin*, a newsletter published by a midwestern Spiritualist minister. Tonight the reading is a "mudra," which is "the Sanskrit word for a type of spiritual exercise that reinforces the thoughts of the mind by the simultaneous use of body positions" (Setzer 1974:v).

> *Jenny:* OK, tonight our inspirational reading is going to be something I learned at the Area Retreat. This is a mudra, a type of meditation using body positions. For this you're supposed to hold your arms up, with your hands outward. Repeat the phrases at the beginning and end after me. Some of you heard this at the Retreat, so you'll know what to do. Ready?

All of us, following Jenny's lead, hold our arms out, with our palms up. We close our eyes. Jenny begins the mudra:

40

Jenny: O God, make me Love!
Unison: O God, make me Love!
Jenny: Collect every cell of my being into your cup of salva-
            tion, and pour me forth into the great, glowing circuit of
            Love in which alone we truly live and move and have our
            being. In my daily life may no portion of my body, mind
            or soul escape being cast into this everlasting current.
            May I be swept along within its melodious surging, and
            thereby fill my place as one responsive part within the
            human whole. May I feel this vital force of empathy and
            compassion even now flowing from my outturned palms
            as a warm, aromatic, nourishing, life-giving energy that
            connects me with all mankind. Present to me continually
            in my mind's eye the faces of those for whom I should
            care, and the faceless mass behind them for whom I
            should also be concerned.
            O God, make me Love!
Unison: O God, make me Love!
Jenny: O God, I sense Love within me!
Unison: O God, I sense Love within me!
Jenny: O God, I AM Love!
Unison: O God, I AM Love!
            (Setzer 1974:3)[12] (Study Group:6/11/75).

We open our eyes and lower our arms, returning to our relaxed positions on Jenny's many couches and chairs.

Jenny then asks, "Do you have any psychic or spiritual experiences to share with us tonight?" We answer in an around-the-room fashion. The first to speak is Louise. Louise has missed some meetings because of a visit to her ailing parents in another part of the country. She reports on her efforts at healing her stepfather, who had undergone surgery, and at "straightening out" her mother and aunt. She used the "White Light" to aid her stepfather's healing. The Pure White Light of the Christ is a manifestation of God's love. It can be used for protection or to improve a situation. It is thought that the White Light vibrates at a high frequency. Anything negative vibrates at a lower rate of frequency, and cannot penetrate the force field set up by the

41

White Light. To put the Light around oneself or someone else, it is necessary only to visualize it "like a spotlight" or "like a fog" surrounding you or the other person (Study Group:2/19/75). If you think and believe the Light is around someone, then it is. Louise enthusiastically reports that she saw "blue lights [blue is associated with healing] around my stepfather's bed at the hospital, just at the time this group was meeting. It was wonderful!"

Louise discussed metaphysics some with her family. She says, "I think I made a believer out of my stepdad" but "it's hard for my mother and aunt to understand."

> *Louise:* My aunt has a 46-year-old delinquent son.
> *Jenny:* Sounds like my brother.
> *Louise:* He's in jail. She asked me to pray for him. I said I would, but she should, too.
> *Jenny:* That's right. Two or three praying are stronger.

Louise relates things that happened to her on her trip in the oblique way common in Spiritualism and metaphysics. She discusses her problems in such a way that a listener without prior knowledge cannot know what her concern is:

> *Louise:* While I was there, I needed to meditate for an answer to something. I went outside among some trees, but my aunt kept calling me and distracting me. I got an answer anyway, that night. It was "Let it be as is."

The next to speak was Louise's husband, Dan. Several years ago, Dan worked in a supervisory capacity, but the firm closed after he had been there for ten years. His job search was then complicated by the backhanded compliment from personnel managers that he was "overqualified" for most available jobs. He works now as a skilled craftsman. His work schedule has prevented him from attending some of the class meetings, but recently he has been laid off from his job. Louise and Jenny surmise that their efforts, in thought and meditation, to bring Dan back into the group may have culminated in his being laid off from work.

Jenny:	Why were you laid off?
Louise:	I prayed that he would be on days.
Dan:	*But* I'm laid off.
Jenny:	Well, I prayed, too, that something would happen to bring you back into the group. I said "Don't let it affect his income, but . . . "
Dan:	I may have to pray that you two will stop praying!

But Dan does not really mind his time off. Supplemental Unemployment Benefits alleviate the financial burden, and having time off gives him time to read and to think. Dan dresses casually, yet presents a studious appearance, and indeed considers himself "studious." Dan has been told by psychics that he has a talent for writing and has taken writing classes at the community college. Tonight he recommends two books he has been reading: *God Did Not Ordain Silence: Many Pray, Few Listen* and *Crack in the Cosmic Egg*.

Jenny then turns to Sara, "Do you have anything, Sara?" Sara explains that she felt she was "with" her friend Louise, when Louise was away visiting her parents:

Sara:	I felt Louise when she was down there. When Dan and I came over here that night I was sitting by the door like a good girl, and I could feel her nudging me [to get farther away from Dan]. And I was with Louise when she was away. I saw her with a woman, her mother, but I didn't recognize her as such because she had changed, aged, so much.
Jenny:	That's interesting. You astralled and didn't realize it.

Jenny has interpreted Sara's experience as an instance of "astral travel." Astral travel is an out-of-the-body experience in which the spirit travels, separate from the body, and can see and hear events.

43

Sara: Talk about astralling, this morning I was meditating, and talking out loud to God, too. "You have nothing to fear" came to me, so I ran around shutting the drapes, turned my chair to the East, and said, "God, God, God, God, God," and I went up, from my legs, and then I calmly came back. But I wasn't afraid. I didn't jump up like I had before. Yet I didn't want to go farther yet.

Jenny: That's 'cause you could still *think*.

Sara: Later today my sister came over. She couldn't figure out what was the matter with me, why I felt so good. I felt wonderful. I could see the sun, but my sister couldn't. She said, "What's the matter with you; it's raining out." I said, "I feel great."

Jenny: You can preprogram yourself to come back in fifteen minutes. Watch the clock and you will.

Sara: I can't find words to express what I feel.

Jenny: True peace and tranquility. Inner peace comes only with God.

Dan: Good-bye world, I'm headed for better places.

Sara is in a good mood tonight—one might almost say effusive —but some evenings she is less so. Sara has borne guilt over the death of a relative. She has felt "haunted" by this person, or at least by his memory. In private consultations, Jenny counseled Sara to accept the fact that the death was not her fault. She instructed Sara to write the names of people who needed forgiveness on pieces of paper, and burn them, in order to "release" guilt and memories. Sara did this, and found it to be successful, although she had to do it twice (because the first time she "didn't really believe"). All this, however, took place in private consultation with Jenny. Within the study group, there were only vague allusions to this problem and cure of Sara's.

Jenny: How about you, Beverly, do you have anything to share?

Beverly, a metaphysical novice, reports that she has nothing psychic to share, but asks Sara how she meditates because, Beverly

44

says, "I can't do it yet." Sara, Dan, and John give Beverly advice on how to meditate. Then Jenny advises: "Pick one phase of your life. Think about it for five minutes. Why is it important? Why do I go back to this? What should I learn from this? What was I really like then? Because I think you have some clearing out to do."

At this point, although Sara's "turn" at describing psychic experiences has passed, she speaks again, picking up where she left off in describing her meditation experience.

Sara:	When my husband came home, he said, "You look good, and happy. What have you been doing?" I said, "I made curtains, and left my body."
Jenny:	I like your honesty!
Sara:	One night this week I knew my husband was eating nuts upstairs in the dark. He asked me, "How do you know I'm eating nuts? How do you know? The light's not on." My husband has had his own experiences, but he won't open up to it. My daughter, Ann, she's eleven, is sensitive and attuned. At school the other day she knew someone was feeling sad even though she was walking far behind them. It's only in the last six months that I've known enough to realize this about my daughter. She's very interested in it.
Jenny:	Your husband is skeptical. I'm always skeptical, too.
Beverly:	Sara has a glow around her tonight.

John, Beverly's husband, is the next to report. He discusses the problems he is having at his job as a plant manager.

John:	I had a fight with my boss this morning. He came saying when am I going to have something done. I said, "I don't know. I don't have enough help." At noon I meditated. Then I felt better. He came back in the afternoon and apologized. He really doesn't know anything.
Jenny:	You have to put him in the Light.
John:	At work I have conflicts with a couple of people. It's out-of-sight-out-of-mind with the general manager. But with

45

	my boss, it's no good. I have good rapport with the men on the floor.
Beverly:	I have to get him out of there, don't I?
John:	I only work there for the money. There are many things I'd rather do.
Jenny:	Melinda?
Melinda:	None.
Jenny:	Just been a peaceful week?
Melinda:	Well, not exactly. Remember I told you I had to go home to a wedding? We missed it. My mom got confused on the time and we got there at the end, instead of the beginning. And the new replacement door on our car rattled all the way there and back.
Jenny:	You should put it in the Light and ask God to remove the rattle (Study Group:3/19/75). What about you, Laura, do you have anything to share?

Laura has just returned from a trip to see her family. She is close to her family. Her mother is deceased, but her father still lives in the home where she grew up. She sees the family whenever she has the chance, thinking nothing of making long trips by car to visit them.

Laura:	I went to C— this week. I just got back at 6:00. I met a lady, a friend of my mother's, who has children ranging from five to seventeen years of age. She has a quiet time for them. I'm going to do that when Keith gets old enough.
Jenny:	That's good. Some people get so they can't stand quiet. In their lives nothing is ever quiet (Study Group:2/26/75). Do you have anything to share this week, David?

David has gained some reknown in the local metaphysical network as a healer. He reports that he was asked to "do something for a cancer patient," a friend of Grace's. David relates that he thought it was a "pretty big assignment" but then he recalled that "it's not me doing it." That is, God is actually doing the healing.

46

God works through the healer. "Healing is God using you like a hose through which water flows" (Study Group:2/19/75). The healer may serve to concentrate, or focus God's energy. The healer may also direct the ailing person's own energy to the unhealthy area. Laying-on-of-hands healing is "asking God to use your hands for his" (Study Group:4/16/75). David reports:

> *David:* There were forces at work to get us there before she had to go to radium treatment. We had twenty minutes with her. The woman was nervous. After I worked with her, her mental state was better.
>
> *Jenny:* If you heal the mental only, that's enough (Study Group: 1/22/75). Do you have anything to share, Grace?

Grace reports on using metaphysical techniques to facilitate her work as a stenographer.

> *Grace:* In the courtroom Friday there was a criminal arraignment. The judge was speaking so fast, I thought I could never keep up. But then I said, "God, you do it," and the judge seemed to be speaking more slowly. The words were going through my head more slowly. The pressure to keep up is sometimes too much. But this aids concentration (Study Group:10/15/75).
>
> *Jenny:* Good.
>
> *John:* Grace, did you get rid of your cold?
>
> *Grace:* No.
>
> *Jenny:* We'll get rid of it yet (Study Group:3/5/75).

Jenny then relates her own "psychic experience of the week." She tells of a message she received during a message circle. In a message circle, a medium gives a personal "message" to each individual in the room, in turn. Message circles are sometimes used as a sort of "party" entertainment. This message circle was held in Jenny's home, and led by Lily, a friend of Jenny's who is a Spiritualist minister-medium.

Jenny: My experience this week was over the weekend. Friday when Lily was here for the message circle, she asked if my son, Ron, had fixed anything lately. I said, "I hope not." He's not very good at fixing things, you see. On Saturday Ron decided to defrost the refrigerator for me—with a knife. He broke all the wires. It would be $150.00 or so to get it fixed. He's out tonight looking for a new one for me. I didn't put him in the Light and say, "Don't touch anything," which is what I should have done, when Lily warned me (Study Group:3/19/75).

By 8:00 we have finished reporting our experiences for the week, and Jenny turns us to the lesson in the book, *Know Yourself*. The first part of the lesson tonight is "Prayer."[13] Those who have brought their books turn to the lesson.

Jenny: What is prayer?

Louise: Talking to God.

David: Isn't prayer really talking it *over* with God?

Jenny: Well, that's where you get prayer and meditation. Prayer is talking to God. Meditation is listening to God.

Sara: It's the presence of God feeling here and now. I can talk to God anytime. It doesn't have to be a certain time, at night or anything.

Jenny: Your whole life should be a prayer.

David: Most people don't go to God with their concerns until it's too late.

Dan: I always start to pray, then I think, "But God already knows this, because God is aware of everything," and I have to change my whole mode of approach.

Jenny: What is ineffective prayer?

Sara: God has only been in my life the last two or three years. I haven't had an ineffective prayer.

David: I think an ineffective drive-up to getting any kind of power to listen to you is one that is negative.

Jenny: Beverly?

Beverly: I can't think of anything.

Jenny: John?

John:	People who ask for the same thing over and over. I'm not going to say, "If You want it this way." Rather, "Ask and ye shall receive."
Sara:	Who's going to say to God, *if* this or that, anyway?
Jenny:	Some people.
John:	It's a psychological out for them.
Dan:	Prayer without belief is a nonprayer. But don't believe you'll get all. There is such a thing as a negative answer, but this is not an ineffective prayer.
Jenny:	I've heard it said that if you ask for something three or four times and it doesn't happen—consider the answer no.
David:	And once you give it to God, don't look over God's shoulder, to see if he's doing it right.
Louise:	I've asked God for things I need. God knows I needed it. Before I met Dan I had five kids to take care of.
Jenny:	Which is the most effective prayer in a group like this, to say, "God, heal so-and-so," or "God, heal all the children in the world?"
Louise:	The specific, because of the force focus.
Jenny:	Specificity, visualizing one person, is best. It's more effective. You can form a mental picture of what has to be done. If you're wishy-washy, for example, "Lord, give me some money," rather than saying what you need it for, it won't work as well. Visualize the bills paid.
David:	You can pray for what you need, but also for what you want.
Jenny:	But you have to be careful that you *really* want it. "Lord, help me deal with each day" is the best prayer. A woman I know prayed that her son wouldn't have to go into the army. She prayed and prayed that he wouldn't have to go into the army. Then he had an accident that caused him to have concussions, and to be blind in one eye. He won't go into the army. He can hardly hold a job. So watch out. This is why I say you have to be careful that you really want it. If you just say you want money, it may come from a death. A thought form has a lot of repercussions. An energy force is in a thought. Through thought we kept a storm from coming down here. Elsewhere it was very bad.

49

> If you watch, you'll see that storms go on either side of this area.

Beverly became concerned about this, and voiced the fear that if a storm was caused not to hit her, then it would hit someone else. Jenny reassured her: "No, you just say, 'Use me as an instrument to keep it from hitting.' It doesn't have to hit anywhere" (Study Group:2/12/75). This episode illustrates a facet of Beverly's character that she does not share with most other metaphysical students. A characteristic of many in the metaphysical world is a self-reflection that often seems, on the surface at least, to manifest itself in self-centeredness. Beverly was particularly devoid of this self-centeredness. Only Beverly was concerned that, by protecting oneself, one might therefore hurt others. Beverly's lack of self-interest surfaced in other ways, too. She listened when others talked. She could remember facts about fellow study group members that others could not. She often brought in stories of people who needed help, whom she had met through her job as a cashier. One of the study group lessons counseled that a person must "love himself first" in order to grow spiritually and to be able to love and help others. Only Beverly needed to be convinced of this, and indeed there was a major effort to convince her that she must "love yourself first." This was the only time I witnessed anyone actively try to convince another of a belief or principle.

Jenny reads from the *Know Yourself* book's lesson on prayer:

> The book says about ineffective prayer: "An ineffective way to pray is to pray negatively, such as 'Dear God I can't get rid of my impatience but I am trying.' This is ineffective. Pray positively. God is a creator and so is man. Man can create or destroy with his thoughts. There is love, truth, and every good attribute all around us. We need to seek it and recognize it. We have the ability to create moods, attitudes and conditions. God is individualized in each one of us. You are one thought. God is undivided in us. It is up to us to tune in with this force and to function within it. If you wish to hear a particular radio program, you must first tune in to the right station. We must tune into this force called God or Cosmic Consciousness or whatever you

prefer to call it. We tune in by meditation on the features of the spirit which are truth, intelligence, knowledge, life and every other positive loving thought. Can we expect God to change us and our conditions if we do not believe it can happen?" (Hayes 1971:33)

Then Jenny reads from her notes on a lecture on the same subject, given by James Bonacci at the area retreat:

Make prayer positive. Positive prayer is receptive prayer. It is affirmative prayer, recognizing that God is a loving Father and that whatsoever we ask, believing, affirming, we shall receive. We do not beg or beseech God. (Bonacci 1976b)

Jenny summarizes the essence of these passages by saying, in her matter-of-fact way, "You have to have faith" (Study Group: 1/29/75).

Jenny:	OK, the second part of the lesson tonight is "Hate or Misguided Love." Most people don't like to admit they have any feelings of hate. What are some of your negative emotions? Where do they come from and how do they manifest themselves? How about you, Louise?
Louise:	I get negative at work. I say, "Change me or change the condition." If I have problems with someone, I always say, "God, change me. Help me as well as the other person." I've prayed to God for guidance to help me understand a neighbor's situation. And sewing calms me.
Jenny:	Dan, how about you?
Dan:	I hate unexpected visitors. I require time to myself. I think it helps me to write a problem down. I have to get it out of my system. I write letters, lots of letters. I used to work for Acme Machine Tool. In 1956 I mentioned a union meeting and they fired me. I typed a four-page letter to the owner.
Jenny:	How about you, Sara?
Sara:	I'm negative a lot. But I'm working on it.
Jenny:	Well, Beverly?
Beverly:	I've been a biddy at work this week.

Jenny:	John?
John:	I have negative feelings toward the corporation and the people there. I manifest it by verbalizing or walking out.
Jenny:	You have to put a Light around your boss. Put him in the proper perspective. How about you, Melinda?
Melinda:	I'm sometimes negative at work, if I don't get enough praise for what I do, or if the people I work around tell me their troubles all day.
Jenny:	You want attention.
Melinda:	Yes, I guess so, recognition. Perhaps it's an ego thing.
Jenny:	And people are drawn to you. People tell you their troubles, their life histories. They might be drawn by your energy. But you can close off.

Jenny advises me to "close my chakras," which are centers of psychic energy in the body. Chakras may open during meditation, or "if you get to feeling too good." But they should be kept closed during everyday activity, lest a person feel too sensitive to the vibrations of others around him. Jenny advises me to "close your chakras by a motion like zipping yourself up. Or cross your arms and legs. Don't feel guilty about it."

Jenny:	Laura, how about you?
Laura:	I get involved with my own thinking. I don't like people who say they'll do something and then don't.
Jenny:	David?
David:	When I get so many interruptions, constantly interruptions, I become negative (Study Group:1/22/75).
Jenny:	How about you Grace?
Grace:	I can be aloof and critical. I need to get to know people well (Study Group:6/4/75).
Jenny:	As for me, I can get angry, though it takes a lot. I can be very, very stubborn. My kids feel guilty saying "no" to me because I never say "no" to them. Sometimes I get revenge —put the knife in and twist. I'm a Virgo. A Virgo is very critical, and has a lot to overcome. But it's the little things that bother us the most, like interruptions, or the toothpaste tube squeezed in the middle. When things bother

52

you, ask yourself, "Will it make a difference five years from now, or one month from now?"

Dan: Or is it important enough for me to destroy this minute of my life over?

Jenny paraphrases from *Know Yourself*:

Many people are quick to find fault or emphasize negative conditions. Others are quick to look at situations as positively as possible, looking at all the alternatives. Where on a Richter scale of negative to positive would you say you are? How positive are you?

The study group members report, in an around-the-room fashion. Sara reports that she is "99.5% to 49.5% positive." Laura is "90% positive. Life is what you expect of it. You cause misery yourself." Dan reports that he is "99% positive." He says he tries to "keep a happy face and a glad hand. If you're happy, this will mirror back at you. If you snarl, you'll end up surrounded by a snarling bunch of people." This is confirmed by Jenny, who says, "That's true. If you give love, you receive love." Everyone else reports being somewhere between "80% positive" to "98% positive."

John and David say they used to be negative, but are becoming more positive. Jenny says, "There are very few things in life which cannot be changed."

Jenny: In the beginning we were all perfect. And we can be again. It's a matter of becoming aware of that divine inner self, that spark that's within all of us. I can always say, "I love the God within that person," even if I am angered by what he is doing (Study Group:1/22/75). I can love that part of him that's part of God, because that's part of me, too (Study Group:3/19/75).

(I saw this concept in action at the SFF National Conference. The conference shared its hotel headquarters with a hardware salesmen's convention. A salesman, somewhat less than sober, wandered into SFF's hospitality suite and asked one of the women present, "Do you love me?" She replied that she loved everyone. He turned to Jenny: "Do you love me, too?" She responded, "I love the God within you." The salesman did not understand, but he was nevertheless impressed with the reception he had received.)

The homework for this lesson was to identify a fault we wished to get rid of, and to think of the positive thing to put in its place. *Know Yourself* advised:

> During meditation each day visualize yourself breathing in the desired quality and breathing out the fault. If you are good at visualizing, literally pump yourself full of God's love and let the overflow push away the unwanted negative fault. . . . This will be a great aid in helping to change our old patterns. Use the energy of God's love, rather than our own negative feelings, to renew our positive energy. The keynote is patience. (Hayes 1971:30)

Jenny:	What is the fault you chose for your homework, and what are you doing about it? Grace, what's yours? (Study Group:1/29/75).
Grace:	My fault is that I don't relax enough. I am either going like Hades, or sound asleep. I'm trying to take time to relax, when I come home from work. And my ceramics class is very relaxing (Study Group:6/4/75).
Jenny:	Good. David?
David:	Procrastination is my biggest fault. I was going to class Tuesday, and I thought I'd be five minutes early. Just as I went to shave, I got three phone calls. I was five minutes late to class.
Jenny:	Were they important calls?
David:	No.
Jenny:	If a person is calling for a reason, if they're blue or something, I don't mind talking. But some people just have nothing else to do, and I call those nuisance calls. What's your fault, Laura?
Laura:	My fault is that I don't always spend money wisely. I'm working on it, trying to keep better track of where it goes.

But I just can't be stingy (Study Group:1/29/75). I send money to a friend who's out of work—no use hoarding it. When I begin thinking about money—thinking "Where will it come from?"—then I get some from here and there (Study Group:2/12/75).

Jenny: Yes, you get what you give. It's a natural law. You have to give to receive. When you give, you should expect something in return. A vessel can only fill up so far, then something must be taken out.

David: You may not get money in return.

Jenny: Right. You might get a bargain here or there, things like that (Study Group:10/1/75). It's a good thing I don't have to worry about money. I'm not at all concerned with the material side of life. What have you been working on, Melinda?

Melinda: My fault is that I tell my husband all the bad things that happen to me, and that's all I tell him. I should tell him the good, as well as the bad. I've been doing that. I even made a list of good things to tell him.

Jenny: Good. John?

John: I've been putting my boss in the Light. I tend to give things to God, then I take them back again. I take over from God. I should give it to Him and leave it.

Jenny: Right. What about you Beverly?

Beverly reports that her fault is when she has a migraine headache, she does not tell John. One of the things John and Beverly are trying to do with metaphysics is to find a way to heal Beverly of the migraine headaches that plague her, but which she tries to downplay. She has seen several doctors of various sorts, including a psychiatrist whom she did not like, and has taken Valium for these headaches. She reported having withdrawal symptoms when she decided to stop taking Valium.

Beverly: I finally told John I had a headache on Friday night. He finished dinner for me, and everyone helped with the jobs around the house. I used some medication. I don't like to take medication, and John doesn't like for me to, but I didn't want to be in bed all day Saturday. And I got better. I don't know why, but it just kills me to tell him I have a headache.

John: Then that makes it worse.

Beverly: Yes, I think it helps to tell him.

Jenny: Sara?

Sara: I asked my family to choose a fault. It took my husband about ten minutes to come out with it. He said I get my defenses, my armor, up too often. I worked on it. I knew when I did it. He told me, too. I'm making progress (Study Group:1/29/75).

Jenny: That's a step in the right direction. All of you should continue to work on it until it's no longer a problem. What are you working on Dan?

Dan: My problem is traffic. I am impatient with other drivers. By saying the word "God," I preempt my anger, and have some control over the other drivers.

Jenny: Saying the word "God" raises your vibrations. There's more a oneness with everyone around you, more harmony. Saying the word "God" raises a negative emotion into a mental state which says—"wait a minute" (Study Group:1/22/75).

Sara: Dan, you should have heard what Louise said about your driving on the way over here.

Louise: I guess that's one of *my* faults. In the car, I want him to go where *I tell* him to go.

Dan: She backseat drives!

Louise: The thing I've been working on is not to be critical of others, and to avoid forming first opinions.

John: That can be a problem. There was a kid in the plant I thought had his thumb up his tail and his head in the clouds. I was going to tell him. Then one day he walked away with a white cane. He was doing filing and deburring. I told the other supervisor about it. I would have really felt terrible if I had chewed him out.

David: But Louise, you have the opportunity to make judgments because of the people who work around you.

Louise: That's true. For example, there's a rule that no relatives can work in the same department. A girl lied to get a job. She denied she was a sister of another cashier. I was training her, and she told me. I thought this was pretty bad, that she lied on the application. But later I recommended her for a place in the office, when the boss asked me, because she had been a good worker, and was smart.

Jenny: I don't think it should make any difference if they are relatives.

Louise: Well, there is a theft problem with employees, and it's often relatives.

Jenny: You have to know when to judge, and when not.

Louise: Well, we're not here to judge people.

Jenny: My fault is that I'm too available. I've been relegating things. It's working. This helps where my family is concerned. They don't get enough attention (Study Group: 1/29/75).

At 8:45 we turned to the ESP experiment for this lesson. Jenny gave each of us a piece of paper and a pencil. Laura volunteered to be the "guinea pig" who would sit in the middle of the room, where all of us could see her. Jenny explained the experiment to us:

There are many different kinds of extrasensory perception. One kind is clairvoyance, another is clairsentience. Clairvoyance is being able to see pictures. Some of it comes in symbols, some of it you actually see. Clairsentience is what we just know. We don't know how we know, we don't see anything, but we just know. Then there's sensitivity, which is feeling something from a person. Now, I want you all to look at Laura, and keep mentally thinking "Laura." View her until you can close your eyes and see a picture of her in your mind. Then go beyond that and see what you pick up when you look at her and think "Laura." See what vibrations you pick up, or what kinds of impressions, pictures, or feelings that may come to your mind. No matter how far out they may seem. Write it down anyhow. For instance, if you suddenly see a parrot, and you think, what's a parrot got to do with the whole thing, or a whirlwind, or anything like this, write it down, because it can have something to do with some part of her life. All right?

For about twenty minutes we look at Laura, concentrate on her, and jot things on our pieces of paper.

57

Jenny:	Everybody about done? All right Louise, let's start with you, and then Laura can comment on the things each one of you picked up (Study Group:1/8/75).
Louise:	I got heat, which is healing, and lightning. I shook my head to see if it was there, when I saw it.
Jenny:	That could be healing too. That's how I send the healing sometimes, psoom! (Study Group:1/22/75).
Laura:	Maybe I need healing for my cold.
Jenny:	How about you, Dan, what did you pick up?
Dan:	Closing my eyes and concentrating about the person, I picked up a rainbow and beneath it a door, but I have no idea what this means.
Jenny:	What did you get? A rainbow over a door?
Dan:	It didn't happen to be in a building or anything else—just a door standing out with a rainbow over the top.
Jenny:	Was it shut?
Dan:	Yes.
Jenny:	OK. Usually the door means an opening. The rainbow is there. This usually represents the presence of God. In other words, a spiritual awakening. All she's got to do is just open the door and go through. She has it closed yet, but she's going to open it. Then what else, anything else?
Dan:	Well, there was also a brilliant rectangle of blue—seemed to be about like 10 inches long, and then a white "L," which was the end of it. I couldn't figure out what that was.
Jenny:	Well, blue represents healing. The average person usually has blue around them, if they're in good health, and well-balanced, and everything is gong the way it's supposed to. The "L" could represent the initial of somebody, or it could represent love.
Dan:	At the end of a blue rectangle. It formed the end of the rectangle. I saw it repeatedly. I opened my eyes.
Jenny:	It's very important to you. May mean you're going to get more from it later. I would say you got quite a bit (Study Group:1/15/75). Sara, what did you get?
Sara:	I pass.
Jenny:	Didn't you get anything? OK, Beverly?

58

Beverly:	I don't do too well on these things. I was thinking about the baby, but I already knew about that.
Jenny:	What about you, John?
John:	I didn't get anything.
Jenny:	Try again. Do you think I'm going to let you get away that easily?
John:	I hear a sound.
Jenny:	Maybe you're developing clairaudience.

John reports that Tom Pix, a Spiritualist minister and medium who is Lily's assistant minister and a friend of Jenny's, also told him that in a message.

Jenny:	Not everybody sees things. Some know, sense, feel, or hear (Study Group:2/19/75).
	How about you, Melinda?
Melinda:	Well, I think her baby's a girl.
Laura:	There's a 50/50 chance.
Jenny:	Are you sure? We just got that it was a boy.
Melinda:	Well, then I got "friend." So it could be that her friend's baby is a girl, then I'm off the hook.
Jenny:	I could be wrong.
Melinda:	No, you're probably right.[14]
Jenny:	David?
David:	No, I didn't get anything.
Jenny:	Grace, how about you?
Grace:	I smelled clover.
Laura:	I've been thinking about a garden.
Jenny:	I picked you up as very strong. In fact you're very unbending at times. Also, you have a very, very strong sense of duty. And your home is your castle. You like things your way in your home.
Laura:	It's a good thing Bob [Laura's husband] isn't here.
Jenny:	I picked up children. And you can't help becoming involved. If somebody is around and you like them, or somebody gives you their troubles, you get involved in it, very definitely. If strangers tell you their life histories,

59

	they are seeing the peacemaker in you. It's a release for them. But you shouldn't become emotionally involved. Just say, "This person has problems, God, help her." And I feel loneliness, but I felt this was in the past, but very deep.
Laura:	Ummmm.
Jenny:	And you're happier now. And I feel lots and lots of light. Many things opening up within yourself now—just beginning to see and feel experiences you never thought possible before.
Laura:	That's really true about being bullheaded.
Jenny:	I didn't say you were bullheaded. I said you were very firm and strong. You rule your home.
Laura:	Well, not all the time.
Jenny:	No, but you like it a certain way. You have preconceived ideas of how things should be.
Laura:	Yes, that's true (Study Group:1/8/75).
John:	This kind of stuff is generalities. If you talk long enough, anyone is bound to relate to something, or else they're dead! I don't put too much stock in it (Study Group: 7/23/75).

John always remained "skeptical" about certain metaphysical ideas and practices. He called some of the things Joe discussed in his classes "hogwash," and dubbed a medium at one of the Spiritualist churches a "fake." Yet John did not try to persuade anyone else of his doubts on this score, for as he frequently said, "Different strokes for different folks." By the same token, no one tried to convince John to embrace that which he, at the moment, rejected. Jenny's reply to John was: "Well, it may help people see themselves, or know themselves. But you don't really need to be psychic to figure out what most people need to hear" (Study Group:2/19/75).

At 9:30 Jenny turns out all the lights, and everyone slides back into their chairs, in preparation for meditation. Most people close their eyes, and sit with their hands on their laps, palms upward. The palms upward gesture allows God's love and energy to flow into and through a person. Jenny softly, slowly, gives us instructions for relaxing, and getting into the meditative frame of mind.

> *Jenny:*   Relax your feet, now stretch them as if you are growing—now relax and let the tension go. Relax the ankles and the thighs, releasing all the tense muscles. Next relax the hips —relax—now the tummy—take two deep breaths, breathe in God's love and energy that are in the air all around us—hold it, feel it—now as you exhale, let the energy flow to the rest of the group. Relax the neck —relax the head (Hayes 1971:31).

Jenny then gives us a "meditation subject" that is meant to aid concentration and provide inspiration for insight.

> *Jenny:*   Dwell on this thought: "Because of my awakened spiritual consciousness and my growing faith in the God presence within me and within all men, there are good changes in my life. I am overcoming suspicions and negative imaginings concerning others and myself. I am consistently replacing such feelings with trust and confidence in my fellow man" (Hayes 1971:31; Study Group: 1/22/75). Now turn your thoughts within. For the next few moments let this thought lift you: I am one with the universe.

The meditation subjects used in the class sessions were often phrases with sacred meaning, like the "I am one with the universe" used here. Other subjects of this nature included: "There is no way to peace, for peace is the way"; "Be still and know that I am God"; or "What a man desires is already within him, but he still wanders here and there in search of it." The meditation subject was sometimes a monosyllabic sound such as "Ohm," or an object such as a candle flame, or a bowl of earth or water (representing the essential elements) on which the meditator fixes his gaze and concentrates. About half the time, Jenny read longer "led meditations," or "mental trips," which the meditators followed. The trips ended with a question, followed by silence, during which the group members meditated on this question. For example, one such trip took the meditators to a room, which they furnished and colored in their own way. The room was meant to represent their own inner selves. While "in" this room, the question "What is my purpose in life?" was followed by several minutes of silent meditation.

Tonight we sit in the silent darkness for about fifteen minutes, and meditate on "I am one with the universe."

> *Jenny:* Come back now. Wiggle your toes and your hands. Open your eyes.

Jenny turns on some dim lights.

> *Jenny:* Did you have any experiences you want to share? Louise?
> *Louise:* I was thinking, if everyone thought healing, there would be no disease. But first you must go within. Then I got this sharp pain at my heart.
> *Jenny:* There must have been something there—love—still unhealed. You healed it just then. You released it.

This exchange between Louise and Jenny may seem peremptory and vague to the reader. But Jenny frequently knows more about members' backgrounds and problems than the other group members do. Study group members discuss problems with Jenny outside the class. Thus the vagueness assures that the person spoken to "knows" what Jenny is referring to, but it is not revealed to anyone else. A characteristic of Spiritualist argot, some of which is used in SFF, is its referential vagueness. One function of this is to shield Spiritualists from prosecution under fortune-telling laws (Zaretsky 1969, 1972). It may also keep group members from becoming too informed about one another's private affairs. In this particular example, Jenny and Louise know specifically what "still unhealed love" Louise has just healed, but the other members may not.

Jenny: What did you get, Dan?

Dan: I saw a field of wheat, in the distance and off to the left, and then the words came to me "this is yours."

Jenny: That's good. It probably means supply, a bountiful supply. Since it was to the left, it means that it's in your future. Ask and ye shall receive (Study Group: 4/16/75).

Dan: And then I felt like I was only in my head. The rest of my body didn't matter. I didn't want to come back. That "one with the universe" is the best thing I ever meditated on.

Jenny: You'll soon go beyond that and be out of your body entirely. Then you just are.

"I are what?" Dan asks, and the class breaks with laughter, as it so often does. Dan can be very stern and serious-looking, but his "one-liner" banter with Jenny bowls the class over with giggles. Dan continues his query: "What about coming back from a state like that? I hardly want to come back now." Jenny assures him that he will come back because he is "tied with the silver cord," which is thought to join the soul to the body.

Jenny: Did you feel the energy, the love of God flowing through you?

Sara: You know what that feels like to me? It starts from my toes and it goes right up, all the way up to here. Sometimes I've had it so strong that it feels like just a vibration all the way through. It feels something like that. It's overwhelming. And it's something that, really, you can just feel it. It starts right down here and you can just feel it. It goes right up through you. I feel so different. If I find myself in any kind of trouble with myself, any kind of problem or anything, I turn myself to God, just tune myself into God. And I just vibrate from my feet right up to the top of my head. I mean all the way through. You can just feel it.

Jenny: It does, it puts you back in tune with all that's around and about you, without all the heaviness and depression, and anxiety. It seems to just wipe it all out.

63

Sara:	There's no medicine on the market—no doctor can do it. There's no words for it. You have to experience it to really know it. If you really experience and you know it, there are no words for it (Study Group:1/8/75).
Jenny:	Beverly, what about you?
Beverly:	I felt relaxed. I'm not really into it.
Jenny:	John?

John feels some of the metaphysical literature and beliefs to which he has been exposed have truly changed his life. He describes a "before" of alcoholic indulgence, ulcers, and high blood pressure, which have now abated.

John:	I was thinking about Sara saying she was negative, during the lesson. I recommend the book *Prayer Can Change Your Life* by William Parker to people. There are self-evaluation tests in the book that are really useful. I used to hide in the bottle. When I began Joe's class, I had a bleeding ulcer, and high blood pressure, and my back was bothering me all the time. Joe's class was a beginning. It raised questions. One nice thing about metaphysics. The things you read are written by humans. All of them have human errors. You can look at it with an open mind and believe what you want to believe, take the best from each one of them, and be able to sit in the class with instructions. You can say, "I don't believe that crap" on one segment. Next breath he says something that might be interesting. So Joe created a lot of question marks in my mind that caused me to do some research on my own. By reading books—*Prayer Can Change Your Life*, which Jenny recommended to me, and other books—I learned more. For me, there's been no smoking or drinking in four months. and I had no withdrawal from smoking this time. My ulcer hasn't bothered me. In fact, as far as I'm concerned, it's gone. My blood pressure doesn't bother me. And I am looking at things a little differently. I'm not concerned with what someone else says anymore (Study Group:1/8/75; 1/22/75).
Jenny:	Melinda, do you have anything you want to share?

Melinda:	I was thinking of that poem, "You are a child of the universe, no less than the trees or the stars" (Study Group: 4/16/75). There were no pictures.
Jenny:	You're going beyond that. So that's why I got what I did for you (Study Group:1/29/75). Laura?
Laura:	I saw a farm. The fields had just been disked. There was grass, and clouds. And I felt one with nature.
Jenny:	Sounds beautiful. David?
David:	I saw blue lights. I don't know what they're trying to tell me.
Jenny:	I would say that's more and more healing coming in (Study Group: 4/16/75). Grace?
Grace:	I wasn't conscious of my body.

Grace's meditation is interpreted as an "out-of-body experience" or "astral travel." Now Laura reveals her skepticism about her own ability, or desire, to astral travel.

Laura:	I never go anyplace, believe me. I stay right here. I can't fathom that tripping around you guys do.
Beverly:	I can't either.
Laura:	That would be like teaching me Chinese (Study Group: 6/4/75).
John:	Different strokes for different folks.

Jenny adds her agreement to John's way of expressing a metaphysical axiom—everyone must do and believe just as his own self or level of understanding allows him to. The metaphysicians claim to maintain a healthy skepticism, even if to the outsider it would appear that they do not.

Grace continues her description of her meditation experience:

Grace:	And I saw the church I went to as a girl. I felt good with it. That church isn't there any longer.
Jenny:	Going to something that's no longer there might mean that you're clinging to the past. We've got to get you going forward now.

Grace:	That's interesting.
Jenny:	It's security for you, knowing that foundation in the past. You've got to expand on that and get going higher and higher. You still have some strong ties to the past. But you're working that out (Study Group:5/14/75). I got things on all of you tonight. I visualized each of you. David, for you I got hands in prayer, but making the shape of a pyramid. Have you been interested in pyramids?
David:	No, not really.
Jenny:	Well, maybe you should be. For Grace, I got a crown, like knowledge opening up. Beverly, I got stars above your head, and the message that they're not as far away as you think they are. You can reach up and take one. For Melinda I got a small gold key and the inscription "There are many doors to open." Dan and Louise, I saw a gold chariot with both of you in it.
Dan:	Who was driving?
Jenny:	I think you still had the reins. It meant that you would get along well together.
Dan:	We've had ten wonderful years. I don't think it will change.

Dan's eyes hold a look of deep affection as he nods toward Louise, whom he sometimes calls his "beloved wife." She returns his affectionate glance.

Jenny:	John, I saw you with the Bible, looking for answers. *And* I saw you spreading the word. You were meant to. Laura, I saw gold coins going out of a purse, and going back in, for you. Sara, for you I got a gold rose, just like a real one, with thorns and all. It was just opening up. The opening means spiritual development. And gold is oneness with God (Study Group:1/29/75).

Now, at 10:00, it is time for the Healing Circle, which will end the class meeting. Members are to list anyone who needs healing physically, mentally, or spiritually. "Needs may involve health, employment, family stress, or any other 'hurdle' currently facing someone" (SFF 1976f). Everyone stands and joins hands.

Jenny: OK, I want you to close your eyes and get that peace and that love right around you. Feel almost like you're standing in a circle of Light. Visualize in your mind, that Light going right around your feet, up through your body, and round and round like a cocoon, until it comes all the way up to your head. Then I want you to take that Light and split it in half and feel it flowing down your arms and to the person on either side of you, and going down through their bodies, healing, cleansing, and making them whole. And as you feel the warmth coming back into your own body, give it out into the circle, until the circle is full, and the Light flows through the circle, until it can no longer hold it. And the Light begins to spread out further, and further. Let's begin with Grace on my right, and have her place anybody's name in the circle for healing who is on her mind. Then when she is finished, she will place herself in the circle. When she's done then we'll go right on around (Study Group:1/8/75).

Eyes are closed. Each member in turn recites the names of four or five people, and then says "and myself." Jenny and David keep lists of people who have asked to be prayed for, and, rather than listing all these names, they say, "All those on my prayer list." (Subsequently John also acquired a prayer list.) As David intones his list: "Jane Allee, James, my wife, all those on my prayer list, myself," his body shakes with each name.

Attesting to her concern for others, Beverly's list includes "the woman who came into the store last week who only has six weeks to live, my mother and father, my in-laws, and those I didn't think of, and myself." There is a protective as well as a healing aspect to the healing circle; the same family and friends, who may not be sick or troubled, are listed week after week as a means of assuring their continued well-being. To this basic list are added names of people who are of concern on a more temporary basis.

67

Throughout the naming of names, Jenny's hands have slowly risen, carrying along Louise and Grace's hands on either side of her, and causing a chain reaction around the circle. Now our hands, still joined, are shoulder high. After repeating her list of names, Jenny ends the healing circle:

Jenny: We praise thy grace, O God, for thou has said where two or more are gathered, there am I also. And so we know before we even ask, that thou has already taken care of that which must be done. Now, in the name of the Son, who taught us all to pray,

Unison: Our Father, who art in heaven, hallowed be thy name. Thy kingdom come, thy will be done, on earth as it is in heaven. Give us this day our daily bread, and forgive us our trespasses, as we forgive those who trespass against us. And lead us not into temptation, but deliver us from evil. For thine is the kingdom, and the power, and the glory, forever. Amen.

Our eyes open and our arms come down, hands still joined.

Jenny: Peace be with you. Peace be with all of you (Study Group:1/28/76).

We loosen hands and step back from the circle.

Louise: My hands get so hot!
Sara: It's not just my hands that get hot!
David: Did you feel that energy coursing round?

The members sit down again and begin to talk informally. Sara is telling about her out-of-the-body experience. Dan is discussing the book *Crack in the Cosmic Egg* with John. Louise is talking about her trip to her folks with Beverly and Melinda. Jenny says, "Sit down here, Grace, let's work on your cold," and begins to "do a healing" on Grace. Jenny runs her hands along a line a few inches from Grace's body and then puts her hands on

68

Grace's head, at the back. David comes over and does the same, from the front (Study Group:6/11/75).

At 10:20, people begin to leave. As we move toward the back door, each person puts a dollar on Jenny's dining table, except Sara, who leaves two dollars.

Jenny, David, and Grace always go to a restaurant after class. Tonight Melinda, Sara, and Laura accompany them. Grace, David, and Sara go together. Jenny, who doesn't drive, rides with Melinda. When we arrive at the restaurant, we look for Joe, Barbara, and Nell, who come here every Wednesday evening after their study group meeting. Nell is a longtime student of Joe. She has driven sixty-seven miles from her home to Joe's classes twice a week for three years. (Joe and Barbara's study group ended in July, and then Nell joined our group.)

Nell is sixty, and is retired from ownership of a small gift shop. She is married to an executive, and is distressed by his lack of interest in the metaphysical world. She participates in Metro Area activities, and attends the Allen County Spiritualist Church. She has become friends with David through this church.

We rearrange the table and gather chairs to seat seven.

Nell:	Hi, Kitten.
Melinda:	Hi, Nell.
Nell:	Hello, David.
David:	And what have you been into tonight?
Melinda:	Nell, what have you done to deserve that?
David:	Don't ask. It would take her too long to answer.
Melinda:	How about the past two things you've done?
David:	That's more like it.
Nell:	He was my father, so he thinks he can say those things to me. Didn't discipline me then and look what happened.

Nell believes in reincarnation, and here she is referring to a prior life, during which she believes David was her father.

Joe begins to describe an event that occurred at an SFF workshop on "regression hypnosis" he attended. During "regression hypnosis" the subject is thought to recall scenes from prior lives. Joe explains that a psychiatrist who was having "family troubles" was "regressed" at the workshop.

Joe: The wife and daughter were jealous of his affection. It was a triangular relationship. So it turns out that the father and the daughter had been lovers in a prior incarnation.

Jenny: That's just what I would have thought. Without reincarnation, how could you explain that relationship?

Jenny and Joe's view of reincarnation is that a discarnate soul chooses its parents (and its body) at some point after an infant is conceived. While living on this earth, a person needs to work through any unresolved problems and conflicts from past lives, and ideally starts on the path to spiritual growth. After death the spirit can continue its growth "on the other side." Continued reincarnation is necessary until the person fully realizes his intrinsic divinity. At this point the person has "broken the wheel of Karma" and need not reincarnate again. He may choose to do so, however, usually in order to teach others. Jenny and Joe do not indoctrinate their students in this "cradle to grave and beyond" philosophy, however, and some students do not share this belief. The pattern of explaining current relationships by reference to prior incarnations, illustrated here by the case of the psychiatrist and his daughter, was typical of Joe and Jenny. Tonight it leads to a general discussion of reincarnation.

Grace: Sometimes I wonder why I am here this time around—why I chose the parents I did (Study Group:4/23/75).

Jenny: Well, I've had a very interesting life.

Melinda: Lives?

Jenny: No, it's all one life, just different manifestations of it.

Laura: I don't know if I believe in reincarnation. I can't see myself as a blob, or spark, of intelligence after death. That's the part I don't like (Study Group:1/21/76). And I wanted to see my family. If they reincarnate before I die, I won't get to see them?

Jenny: No, you'll see the personality they shared with you in this life.

Nell: I definitely believe in reincarnation. I think it explains a lot. Do you believe in reincarnation, Melinda?

Melinda: Well, to me it's a theory, as good as any other, but a theory.

Jenny: There's been nothing in your life to make you believe in it.

Melinda: Right (Study Group:5/28/75). David, what were you talking about before class—something about court?

David explains that he is a plaintiff in a lawsuit concerning an injury he sustained while working at his security job. He is undecided whether to settle out of court for a lump sum, "or go to court and ask for some different arrangement." David explains that he has fifteen days to make his decision and has consulted Jenny and five other mediums and psychics. "They were about evenly divided. But all in all the consensus seems to be a bird in the hand is worth two in the bush" (Study Group:1/28/76).

I ask David whether he uses his psychic abilities in his counseling work. He replies: "No, I don't like to think that I do. Yet I know that I do get impressions. I just don't talk about this kind of thing. Some of those men have had so many wild alcohol-induced hallucinations, this would really confuse them. They wouldn't know what to think!" (Field Notes:4/10/77).

Laura exclaims that she had "better be going home" because her husband, Bob, has to leave on a business trip in the morning.

Laura: He's had to go on several trips lately. He had to leave last Friday, and I was moping around. He didn't want to go. I didn't want him to go. Finally I said, "Why don't Keith and I go with you?" Bob said, "Would you really like to? I thought of that earlier but didn't say anything." So we went with him, and had a good time.

David: Isn't that called programming?

71

Jenny: Yes, pre-programming. You sent thought waves into the ethers. He picked them up.

Laura: Oh, so he thought it was his idea. That's clever— because I didn't know I was doing it.

Jenny: That way there's no guilt. He either accepts it or rejects it (Study Group:3/12/75).

Grace: Laura, I hope you didn't get your cold by sitting next to me. My cold has lasted so long.

Jenny: That's another example of programming. Don't say "my cold." You shouldn't claim it. You're programming yourself to keep it. It's that same energy force that's in a thought—the repercussion of a thought form I was talking about earlier. I hear mothers telling their kids "Put on your coat or you'll get a cold." They're programming them to catch one.

Sara: Louise is always telling her mother-in-law not to say "*my* arthritis, but *the* arthritis."

Nell: I know a woman who was always saying. "This gives me a pain in the posterior" about everything. And do you know what? She got hemorrhoids! (Study Group:6/11/75)

Jenny: Every ailment has a mental component.

Sara: Jenny, I wonder how much money we've all saved that would have gone to psychiatrists by coming to your classes.

Jenny: Well, it's like I say, in the old days, neighbors were friends, and people used to talk over the back fence and iron out their problems. They talked them over and got them out. Talking over the back fence was the best psychology ever. Now our pace is too fast to even *know* the neighbors. Today neighbors are often not close, and people don't want to air their dirty linen in public. But we have to get the problems out. If we don't, we just build more webs. People have to face it. They can go to psychiatrists or psychologists, but they are expensive, and fallible. So people come to groups like this, and to me.

Sara: I think this class has changed all of us—changed our outlook.

Grace: Yes, I do too.

Laura: Yes, I agree.

72

Sara: I think everyone has helped everyone else. At least everyone has helped me.

Jenny: Everyone has helped everyone else. Or we wouldn't have the harmony that we have (Study Group: 4/16/75). Well, I have some people coming tomorrow morning, and it's 11:30, so I expect I'd better be getting home. As it is, I'll have to say, "OK God, I have to sleep fast tonight."

The group breaks up to go their separate ways. During the week the members will not see each other, except for Sara and Louise, who are neighbors, and David and Louise who attend the same Spiritualist church. Beverly and Laura may call each other. Laura, John, David, or Louise may call Jenny in mid-week.

The "help" everyone has given everyone else mentioned by the group members is purely "spiritual" in nature. Psychologists would say it is "social support." These group members are not part of a community of devotees in which financial burdens or work load is shared. Even in situations where it seems it would be warranted, physical or monetary aid is neither expected nor forthcoming. (The one exception to this is that the group members do share rides.)

For example, one evening Lorraine, who attended our study group for a short time, mentioned that her house was a "total wreck" and if she could just get it clean once, she thought she could handle keeping it clean. I thought to myself, "Maybe we should all go over to her house and clean it one day. It wouldn't take long with all of us working." But before I could assimilate this thought, Jenny said to Lorraine, "Put your house in the White Light, and try something a medium friend of mine does. She 'declares divine order' and that seems to help. Also, get yourself on a schedule. When you wake up in the morning, make the bed first thing, then do the dishes, etc." Thus Jenny offered spiritual, as well as practical, advice. The group members offered to help Lorraine put her house in the White Light. Lorraine also had a puppy that she needed to give away, and again, the thought ran through my mind, "Maybe one of us should offer to give the dog a home, at least for a while." But again, Jenny advised the woman, who had placed an advertisement in the newspaper, to "put the dog in the Light, and someone will come for him."

The most extreme example occurred one evening when Sara was afraid one of the tires on her car was going flat. John offered to exchange the car's spare tire for this problem tire, but Jenny said, "No, we'll put it in the Light"; and indeed, John did not change the tire.

Even social support has its limits—if it begins to interfere with one's own life. If a person becomes an "energy sapper" so that listening to his problems begins to be a burden to you or to interfere with your own functioning, then you should "close off."

For Jenny, of course, this use of spiritual solutions is not a *denial* of more active pragmatic solutions (as it was for me). In fact, she sometimes did join practical advice to spiritual counsel. To Jenny, there is simply no need for more work once the spiritual solutions are in place. Jenny was probably wise to cause Lorraine to work out her own permanent solutions instead of temporarily relieving her of her problems, as my solutions would have done.

This "Know Yourself" class ended in January 1976, when the group had finished the last lesson in the book, despite the protests of group members who wanted it to continue. In May 1976 Jenny began a healing class that Louise, David, and Grace joined. Laura also met with this class until June, when she moved to another part of the country. Laura returned to visit Jenny, John, and Beverly at Christmastime in 1976, and Beverly reciprocated her visit. In 1977 Jenny began a Bible class, which John, Beverly, David, Grace, and Sara joined. In July 1977 David was attending this class regularly, and Grace and Sara came to it when their jobs and family duties permitted time.

SUMMARY: CHARACTERISTICS OF STUDY GROUP MEMBERS

As the preceding description of the study group showed, the members have several characteristics in common. It might be well first, however, to make clear that there are some characteristics, once thought to be common for religious seekers, that the study group members do *not* share. They are not poverty-stricken, or even deprived relative to their peers. They are not deviants, following life-styles that are not the norm in American society, nor are they seeking an alternative to that society. Empirical studies have now laid to rest the claim that only society's "marginal" people—the "deprived, disorganized, and deviant" in Hine's (1974) terms—have marched out of the pews into the sensuous pools of Esalen or the transcendent splendor of meditation (e.g., Bird 1978; Hine 1974; McCready 1976; Wuthnow 1976). My observations support the findings of these studies.

Neither are these religious experimenters young, standing on the brink of creating their families, their place in the community, and their identities. They range in age from thirty to sixty-six, and all are established in family and community life.[15]

A characteristic the study group members do have in common is that they have pondered the great questions of life and death. Why am I here? Where do I fit in? Is there life after death? Does God exist? The members say they came into the group because they "wanted to know what this world is all about," or were dissatisfied with what they "knew about their relationship to the higher power" or had wanted to lay to rest "confusing questions of belief" (Study Group:7/2/75). Their reflections have led to the conclusion that there must be "something more" to life than "meets the eye" (or any of the other senses). Many have had extrasensory experiences such as déjà vu, a premonition, or communication with a deceased relative, which suggested to them that indeed there is something more. Some came to SFF seeking explanations for these experiences (SFF 1975b,e).

In their approach to finding answers, they have manifested the autonomy a differentiated society allows. They have tapped a variety of wells—Protestant denominations, the Catholic church, and metaphysics—in their search for answers. Spiritual Frontiers Fellowship supplies answers for these questions. The answers, drawn from many different religious traditions—from Gnostic

75

Christianity to Hinduism—are suggested in such a way that the group member can formulate his own understanding of them.

Another characteristic these metaphysical students share is guilt engendered by circumstances in their lives that had "fragmented" them. Six of their lives have been touched by divorce, two profess to be recovered alcoholics, one's job is subject to economic downturn, another must create a new home for her family frequently. Throughout the life of the study group, the members discussed guilt over past (sometimes very far in the past) perceived misdeeds. The members discussed long-standing guilts—guilt stemming from previous marriages, the disruption of their children's lives, their own (more imagined than real) mistreatment of stepchildren. Guilt was produced by overindulgence, a death in the family, or a child's wayward ways. As John said to me, "You're taught [guilt] at a very early age. You learn you can do this and this and that, but if you go beyond that, you're going to hell. You learn that very early. It sticks with you."

The study group offered explanations (usually cast in a spiritual light) for the circumstances surrounding these deeds, ways of "releasing" (also spiritual in nature) the guilt, and the assurance that the seeker could still find salvation.

Spiritual Frontiers Fellowship offers both a genuine search for meaning, and practical ways of dispelling guilt or dealing with hypertension and drinking. Answers to life's grandest philosophical questions can be found in the metaphysical milieu; and these answers are presented in much more specific detail, and proffered in a tremendously more optimistic tone, than those espoused by the Methodist or Baptist minister from his pulpit. But solutions for life's most mundane irritations—headaches, backaches, little sons who won't take naps—are also found in metaphysics. Indeed, the study group offered ways of curtailing the hostility caused by the "toothpaste tube squeezed in the middle," ways of alleviating physical pain, and things to do for things we can do nothing about.

This study contends that metaphysics, as exemplified by

Spiritual Frontiers Fellowship, is a particularly apt solution for the middle-class search for meaning in our time. It apotheosizes the autonomy characteristic of our society by offering an individualistic epistemology for finding meaning. A metaphysical student can formulate his meaning for himself, and take it with him wherever he goes. The symbol of meaning (the divine inner self) is cast in a spiritual idiom, and therefore meets the criteria for an unempirical, unfalsifiable center for one's being. At the same time, SFF perceives itself as scientific and modern.

Metaphysics does not require changes in the middle-class lifestyle. There is talk of the benefits of a vegetarian diet because eating meat "lowers vibrations," but there is no need to become a vegetarian or a celibate to embark on the metaphysical path to meaning. Metaphysics requires only "spiritual" commitment to a tenuous and short-lived community. There are no communal efforts that depend on people's willingness to give physical or monetary aid to one another, where human frailties may spoil the "spirituality" of the community. Metaphysics is a "no-fail" answer to the meaning problem. There are no prophecies to fail (Dohrman 1958; Festinger, Riecken, and Schacter 1956). There is no vision of a utopia that stands in opposition to the American dream.

The chapters to follow delineate the kind of response Spiritual Frontiers Fellowship makes to the conditions of modern society discussed earlier: autonomy, meaninglessness, separation among people, rationality. Each chapter will employ examples derived from this chapter. Chapters 3 and 4 will analyze Spiritual Frontiers' individualistic epistemology, and the individualistic structure that supports it.

1. All names of people and places are fictitious. Any resemblance to actual persons or places sharing these names is coincidental.

2. This distinction is common in metaphysical groups (Truzzi 1972).

3. "All [the metaphysical groups] consider their philosophies to be scientific

as well as religious. They seek to be united with their God as Principle or Law through the understanding and utilization of spiritual or psychic laws. By their use they believe they can gain health, prosperity, peace of mind, or inner occult development according to their respective goals" (Judah 1967:13, point 3).

4. This is characteristic of metaphysical groups. "Nearly all [the metaphysical organizations] became united in the central belief that the inner, or real, self of man is divine. Each has his spark of divinity" (Judah, 1967:13, point 2).

5. All the metaphysical groups make a place for "the moral teachings of Jesus. . . . Jesus is the way-shower, one who was more aware of his divine nature than others, and who therefore has pointed out the path" (Judah 1967: 14, point 5).

6. In "all metaphysical philosophies . . . one is asked less to believe than to test the principles to be demonstrated in his experience" (Judah 1967:14, points 8, 10).

7. The activities of the areas differ, depending on the energy of the leadership and the size of the following. They range from sponsoring 3 public meetings per year to holding monthly meetings and 1 or 2 weekend seminars and retreats per year. The Metro Area holds monthly meetings from September to June, sponsors an annual three-day retreat, and publishes a monthly newsletter. Fifty to 75 people attend Metro Area meetings. The retreat draws in excess of 100 people.

The lectures given in the Metro Area's 1975–76 season were: (1) Reincarnation vs. Resurrection, (2) Practical Techniques for Healing, (3) Organic Gardening Made Easy, (4) The Importance of Dreams in Spiritual Growth, (5) The Philippine Healers, (6) The Battle of Armageddon: True, False, or Otherwise, (7) Illusion vs. Reality: The World of the Mentalist, (8) Cosmic Consciousness: Our Oneness with God, (9) Creating a World of Light, (10) The American Indian —Medicine Man—Mystic.

8. See Appendix B for SFF's *Principles, Purposes, and Program*, 1974.

9. The 1976 dues structure was: individual—$15.00; student—$5.00; retiree (over 65)—$7.50; husband and wife—$20.00; contributing—$50.00; patron— $150.00; donor—$250.00; life member—$500.00 payable within two years; joint life memberships—$750.00 for husband and wife. SFF reported a membership of 7,835 in May 1975 (SFF 1975d).

10. SFF can be said to have two major goals: (1) awakening interest in psychic phenomena and spiritual healing in the orthodox churches, and (2) encouraging individual spiritual growth. This study is concerned with individual spiritual growth, and does not evaluate SFF's success in bringing interest in "mystical, psychical, and paranormal experience" into the established churches (SFF 1974). Judah (1967:71) indicates that there has been some success in this endeavor. He notes that "the Spiritualistic emphasis upon psychic healing has affected to an extent the renewed interest in healing among some Protestant churches. Probably the greatest influence has come from the Spiritual Frontiers Fellowship." His list of people whose work has been prominent in persuading the churches not to discount spiritual healing includes the healers Ambrose (now

deceased) and Olga Worrall, Methodist minister and author Dr. Albert Day, and Congregational minister and healer Alex Holmes, all of whom are SFF leaders. Judah (1967:89) also states that SFF's "influence may be greater than its official size." Part of this influence is due to the distribution of the *Spiritual Frontiers* journal to theological seminaries, and publication of articles by SFF members in official denominational organs. SFF leaders often lecture in Christian churches and seminaries. Some of the more-well-known leaders, such as Olga Worrall and psychologist Lawrence LeShan, author of *The Mystic and the Physicist* and *How to Meditate*, are frequent guests on television talk shows. Through these media, SFF's interest in prayer, healing, and immortality are spread beyond its membership and into the established churches.

11. These ten people formed the nucleus of the group. The study group was closed to newcomers after the fourth week. We were, however, joined in July and September by two women who had just graduated from other study groups, who had attended Joe's classes, and who were friends of Jenny.

12. This mudra is from *Love + Joy + Peace and Other Mudras for the Masses: A Spiritual Development and Protection Exercise that Utilizes Hand Ritual*, by the late J. Schoneberg Setzer, an SFF leader. The exercise contains 19 other mudras, with different hand positions and passages, for joy, peace, patience, kindness, goodness, faithfulness, gentleness, self-control, faith, hope, truth, beauty, determination, courage, strength, life, light, and eternity. This spiritual exercise can be performed alone or in concert with others, as reported here.

13. Two lessons are included in this description: one dealing with spiritual concerns ("Prayer"), and one having a more mundane focus ("Hate or Misguided Love"). Each meeting actually contained just one lesson.

14. The baby, born in July, was a boy.

15. A comparison of the distribution of occupations among these ten study group members (including Nell and excluding me) with the distribution of occupations among the population of the two contiguous counties where study group members reside shows that white-collar occupations are overrepresented in the study group (70%, as opposed to 54% white-collar for the general population of the two counties [U.S. Bureau of the Census 1973]). (Since occupation is primarily important as a measure of socioeconomic status, study group women who were homemakers were categorized by the spouse's occupation, and retired persons were categorized by their former occupations, in order to make this comparison.) The study group members seem to have a high rate of divorce. Of the 16 marriages entered into by the ten group members, six, or 38%, had ended in divorce by 1976. Yet this is not a higher rate of divorce than is found in the general population of the United States. It is estimated that 45% of all U.S. marriages end in divorce (Reiss 1976). Thirty-one percent of the study group members' *first* marriages had ended in divorce, as compared to 33% for the U.S. population (Reiss 1976). In the state that was the home of the study group, 10% of the population had the status of "separated" or "divorced" *in 1975* (U. S. Bureau of the Census 1976). In comparison, none of the study group members were divorced or separated at that time.

3

An Expression of Autonomy:
Individual Exegesis

At the outset I argued that social fragmentation led to a sense of individual autonomy. Individuals in modern society feel free to choose from a myriad of life-integrating principles and styles. New religious movements respond in a variety of ways to the crises of choice that autonomy leaves in its wake. Some respond by taking away the autonomy—by providing the individual with an authoritarian leader and a structured community of believers. Spiritual Frontiers Fellowship, and its sister groups in the American metaphysical movement, do not respond in this fashion, however. Instead, SFF expresses and legitimates autonomy, and even deifies the independent and individual "self."

Spiritual Frontiers and the other groups in the metaphysical movement are examples of the highly individualistic forms of religion discussed by Bellah (1970) as "modern religion" and Luckmann (1967) as "invisible religion." Bellah and Luckmann argue that this form of religion evolved concomitantly with modern industrialized society, where institutional segmentation has made life an "infinite possibility thing" (Bellah 1970:40) and religion a matter for the "private sphere" (Luckmann 1967:97).

SFF's basic philosophy is that each person must find his own path to truth, and it presents a variety of beliefs and viewpoints from which its member may select. The individual is free to fashion his own meaning from this array, accepting some concepts and rejecting others.

By their emphasis on individual interpretation, the metaphysical movement groups make a "contribution to the evolution of contemporary religious forms" (Zaretsky and Leone 1974:xxxv). The evolution of religion embodies a trend toward differentiation and a trend toward individualization (Bellah 1970; Luckmann 1967; Zaretsky and Leone 1974). The Protestant Reformation represented a step in this evolution, for then "the channels to God were democratized." However, the form and substance of the Deity "remained prescribed by the churches." The new reformation represented by the metaphysical groups allows the individual to decide for himself what the nature of the supernatural is, and what it means to him. The metaphysical groups have, thus, "democratized theology." The Protestant Reformation offered every man access to the supernatural, thus making every man his own priest. The metaphysical groups make every man his own theologian (Zaretsky and Leone 1974:xxxi, xxv). The participants in this new reformation have no need for a Saint Thomas Acquinas or a Maimonides. They would be viewed as intruders on the individual's freedom to interpret.

SFF manifests individual exegesis in principle and in practice; its *Principles, Purposes, and Program* (SFF 1974:Part 4, point 9, emphasis mine) says: "SFF holds that the only essentials are loyalty to the truth *as one perceives it*, and willingness to venture out in obedience to it."

Study group leaders are advised that "each member of a group should feel free to work out his own interpretation of psychic phenomena (or any of the other topics discussed in SFF groups, such as spiritual healing, survival of the soul, spirit communication, reincarnation, or astrology), accepting only what he can honestly integrate with his own experience and conviction" (SFF

81

1971:37). At an SFF leadership conference, where national leaders give area and study group leaders ideas on resource materials and group management, a national leader said:

> What we should attempt to do in our study program is . . . to try to give people the opportunity to become their own authority. . . .
> And the more we are exposed to a variety of ideas the better equipped we will be to make our own determinations. (SFF 1975c)

The operation of individual exegesis is shown in Joe's admonitions to his metaphysics class members that they should not simply believe what he says, and by his assertion that there is no one path to spiritual growth. At least once in each session of the metaphysics classes, Joe exhorted the members to "learn to listen from within yourself and know" or to "test what we tell you. You gain knowledge through us, wisdom through yourself."

In Jenny's study group, John said, "The nice thing about metaphysics . . . is you can look at (the things you read and hear) with an open mind and believe what you want to believe, take the best from each one of them" (Study Group:1/8/75). I once asked John if he understood everything in Joe's classes from the beginning. He replied:

> If you're asking me if I believed everything, no I didn't. I still don't, but I've filed it away. . . . There are kooks writing about this sort of thing, and you have to read it and choose for yourself. Pick and choose for yourself. (Study Group: 6/11/75)

This method of picking and choosing is what is expected of metaphysical students. Leaders advise that students accept only what makes sense to them. Jenny said, "You have to figure out what to keep, and what to throw out" (Study Group:9/10/75). John's method of "filing away" in his mind concepts that he does not yet accept is part of the methodology of finding meaning in metaphysics. Joe said:

> Don't believe a word that I'm teaching you until you experience it. Gather in the information. Don't reject it. Don't throw it away. But

place it to the back of your mind, because at this time you may not fully understand it. (Metaphysics II:2/10/75)

At a later stage in his development, John may believe the things he has "filed away" but does not now accept.

Individuality is illustrated by the study group members' tolerance of one another's beliefs and disbeliefs concerning reincarnation and out-of-the-body experiences. John often said, "Different strokes for different folks," or "I can't relate to that." Laura maintained that having an out-of-the-body experience would be like "learning Chinese" for her, and that telepathy was "out of her realm" (although she could do psychometry). No attempt was made to convince group members to accept whatever they were rejecting.

PERSONAL EXPERIENCE AS THE CRITERION FOR TRUTH

The only valid criterion recognized by SFF for establishing one's own truth is personal experience. A metaphysical student should never accept another's authority as the basis for belief. The "internalization of authority" is characteristic of metaphysical movement groups (Bellah 1970:223; see also Judah 1967:14-15, point 8; Zaretsky and Leone 1974b:xxviii, point 19). Arthur Ford, one of SFF's founders, alluded to the preference for personal experience over theological doctrine in a lecture at the 1967 National Conference of SFF.

Who am I, or who are you, or who is anyone to question another man's experience? I had rather hear some person tell me something that has grown out of a first-hand experience that has been meaningful enough to change his life than to listen to a man who speaks only from a theological or dogmatic standpoint. (Ford 1967:10)

That one should not simply accept a teacher's authority was a constantly reiterated theme in Joe's metaphysics classes. "Don't let others lead you. Listen to God. Meditate and let God show you. Don't believe everything I tell you. . . . Test what we tell you" (Metaphysics I:11/4/74). The student is to "test" what he hears and reads, and to remain "skeptical" (SFF 1975c). Even the leaders who are most steeped in metaphysical beliefs consider themselves "skeptical." Jenny said "I'm always skeptical, too" when Louise complained about her disbelieving family.

The way to "test" or discern truth is by intuitive religious experience (Judah 1967:15, point 10). A message or insight received while "meditating and letting God show you" would serve as an experience capable of validating truth. It would be seen as an "experimental demonstration" of this truth. Jenny understood that I did not believe in reincarnation because, as she said, "there's been nothing in your life to make you believe in it." Presumably, if I had had such an experience, I would have accepted reincarnation as true. An experience that would establish the "truth" of reincarnation would be a vision in which a person saw himself in a past life. This could occur in a dream, in meditation, or in "regression hypnosis." Or a metaphysical student might be strongly attracted or repulsed by another person. Perhaps the person reminds the student of someone else he has known. If not, then how are these strong negative or positive feelings to be explained? It is assumed that these two personalities have "been together before" in a prior life. Their relationship in this past life is the basis for the present attraction or repulsion. By meditating on this, the student may be able to discover when and where they were together before, and what their relationship was. This kind of experience is capable of validating the theory of reincarnation for the student. Reincarnation is then added to his repertoire of beliefs.

Validation of beliefs may be achieved through spiritualistic phenomena (Judah 1967:15, point 10). As an example, immortality was "proved" to Nell when her deceased mother appeared to her in a "materialization" at a Spiritualist camp. (In a "materialization" the form of a person who is "in spirit" appears in a fog-like white substance.)[1] Several other spiritualistic experiences capable of validating the belief in immortality were noted by Robert Ashby (1974), the late research director of SFF, in a study

84

of attitudes toward survival (immortality). The study was based on an analysis of responses to questionnaires (N = 442) distributed during the three national SFF retreats in 1972, and mailed to some areas. The respondents were asked, "Which sort and what amount of evidence would be (or was) necessary to convince you of the reality of survival?" The answers included the general categories of "Experiential Proof" and "Evidential Communication" as well as several specific types of experience: meditation/ awareness, out-of-body experiences, reincarnation, automatism (for example, automatic writing, during which a person's hand is thought to be led by a spirit), apparitions, revived dead (accounts of supposedly dead persons who have revived), and spiritual communication and guidance.

The results of the survey demonstrate that metaphysicians believe "experience is the best teacher." These experiential categories, taken together, accounted for 52 percent of the answers.

The other, nonexperiential, categories of evidence, ranked in order of importance, were "Personal Belief or Conviction" (Ashby [1974:141] says "those who listed 'Personal Belief or Conviction' (11%) quite possibly base that conviction on personal experiences of an evidential type which they did not detail in the response."); "Scholarly/Educational"; "Religious Belief"; "Vicarious Proof"; "Scientific Research and Technology"; and "Theoretical/Philosophical." All these categories (plus an "Other" category) accounted for only 35 percent of the responses. (Thirteen percent of the respondents had "no reply" to this question.)

Experience in the use of psychic powers can also be used to verify beliefs (Judah 1967:15, point 10). The development of one's own psychic abilities "proved" the existence of these abilities. If a person can "do" psychometry (receiving messages about a person by holding an object that belongs to him) or if one has "seen" things clairvoyantly, then these phenomena must exist.

The amelioration of health conditions is used to "prove" spiritual healing (Judah 1967:15, point 10). If a person is ill, undergoes a healing, and feels better, this is an experience capable of validating the efficacy of healing. In Metaphysics I class, Laura had requested healing prayers for a cousin who had been in a coma for a number of years. She and John continued to put the cousin in the healing circle in the study group, and Jenny once accompanied Laura to visit her. Laura reported any improvement in her cousin's condition. These improvements were "proofs" of the efficacy of healing.

Often, the things discussed by Jenny during the sharing of psychic and spiritual experiences portion of the class were healing success reports in which a member of the metaphysical network, or a relative or friend, had been helped through spiritual healing. Sometimes these reports were quite dramatic. For example, Jenny said that the husband of a member of Joe and Barbara's study group had been told he had cancer. The group put him in prayer, and "when he was operated on, the cancer was gone. He also had an old war injury which had partially collapsed a lung. Now his lungs are working also. I told them when God gets in there he isn't going to do any half-way job" (Study Group: 3/26/75).

The closer the healing is to you personally, the greater the "proof" value it has for you. Hearing a report of healing is not as good as witnessing a healing in your own family or friends. The most compelling of proofs is being healed yourself.

The amelioration of material conditions could also validate beliefs (Judah 1967:15, point 10). The Law of Cause and Effect, expressed as "you have to give to receive," was validated for Laura, as reported in chapter 2, when she stated that she sent "money to a friend who's out of work—no use hoarding it . . . then I get some from here and there." Later in the year, the same law was validated for Sara when, after she began tithing to a church, she was able to buy some things she wanted at bargain prices. "Nothing like that has ever worked for me. Not until I started tithing" (Study Group:10/1/75).

Jenny said about a number of things, from meditating to relieve anxiety to saying the word "God" to dispel negative thoughts, "Try it. It works." If the student tried it, and it did work, then his belief in the practice, and the principles behind it, was verified.

A RATIONALE FOR INDIVIDUAL EXEGESIS:
BELIEF IN THE GOD WITHIN

SFF's two central beliefs—that "God is within," and that direct and ongoing communication with God is possible—provide the rationale for the individual's freedom to interpret. Joe asserted that each person has a divine inner self, and so "we are all men of God." SFF's *Principles, Purposes, and Program* (SFF 1974:Part 2, point 2) upholds this point of view with this statement:"Man is a creature of both the physical and non-physical worlds, and in spiritual experience becomes aware of his true heritage as a child of God with unlimited capacity for growth."

The central belief that the inner self of man is divine is shared by all the metaphysical organizations (Judah 1967:13, point 2 Zaretsky and Leone 1974b:xxiii, point 1). This is also the nature of God as expressed in Hindu theology, but it is doubtful that most of the metaphysical movements borrowed this view directly from Hindu philosophy. A likely origin for infusion of Eastern ideas into American metaphysics is Madame Blavatsky's Theosophy (see Ellwood 1973, 1976).

The metaphysicians see their view of God as very different from that espoused by "mainline" Christianity. Joe said, "We see God as in here [touching his heart], within us. 'Church Council Christianity' puts God way out there, away from us" (see also Needleman 1977). There are times when God is addressed as if He is "out there," as when Jenny raises her eyes skyward and says, "This one's for you, God" concerning a particularly recalcitrant problem, or when she says, "OK God, I have to sleep fast tonight," when she has only a few hours to sleep and needs to wake refreshed. Still, this is a friendly, involved, protecting God, a force that can come forth with aid, and not a disinterested and awesome transcendent God. Yet God is sometimes spoken of as the "God-Force" or "Cosmic Consciousness" (Hayes 1971:33). Judah (1967) notes that God is perceived as both immanent and transcendent in the metaphysical groups. It would not be considered inconsistent to view God both in a friendly, fatherly way, and in an impersonal mass-of-energy way. "God is actually energy, pure energy, but to make it understood there has to be a manifestation, or personification" (Johnson 1976a). Joe said, "God has many forms."

The belief that God is within provides the rationale for direct communication with God, and thus for the individual's freedom to interpret the shape and significance of God in his own life.

Communication with the God within is achieved through the rituals of prayer and meditation. "Prayer is talking to God, or one's divine inner self. Meditation is listening to God." Through "altered states of consciousness, which are their ritual property, [the metaphysical participants] maintain constant contact with the divine" (Zaretsky and Leone 1974b:xxix, point 24). Recall that meditation can serve as an experience capable of establishing truth. A message received in meditation has its source in the divine inner self. That is, it comes from God. This message, or insight, is, in fact, revelation.

> SFF holds that the doors of revelation are never closed; God is still speaking, and by the disciplines of study, prayer, and healing our generation may learn more of those truths which Christ said his disciples were "not yet able to bear" (SFF 1974: Part 2, point 6)

The rituals of prayer and meditation are particularly well-suited to serve a religious philosophy that emphasizes individualism and internal authority. Prayer and meditation are the ultimate in individualistic rituals. These rituals are meant to be simple, available to everyone. They can be performed without ritual specialists, ritual paraphernalia, or ritual time or space. They are portable rituals: all that is necessary to their performance is one's own body, mind, and soul. They can be performed as personal needs for communication with the divine require.

ALLOWING INDIVIDUAL EXEGESIS: THE CREEDLESS RELIGION

The principles of individual exegesis and personal experience as the authority for truth suggest that SFF should not be dogmatic in the presentation of its beliefs. This is indeed the case. SFF considers itself "creedless," as do the other groups in the American metaphysical movement (Judah 1967:12-13, point 1; Whitehead 1974).

SFF "does not formulate any doctrine or espouse any opinion" (SFF 1965; see also Ethics and Religion, 1974). The *Journal* of Spiritual Frontiers Fellowship attempts to present a diversity of opinion: "Every article presents some important truth that the author, being human, inevitably links with a modicum of error. As the articles grind together, they mill the truth" (SFF 1971:19).

SFF's only statement of its credo is *Principles, Purposes, and Program.*[2] Even within this statement, there are indications of openness to change. The statement delineates SFF's three main areas of concern: prayer, spiritual healing, and personal immortality, and then says:

> More important than even these special concerns which may change
> from time to time, is a pioneer spirit which always looks forward to
> further steps in understanding and experience. SFF recognizes that
> no individual or institution can both stand still and follow truth
> (SFF 1974:Part 1, Point 3)

In a lecture at the national conference in 1967, Arthur Ford described what SFF "really stands for . . . free inquiry, free thinking, free investigation, and the religion based upon experience rather than dogma" (Ford 1967:18).

The conviction that the group has no dogma is so strong that it in itself acts as a dogma. In a section entitled "Ground Rules for Study Groups," the *Procedures Guide for the Formation and*

Conducting of SFF Study Groups[3] (SFF 1976e:5) says: "*No person* should have the privilege of argument with the intent to convince any other person of his/her point of view." If a speaker came into a group and prefaced his remarks with "You must believe and follow what I am about to say in order to grow spiritually," I believe he would be sanctioned. Much more likely is that a person would begin a speech with:

> I'd like to preface my talk with a statement I make to my prayer therapy groups. . . . We, the teachers, are not the ones with the answers for you. . . . The answers for you, are, of course, with you. I just want to take some time tonight to share with you some of my experiences, and of course my opinions. I don't expect you to believe eveything I say, not as necessarily true for you. But if you could find something in what I have to share with you, and it's useful to you in your life, I will feel that I have succeeded. And that is what I hope always to accomplish, as a teacher (Bonacci 1976b)

With this kind of introduction, the speaker's views are readily listened to, and tolerated, if not accepted as one's own.

SFF perceives its role as that of a disseminator of a wide variety, a potpourri, of information. This function is fulfilled by means of a mail-order bookstore and library, the lectures and workshops presented at conferences, retreats, and area meetings, and the lessons given in the study groups.

Area and study group leaders attending the leadership conference were told:

> Our study program should be an attempt to expose your people to as many different points of view as possible. . . . So that, we are not saying this is the SFF position on healing, or this is the SFF position on human survival. SFF does not have a position. We have a variety of people who have a variety of viewpoints. And we have a kind of free market place of ideas. We don't have one core orthodoxy.
>
> We have a philosophy of wide exposure to a free market place of ideas, and to encourage people to come to their own conclusions, make their own decisions. We'll offer them options (SFF 1975c)

The potpourri is, of course, not an infinite one. The same books tend to be recommended. There is a network of speakers who speak on a lecture circuit of metaphysical group functions. Yet, Jenny's study group discussed forty-six different lessons on topics ranging from healing, prayer, meditation, spirit communication, reincarnation, and telepathy, to self-inquiry, self-realization, self-doubt, and depression. If a group member also attended monthly Metro Area meetings, in the course of a year, he would have heard ten lectures by ten different speakers, with titles running from "Reincarnation vs. Resurrection," through "Practical Techniques for Healing," to "Organic Gardening Made Easy." If he also attended the area winter retreat, he would have heard five more lectures by two speakers, and participated in four two-hour experiential workshops. For his workshop experiences, he could choose to participate in yoga, acupuncture, healing, self-hypnosis, palmistry, tarot, or astrology, among others.

The disclaimer attached to announcements of all SFF-sponsored activities symbolizes the concept of offering a variety of ideas and viewpoints:

> Spiritual Frontiers Fellowship is an eclectic organization, bringing together individuals of diverse backgrounds and interests. As a service to our membership and the general public, programs are offered that include a wide variety of topics. The use of any speaker, program, or resource material should not be interpreted as an endorsement by SFF of theology, philosophy, theories, or methods, nor of any organization with which the speaker or writer may be identified (SFF 1976c:3)

Spiritual Frontiers Fellowship is based on the principles of individual exegesis and internal authority, which I have interpreted as an expression of individual autonomy. The belief in a God who dwells within provides a rationale for the individual's ability to discover his own truth. Direct and constant communication with this God is maintained through the highly personal rituals of prayer and meditation. Thus, SFF's individual exegesis expresses and legitimates the individual autonomy that results from societal fragmentation. The next chapter demonstrates that the nature of its membership requirements and organizational structure are also conducive to individual exegesis.

1. "The theory behind materialization is that a spirit must first lower its rate of vibration to conform to that of the medium's physical body. Then the astral, or inner, body of the entranced medium is projected from its physical encasement. Finally, the astral body is used as a frame upon which helping spirits mold ectoplasm into the likeness of the spirit to be materialized and made visible. Ectoplasm, which is described as a white or gray substance of fine material particles, flows forth generally from the nose and ears of the medium. At the end of the materialization it can be withdrawn and disappear into the medium's body in a fraction of a second" (Judah 1967:68).

2. See Appendix B for the text of *Principles, Purposes, and Program.* This statement was written at the time of SFF's founding, in 1956, and was slightly revised in 1974.

3. The national office publishes four documents that outline SFF's organization and governance: (1) Constitution and By-Laws of the Spiritual Frontiers Fellowship (9 pages) (SFF 1973a); (2) Spiritual Frontiers Fellowship By-Laws (Local Organizations) (6 pages) (SFF 1973b, 1976a); (3) The Handbook of the Spiritual Frontiers Fellowship: A Guidebook on Policy and Practice for the Use of National Executive Council and Committee Members, and of Local Chairmen, Officers and Committees (54 pages) (SFF 1971); and (4) The Procedures Guide for the Formation and Conducting of Spiritual Frontiers Fellowship Study Groups (31 pages) (SFF 1976e).

4

Fostering Individual Exegesis: Individualistic Structure

Spiritual Frontiers Fellowship is structured so as to allow and encourage individual exegesis. SFF has loose membership requirements that allow participants to search for their truths where they may. The Fellowship is nonhierarchical in organizational form, and antiauthoritarian in its style of leadership. These structural elements facilitate individual exegesis.

NONEXCLUSIVE MEMBERSHIP

Spiritual Frontiers Fellowship does not require that the individual's search for his own truth be confined to SFF alone; membership in SFF does not preclude membership in other spiritual organizations. In fact, membership in several organizations, either simultaneously or serially, is characteristic of metaphysical students (Wallis 1975; Whitehead 1974; Zaretsky and Leone 1974b; see also Balch and Taylor 1977 re the "cultic milieu"). Each year SFF gains one-third new members and loses one-third old members, demonstrating the rate at which individuals "move through" the organization. Thus, the potpourri of ideas and principles one person may be exposed to does not necessarily stop at the boundaries represented by SFF activities.

The "membership histories" of our study group participants reveal "multiple memberships" in metaphysical groups. Six members attended Spiritualist churches occasionally or regularly. David participated in the Sunday services of one Spiritualist church as a healer, and was on the board of directors of another one. Three had been members of the Association for Research and Enlightenment.[1] Laura received literature from the Unity School of Christianity. John belonged to a metaphysical book club.

A long list of metaphysical group memberships is common in the credentials of lecturers and workshop leaders at SFF activities. A retreat brochure contained this biographical sketch of a workshop leader:

> Dr. D—, a prominent architect[2] in C—, a member of the Executive Council of SFF, is a longtime student of the paranormal. . . . He is a member of the Institute of Noetic Sciences, A. R. E., Fellowship of Spiritual Understanding, ESP Associates, Academy of Parapsychology and Medicine, author of articles on architecture, individual liberty, and paranormal subjects, and popular workshop leader.

The main reason exclusive membership is not required of SFF members is that it would be disconsonant with a philosophy that the individual is his own authority for truth. If an individual internalizes the concept that he must find his own path to truth, and that this can be found in many sources, he is likely to feel the more groups he participates in, the better.

There are other elements that contribute to the necessity to maintain ties with more than one spiritual organization. Zaretsky and Leone (1974b:xxv, point 9) point out that some of the metaphysical groups do not offer life cycle rituals. SFF offers no such rites and no special observations during the Christian religious holidays at Christmas and Easter. For these occasions the members of the study group attended orthodox churches, or Spiritualist churches, or both. SFF's policy is that it does not want to *replace* the church in the lives of its members, but to supplement it (SFF 1974:Part 4, point 3). (Nevertheless, SFF members do not, as a rule, attend church regularly, although they may go for special events.)[3]

Another reason ties with orthodox churches may be desirable is that the activities of the groups in the metaphysical movement are

94

generally not a family affair. The registration form for a SFF national retreat stated: "This retreat is for mature young people and adults. No accommodations are available for children" (SFF 1976b). Another national retreat did have provisions for a young people's seminar in 1976, but "young people" means persons of college, or at least high school, age. The same lack of family activities is evident at the area and study group levels. There were some children present at the Metro Area 1975 winter retreat; but there were no activities planned specifically for them, and they did not attend many of the lectures and workshops. Joe and Barbara told me they were taking their two oldest children, aged fourteen and thirteen, to the 1976 area winter retreat, but the fact that this was noteworthy suggests that is was unusual. In the study group, only Beverly and John and Dan and Louise participated as couples. Jenny and Grace were widowed, and Laura, Sara, David, and I were married but attended the activities alone. Four more women who attended for short periods of time (three joined after other study groups ended, one left to join a more convenient group) were all married but attended the study group alone.

Another element that requires membership in several spiritual organizations is the fact that some of the metaphysical groups "deal with only a limited range of the supernatural. To fulfill the whole range of human requirements, it is necessary to seek membership in complementary groups" (Zaretsky and Leone 1974b:xxv, point 9). For example, some SFF members also belong to ARE because they feel these two groups complement each other. They are very similar in philosophy and goals, and ARE publishes more books and lessons than does SFF. SFF concentrates more on the psychic than has ARE, whereas ARE has a highly developed program of dream interpretation, lacking in SFF. A major concern for SFF is healing; ARE's stand on healing is complicated by a belief that healing may disturb karmic responsibilities. A person could, therefore, gain information on the psychic and healing from SFF, and information on dreams from ARE.

Participation in several groups simultaneously is facilitated by

95

the varying degrees of participation and commitment commonly allowed in metaphysical groups (Truzzi 1972; Wallis 1975). A person's commitments can be parceled out as he sees fit. Jenny was involved in SFF at all levels: leading study groups, holding a position on the Metro Area steering committee, participating in national meetings. She was also a member of the Association for Research and Enlightenment, but her membership was "inactive": she merely received ARE's literature. Laura attended the SFF study group and some area activities. She also received Unity's publications, but did not participate in local Unity activities. The form of involvement in metaphysics can be fitted to individual needs. Solitary study and meditation is one form, gregarious fellowship another. One can become a dependent follower, or a depended-upon psychic professional.

Within the groups I studied, the least-committed persons were those who attended just one of Joe's metaphysics courses. Some of the women who attended these classes attended an adult education course each term. One term they might take "College Psychology," one term "Metaphysics," and the next "Slimnastics." For others this class was a stepping-stone to further participation in metaphysics. They might study on their own and take more metaphysics classes, or they might set up a client relationship with Jenny or Joe, or join SFF.

The least-committed SFF member would pay dues to the national organization, receive the national *Newsletter*, and use its bookstore and library. Participation would consist entirely of correspondence with the national organization. It would not require participation in any activities at either the area or study group level. This type of participation is exemplified in a letter written to the SFF *Newsletter* (SFF 1976d).

In correspondence in March I had mentioned to you my many years as a member of SFF, making extensive use of the library and enjoying the *Journal* and other mailings. . . .

My husband and I have had joint membership for the last few years and we attended the recent conference together, the first time either of us had been with an assembled SFF group. It was a very special and most enjoyable three days.

Some metaphysical organizations, such as Astara, are virtually mail-order concerns. Although Astara holds a small Sunday service in its headquarters in California, by far its major influence is through selling lessons and books by mail. Marty (1970:228), in a study of the magazines of the occult, even states that the groups in the "occult establishment" lack a communal impulse. He perhaps overstates the case, since he studied the magazines of the occult establishment and not an organization that has group expressions, like SFF. Still, it is important to note that large numbers of people participate on this mail-order level. Marty (1970:230) says the occult magazines "satisfy the religious needs of many thousands or millions—we cannot even begin to guess at the number—who have turned to their myriad advertisements, books, products, and claims."

In SFF a slightly-more-committed person would attend the program of an area group, if there was one close enough to his place of residence. Generally, area meetings take place monthly or less frequently. A more-committed person would join a study group. Study groups usually meet once a week, or at least biweekly. Some study groups are ongoing and have no specified ending date, but most have a definite life-span. Study groups based on the lessons in *Know Yourself* last one year. At the end of the year, a person may end his involvement; may pursue his metaphysical interests on his own, through meditation and reading; may join another study group concentrating on a different subject (meditation, healing, or giving messages, for example); or he may begin a study group of his own.

Another type of participation in SFF is attendance at the retreats, seminars, and conferences. Some people spend their summers traveling from spiritual retreat to spiritual retreat. One young woman at the 1975 Metro Area retreat, a teacher, said she was going to travel by car in the summer to the three SFF retreats in Minnesota, Pennsylvania, and North Carolina, to the ARE headquarters in Virginia Beach, Virginia, and to Unity Village in Missouri.

The most-committed individuals are those who become leaders. Leaders at the study group level are often also leaders at the area level. These people devote considerable time and effort to the organization. The leaders may be asked by other areas and other metaphysical organizations to lecture at their programs. They may be asked to hold workshops or to be psychic consultants at retreats. It is generally these most-committed members who hold multiple memberships in metaphysical movement groups.

SFF does not even require membership for participation in most of its activities. Membership is required in order to use the mail-order library, and for attendance at national retreats, but not for participation in area activities or study groups. In Jenny's study group, only four of the members actually joined SFF: David, John, Beverly, and I. Little attention was paid to the fact that the study group was affiliated with SFF. Jenny did always participate in area meetings, and David, John, Beverly, Laura, and I occasionally attended them. Interest in SFF was at its peak just before and after the Metro Area winter retreat and the national conference. Five of us in the study group attended the three-day area winter retreat. Only Jenny and I attended the 1975 national conference.

The study group was listed as an SFF study group in the area *Newsletter*, but it was not labeled as such by the group members. They called it "Know Yourself class," "Jenny's class," or "Meditation class." Members joined the class because they knew Jenny, or knew someone who knew Jenny. They would have attended the study group whether or not it was affiliated with SFF or any other organization. The study group and its members had only tenuous ties to the higher levels of SFF's organization. This is the usual state of affairs, and it demonstrates the nonhierarchial nature of SFF's bureaucracy.

98

NONHIERARCHICAL STRUCTURE

SFF's three organizational levels, national, area, and study group, are loosely articulated. Bateson (1972:96) has defined a pure hierarchy as "a serial system in which face-to-face relations do not occur between members when they are separated from some intervening member; in other words, systems in which the only communication between A and C passes through B." The organization of Spiritual Frontiers Fellowship is certainly not hierarchical in this sense. A person can participate in SFF on any or all of its three organizational levels, in any combination, although official membership can only be obtained through the national office.[4]

Although the national level provides literature and sponsors retreats, which draw 200-700 people each, it is often required to defend its existence because the members who participate at the area or study group levels do not believe the benefits they derive from SFF emanate from the national office (Althouse 1976d; Fenske 1975).

The seventy-three area organizations in thirty- five states are autonomous and self-supporting financially.[5] Their activities range from sponsoring three meetings a year to holding monthly meetings and a few weekend retreats. The Metro Area, for example, holds monthly meetings (except in July and August) with attendance of 50-75 people, publishes a monthly newsletter, and holds a three-day retreat in the winter of each year in which more than 100 people participate.

The areas maintain a great deal of autonomy regarding the content of their programs (SFF 1971:26). The principle of local autonomy in programming was affirmed at a leadership conference when an area leader asked a specific question: "How many meetings per year should be called in an Area?" The national leader moderating the conference replied:

> This is where Spiritual Frontiers is trying to stay open. And I believe every Area, every study group, develops its own personality. It depends on where you're at, what you're doing. If four meetings a year

99

work, OK. If three meetings a year work, OK. . . . Find out what
people want. (SFF 1975c)

The national organization does have some control over area
leadership. Areas are governed by chairpersons. In the larger
areas the chairperson is assisted by a steering committee. These
leaders are usually elected by the SFF members in that area, but
the chairperson's nomination must be approved by the national
office. In practice this procedure is a "rubber stamping" of a person chosen by the area, yet it probably does serve as a screening
device for persons who would not be acceptable to national
leaders. For example, an area would not be likely to tender the
nomination of a person who was strongly antichurch, since the
national leaders want to maintain SFF's original purpose of
reawakening the Christian church to psychic phenomena. Neither
would an area be likely to nominate a person whose philosophy or
life-style might mar the dignified image SFF wishes to project.
Area and study group leaders at the leadership conference were
warned to

remember our purpose, bringing the psychic back into the church.
The   leader you choose should be a church member, should attend
a church. It leaves a bad image if the leader is an astrologer, when
people ask, "What church does he belong to? What is his occupation?" (SFF 1975c)

(In fact, the national leadership manifests this "church member"
ideal to a greater degree than does the area leadership.)[6]
The study groups are even more autonomous than the areas.
The national office publishes a book on how to form study groups
(*The Procedures Guide for the Formation and Conducting of
Spiritual Frontiers Fellowship Study Groups* [SFF 1967e]), but
this is meant to be a manual of suggestions and not a set of hard-
and-fast rules. The *Procedures Guide* reflects a desire to keep
study groups from becoming too formal and organized. A group
of eight to twelve persons is recommended because this "allows

100

for maximum inner growth with minimum outer organization" (SFF 1971:34–35; see also SFF 1976e).

The autonomy of study group leaders was demonstrated in 1975 when the national office attempted to impose membership quotas on study groups. National leaders legislated that three-fourths of the members of a study group must be SFF members. This was done in part to encourage study group participants to join SFF, and thereby expand the coffers with their dues[7] (40 to 60% of SFF's income derives from dues); it was also an attempt to discourage exploitation of the SFF name.[8]

The idea of a membership quota was not well received by study group leaders.[9] They felt that memberships should follow, or arise out of, participation in study groups. Study group leaders are often charismatic psychic professionals, like Jenny, who could lead study groups and development classes that would be popular whether or not they were sponsored by SFF.

The dissatisfaction with the quota rule was widespread enough to cause the national leadership to revise it.[10] The national and area organizations have no means of policing study groups (national does not have a list of study group leaders, for example), and so directives concerning them can, in practice, be ignored.

ANTIAUTHORITARIAN LEADERSHIP

SFF is antiauthoritarian in its style of leadership. There is no charismatic leader at the national level, and SFF has taken steps to avoid one. The two founders still living participate and are respected, but not revered.[11] The president is elected,[12] and is more a functionary than a "leader". SFF by-laws restrict the president to two two-year terms. According to one former president (Althouse 1976c):

> Limiting the tenure of the President helps to keep SFF from being identified as any one person's "thing." SFF has never been a "one-person show." We have had fine leadership in SFF, but no one leader is identified as the source of our life together.

101

President Althouse (1976c) noted that Arthur Ford, a popular medium who helped found SFF, had the "adulation and personal following" that would have allowed him to tie "SFF to his own 'personality cult.'" Ford was a noted Spiritualist medium, and a minister of the Disciples of Christ Church. He was one of the mediums who helped Bishop Pike in his endeavor to contact his deceased son (Heron 1967; Pilleggi 1970). Ford also gained notoriety by claiming to have broken the code the magician Harry Houdini had prearranged to prove or disprove life after death. But, says Althouse (1976c), SFF did not become an "Arthur Ford movement," and Ford "always rejected that role."[13]

Leadership on the area level is of the functionary type, as well. The Metro Area is governed by an area chairperson and a steering committee elected by SFF members present at a business meeting. Since the area has no staff, unlike the national, all the work of program planning, securing speakers, advertising meetings, and preparing and mailing the newsletter falls on the shoulders of the steering committee. They are an energetic group and so tend to be reelected.

The norm is that study group meetings will be run democratically. The study group leader is merely to "guide" the members.[14] The SFF *Handbook* (SFF 1971:34–35) says groups should eschew "a leader on whom all depend as an authority." Instead, "the leader is a convener or catalyst, in whose presence the group's life develops." The *Procedures Guide* (1976:5) labels the leader "the facilitator." In *Know Yourself* (Hayes 1971), the leader is called a "moderator." The first passage the moderator is to read to the group members at the first meeting concerns his relationship to them. Jenny paraphrased this passage:

> Tonight, I will be your moderator. And from here on, you'll see that I'll sort of guide you at times, but you're going to be doing a whale of a lot of it all by yourself. The more you do yourself, the more you learn. As you know, as anybody knows, you can sit and listen to somebody lecture, but until you start practicing it, getting things actually going within yourself, it doesn't do a bit of good to sit there

and have somebody else tell you how to do something, or what to do. (Study Group:1/8/75)

The decentralized, autonomous, and antiauthoritarian nature of SFF's structure does function to promote individual exegesis, but it is not without its disadvantages when observed from the viewpoint of the continuing life of the organization. At present the national office feels it faces a dilemma. On the one hand, SFF wants to project a dignified and scholarly image.[15] This requires some rules, and some structure to provide a means of upholding the rules. This was illustrated by the attempt to impose membership quotas on study groups in order to protect its image and financial condition. With the present, nonhierarchial structure, the national office was, in effect, unable to accomplish its aim. The size of SFF's operation and the scope of its services to nearly 8,000 members also necessitates some structure. SFF wishes to provide its members with a mail-order bookstore, library, newsletter, and journal. It wants to create opportunities for the members to meet together at a conference and retreats held around the country annually, as well as at area meetings and in study groups.

On the other hand, SFF wishes to maintain the democratic and decentralized form that is most consonant with its philosophy of individual exegesis. This dilemma was voiced by a national leader at the 1975 leadership conference (SFF 1975c): "How do we remain an eclectic open-ended organization, within a structure?" Thus far, SFF has solved the dilemma by retaining a non-dogmatic, nohierarchical, and antiauthoritarian stance (cf. SFF 1974: Part 4, point 8).

The principles of individual exegesis and internal authority are well served by this democratic structure. The individual's freedom to interpret dictates that SFF must remain creedless, offer a variety of information to its adherents, and avoid officially endorsing any particular person or idea. Since the individual is his own theologian as well as his own priest, organizational structure must re-

103

main loose and decentralized. The many levels of commitment available in SFF afford flexibility to its members, and allow for membership in several goups simultaneously. All these elements of structure are conducive to individual exegesis, the metaphysical movement's expression of individual autonomy.

We have seen in the last two chapters that Spiritual Frontiers manifests individual exegesis in principle, in practice, and in organizational structure. This I have interpreted as an expression of the individual autonomy that modern society embodies. The chapter to follow describes the identity that SFF ultimately offers its adherents, in the form of the powerful identifying metaphor, "I am God."

1. Jenny is an "inactive" member of ARE. It is interesting that Jenny's original commitment to SFF was somewhat accidental. She was debating whether to join an ARE or an SFF study group, and chose the SFF group because it met at a more convenient time for her. Her membership in SFF and subsequent involvement in area and national activities were consequences of joining this study group.

2. Note that the credentials include professional success. College degrees are also listed in these biographies.

3. None of the study group members except Jenny attended church regularly (Jenny was an elder in her Presbyterian church). That this was common was affirmed by other study group leaders (SFF 1975c), and by a national leader, who wrote, "Quite a number [of SFF members] do not regularly attend church now but have been drawn to SFF because they are seeking the 'truth,' and their church would not give them the growth stimuli they needed. SFF is church oriented without the dogma, creed, and stuffiness" (Perkins 1976b). The national and area leaders, most of whom are active church members, are exceptions.

4. To be a member of SFF, it is necessary to pay annual dues to National: see chapter 2, footnote 9 for the 1976 dues structure.

5. The national office does not finance area activities. Some prosperous areas give the national office a portion of the profits that they realize from their programs. Metro Area does this.

6. All 40 of the candidates for national office in 1975-76 and 1976-77 were church members (42% were ministers, and another 38% were active church

members [committee chairpersons, etc.]). In contrast, 10 (22%) of the 45 area chairpersons for whom data were available (from a possible 73) were not affiliated with an orthodox church (SFF 1975a,c). The denominations most heavily represented in this sample of leaders were Methodist, Presbyterian, Episcopalian, Congregational, and United Church of Christ (SFF 1975a,c). The rank-and-file members often do not attend established churches regularly (Perkins 1976b, SFF 1975c).

7. A national leader said: "What this is tackling is freeloading. . . . A person who wants all the advantages. We're providing the organization and so forth, but they don't want it. Tell me another organization that you can attend their meetings without belonging to it. We need to push this more. We need to push it more budget-wise, too" (SFF 1975c). National leaders at the 1975 leadership conference also suggested that area leaders were too lax in allowing non-members to attend area activities and receive area newsletters. Again, this was primarily an economic concern. Area leaders, however, resisted restricting activities to members. They maintained that allowing participation was a good means of recruitment, and were willing only to charge slightly higher admission fees to nonmembers.

8. A national leader explained to area leaders: "Last October the Executive Committee did take some action to gain some—"control" is the wrong word—to have people understand what we're in when we're in Spiritual Frontiers Fellowship. Because we do have people who expoit, and I can see it no other way, exploit, Spiritual Frontiers Fellowship. We have people who call their groups Spiritual Frontiers Study Groups and they are not Spiritual Frontiers Study Groups. It's somebody who's got a hobby horse. They want to ride that horse. They want to get it under some good umbrella, and they're out on an ego trip. Now that's about as bad as I can make the picture. Nevertheless it occurs across the country. Some of them even set it up so it becomes a source of income for them. So we had to face the thing. What makes a *bona fide* study group? This applies to whether you allow them to be listed as Spiritual Frontiers Study Groups in the newsletters of your Areas. There is no control *we* have over them, but *you*, in putting out your newsletter, can certainly draw a line at this particular spot" (SFF 1975c).

9. A gathering of study group leaders at the leadership conference expressed dissatisfaction with the quota rule:

National
Leader: "The legalism of being a study group leader is far less important to me than the dynamics of being a study group leader. You're working with people. You're working with responsibilities, and development. You know, it's great to say we need exactly three-fourths members, but then if you're one less than three-quarters—you know, that's not in the spirit or intent of the founders, or the ongoing goals.

105

Study Group Leader #1:	It would be ideal if you can get that many people. But now, the people in my group are just not at this point.
Study Group Leader #2:	When I received that news, it frightened me.
Study Group Leader #3:	Yes, it did me, too. I thought, "Well, if I can't do it within SFF, Then I'll do it on my own." (SFF 1975c)

10. The rule was revised so that if a person wished to continue membership in a study group after six months, he would need to join SFF. This attempt by the national office to centralize authority and control could be analyzed in Wallis's (1974) terms as a move along the continuum from "individual cult" to "authoritarian sect." Wallis cites other groups whose moves in this direction failed: Spiritualism, Theosophy, and New Thought. SFF failed for the same reasons Wallis cites for these groups' failures: (1) a strong belief in individual exegesis, vitiating any leader's attempt at control, and (2) a "spontaneous" founding by a group of interested people, leading to decentralized leadership and no charismatic element. I would add to these reasons the simple lack of communication between study groups and the national office, or, for that matter, between study groups and area leadership.

11. I often heard criticism directed toward ARE, which did have leader figures in the persons of the deceased Edgar Cayce and his son, Hugh Lynn Cayce. The criticism was that the group had wrongfully deified Edgar Cayce by placing him posthumously in this role, and that Cayce himself would not have considered it proper.

12. A move in the direction of greater democracy in the election of the national administration (executive council and officers) was taken in 1976. Until that time, national officers were voted upon by the SFF members attending the business meeting at the annual national conference (about 500 of SFF's 8,000 members attend the conference). In 1976 a mail ballot, sent to all members, was instituted. The old procedure had been a matter of contention among the membership. Jenny exhorted those of us from the Metro Area who were attending the national conference in 1975 to "be sure to go to the business meeting. That's where we vote for officers and executive council. Most people don't know that and don't go to it. SFF leadership always has the people it wants picked. Last year we finally got them to let us make nominations from the floor. Before that they wouldn't even allow that." She said the already-chosen candidates were "the famous people, the authors." This procedure was probably promoted by SFF's desire to protect its image by discouraging psychics and astrologers from holding leadership positions. The new mail ballots are to have multiple nominees for each position, and space for write-in votes. (The nominations committee has complained, however, that the membership does not participate at the level of providing names and information on potential candidates, making it difficult to present a large slate on the ballot [Althouse 1976a,b].)

13. Other SFF founders were Paul Lambourne Higgins, a United Methodist minister; Albin Bro, missionary and educator; and Dr. Bro's wife, Margueritte Harmon Bro, author and lecturer. Dr. Bro died in 1956, Ford in 1971, and Mrs. Bro in 1977.

14. It is in study groups that charismatic leadership is most likely to arise. The evidence of Jenny's charismatic leadership is discussed in chapter 6.

15. "SFF is honored to be considered one of the most 'level headed' of the many organizations springing up in this field" (SFF 1975d).

5

Self-Realization in Spiritual Frontiers Fellowship: Spiritual Growth

The fragmented and diversified nature of modern society has the effect of moving the locus of myth and meaning from the community to the individual. Referents for establishing identity are located, not in the community, as they are in more primitive societies, but in the individual. "In modern society . . . every person finds his Holy of Holies where he may." Universal symbols that "have about the same wealth of meaning for everybody" are lost (Langer 1942:287–88).

The self is the focus of "modern" religion. The private history of the individual is the locus for myth and the source of ultimate significance in industrial society (Bellah 1970; Campbell 1968; Luckmann 1967; van Baal 1971).

The process of uncovering the ultimate significance located within oneself is self-realization. It is self-realization that, according to Luckmann (1967:10), "represents the most important expression" of modern society's "ruling topic of individual autonomy" (cf. Bellah 1970:227).

Self-realization is the goal of metaphysical aspirants. For all their individualism and emphasis on the self, however, the metaphysicians are not completely man-centered. They have left the community out of their religious equation, but they have not omitted God. For the self they are seeking to know is the *divine* inner self.

The idiom used in Spiritual Frontiers Fellowship to describe the process of self-realization is "spiritual growth." Spiritual growth is conceived as an increasing awareness of one's divine inner self. A goal of Spiritual Frontiers Fellowship is to "increase within the individual an inner sense of awareness which leads to personal development" (Rauscher 1970; see also Perkins 1976a; SFF 1971). The emphasis on finding meaning from within oneself is demonstrated in Arthur Ford's (1967:9-10) address to the 1967 national conference.

> Today the Holy Spirit is active as it has not been, probably, at any time in the history of the Church. It is active because people are frustrated, disillusioned, and in a great many instances, without any hope. They are turning not always to those who are supposed to know the answers, but they are turning inward, and within themselves are finding the source of strength and the answer to their dilemma.

SFF deals with the identity problem by pointing out individual paths to spiritual growth. The principles of individual exegesis and the authority of personal experience dictate that no one path to spiritual growth is to be advocated. Under the influence of the overriding individualism of the group, the very phrase "spiritual growth" constitutes a multivocal symbol, perceived in different ways by different people.

At its simplest, spiritual growth corresponds to the level of experience "in this work" (i. e., experience with metaphysics).

> Each individual in a group who has unique needs is trying to find his or her way toward a kind of spiritual maturity. (SFF 1975c).[1]

Spiritual growth is thought to progress in "phases" consisting of:

109

1. Intellectual inquiry—this phase usually begins casually and leads to reading books, attending talks and meeting persons with a similar interest.

2. Psychic experience—this phase often hits a person with an impact, and comes through a visit to a medium or some other vivid personal experience. One does not get all the answers, but from that time on knows the unseen world is real and vital.

3. Spiritual dedication—this level is the natural outgrowth of the others. Intellectually and emotionally satisfied, one awakens to the realization that we are spirits now; that our earthly existence is but one stage and we can continue to grow spiritually here and hereafter. With this new enlightenment and guidance that comes with it one draws closer to God through meditation, prayer, and worship. Such an explorer comes ultimately to a state of willing obedience in which the small personal "self" is yielded up to God and he enters with confidence into the full life that God prepared for man on earth.

These phases of growth may come quickly or may take a lifetime. (SFF 1971:22–23)

Joe, who is influenced by Astara, has a more complex view of spiritual growth. Joe sees spiritual growth as "soul evolution." Soul evolution is a process by which a person passes through seven levels of awareness, from the awareness of only the material existence, to an awareness that "I and the Father are one." The seven levels of awareness correspond to seven planes, which are arranged hierarchically. The lower three planes are the three worlds of man: Physical, Emotional or Astral, and Mental. The three higher planes are the three worlds of God: Nirvanic, Monadic, and the Divine Godhead (Christ Consciousness or God Consciousness). A plane called "Intuition" lies between the two sets. Each person exists on all seven planes simultaneously, but his awareness of this depends on his respective level of "soul evolvement." Persons whose souls have not yet evolved will be aware of only the lower planes. As soul evolution progresses, awareness of higher and higher planes is achieved. The seven levels also correspond to seven chakras (centers or vortices of psychic energy) in the body. Each center is located in a particular

plane along the spinal cord. The chakras are also arranged hierarchically, and they are labeled, from lowest to highest: Root,
Spleenic, Navel, Heart, Throat, Brow, and Crown. As a person's
soul evolves, he "opens up the chakras." Earliest man's energies
were concentrated in the Root chakra. At present, most of
humanity's energy is centered in the Navel, but a few have moved
on toward "thinking with the Heart," and even fewer with the
Throat, and so on up the pyramid (Metaphysics II:5/12/75).

Reincarnation also plays a part in Joe's theory of soul evolution. Spiritual growth occurs through a series of incarnations on
this earth and lives "on the other side." The number of lives required for the evolution to occur varies. Persons who reach the
highest level have transcended, or "outlived," the Law of Karma.
At this stage the soul is not required to incarnate on earth again,
although it may choose to do so in order to lead others. Souls that
have reached the highest level and have chosen to reincarnate are
great spiritual teachers, such as Jesus Christ, Buddha, and
Mohammed.

In contrast to Joe's view, *Know Yourself* defines spiritual
growth in much more worldly terms. In a section called "What
does it take to grow spiritually?" it says:

> Spiritual growth is a process of becoming a better person on this
> physical level through your relationships with other people. . . .
> Spirituality is . . . an internal actualization of truth, love, wis-
> dom and knowledge flowing from the individual in his everyday life.
> (Hayes 1971:90, 142)

Jenny's view of spiritual growth is also a pragmatic one. Jenny
described how the study group would promote spiritual growth:

> We concentrate on getting you to know yourself spiritually. That's
> what the classes are all about. To learn the inner you. . . .
> We will study five different areas of development:
> Healing. You'll be learning how to heal yourself as well as reaching
> out and helping those around and about you.

111

Prayer is also very essential. Prayer is talking to God. It doesn't have to be a big elaborate thing. It's that which comes from your heart that counts. . . .

We will be doing some ESP experiments, to teach you some sensitivity, so you will be sensitive one to the other.

And we will be getting into meditation. This is listening, getting to know your inner self, what you really are, and beginning to expand within yourself. . . .

Also, we will look at the effect that your attitude has upon how you react to other people; what you need to get for yourself. This is a part of the healing process. We always stress that there are three main sections to healing: the body, the mind, and that which is beyond the body and the mind, the soul. . . .

God made you to begin with perfect, and we think that everyone should become as perfect as they possibly can to be one with God again. (Study Group:1/8/75)

The manifestations of spiritual growth are, according to *Know Yourself*, more positive relationships and attitudes (Hayes 1971:90–91). Thus, the metaphysicians apply the teaching "By their fruits ye shall know them."

This notion of positive change in personal attitudes and relationships as the fruits of spiritual growth was expressed in answers given in the study group to the question, How can a person tell if he himself or another person is spiritually evolved?

Sara: Spiritual growth is a change in attitude, a change in life. It's knowing truth, knowing life. It's an evolutionary change. In me there's been a complete change from ten years ago to the present. The past is gone. It's a new life.

Jenny: By the fruit of the spirit. Attitude. They are kind, loving, and radiate something you want to be near. They would be gentle, kind, positive. That's what a spiritual person is all about. A spiritual person is manifesting God within him. It has nothing to do with church. If you ask them a question like how God manifests Himself in their lives, they'll tell you. (Study Group:6/18/75).

The *Know Yourself* book answered this way:

> The best way to evaluate if you are growing spiritually is to ask your family or those closest to you. . . . Turn to those that know you best, your family and your friends, and ask them. . . . What would they say? Have they noticed a change in your attitude, your ability to cope with situations, your willingness to give and share? Have they noticed your increased sensitivity and awareness? Have you noticed a change? (Hayes 1971:84)

In a lesson on spirituality, study group members were asked to write an answer to the question, "What is your idea of a spiritual person?" The answers reflect both "knowing God" and increased concern for other people. A spiritual person

reflects radiance from God and nature;

knows God;

obeys God's laws;

lives by the law of love, and loves thy neighbor as thyself;

puts God first and is concerned with his fellowmen and with nature;

knows God. He knows he's not just a body or a mind.

You'd know the spiritual person by his works. (Study Group:6/11/75)

Spiritual growth, then, is the process of coming to "know God," by identifying with the divine inner self.

GAINING IDENTITY THROUGH SPIRITUAL GROWTH: I AM GOD

A metaphorical relationship with the divine lies at the base of the identity gained through spiritual growth. Recall that in chapter 1 it was posited that rational reasoning serves to separate the thinker from the object of his thought, and thus mitigates against a unifying identification with something "beyond oneself" (Klapp 1969; Rappaport 1977). The inevitable felt separation of the human from the world around him (of which he actually is a part) arises from his ability to use symbols. The ability to objectify his experience into symbols causes the symbolizer to perpetually be the subject "totally different from his world, the world of objects." Conscious, rational reasoning reminds man "again and again of his otherness" (van Baal 1971:220,226), and does not provide him with the sense of union that identifies.

The use of metaphor ameliorates the separation of subject and object. By the use of metaphor, we can objectify ourselves. That is, the subject takes the point of view of "the other" at the object end of the copula. The process of identification involves moving "from the preoccupation with the predicate back across the copula to an understanding of the subject and its difference" from the object. Metaphors can provide identity to "inchoate (i. e., inadequately identified) subjects." "Metaphors move us, and their aptness lies in their power to change our moods, our sense of situation" (Fernandez 1974:122,129).

The metaphorical relationship with the divine found in SFF can be expressed as:

God is my inner self,
My higher self is God,
I am God, or
I am

The metaphor is used two ways. In the first instance, "God" is the subject. God is "located" in "my inner self." God is "in the kingdom within, His kingdom, in our very own mind or consciousness" (Parker and St. Johns 1957:92). This metaphor is derived from Joe's insistence that "God is within. . . . God is in here [touching his heart],within us." "God is my inner self" is the first metaphor that needs to be accepted by the metaphysical student. By accepting this metaphor, he is accepting the belief that God dwells within, and is readily available to meet individual needs for communication with the divine. This metaphor establishes that God is within.[2]

114

An aid to accepting this metaphor and enhancing the communication with the divine is the concept of a benevolent, all-good God (Judah 1967:14, point 7). Dr. William Parker, a psychologist, founder of a New Thought church, and SFF leader, found that the image of a benevolent God was important in his prayer therapy work (Parker and St. Johns 1957). Parker found that the first step to improving one's life through prayer was the acceptance of a "God of Love" concept. More abstract concepts of the divine, and especially the image of an "avenging Heavenly Father," were difficult to approach with quotidian problems. Parker's student James Bonacci (1976b) reiterated God's "goodness" and we might say "helpfulness" in a lecture on "Prayer and Meditation for Wholeness" at the 1976 Metro Area winter retreat: "The first, and I think most important, premise in prayer and meditation is to know that God is a totally creative and good force working within us and around us."

In the second metaphor, "My higher self is God" or "I am God," "my higher self" or "I" is the subject. This metaphor establishes the divinity of one's own inner self. I have derived this metaphor from SFF's concept that each person has a spark of divinity. The propositions that God is within and that each man has a spark of divinity are basic because they form the foundation for "spiritual growth," which is fundamental to the metaphysical philosophy. Although each person may travel his own path to spiritual maturity, if he was not interested in "growing spiritually" he probably would not stay in the group.[3]

Accepting the "I am God" metaphor, becoming increasingly aware of the divineness of one's inner self, is spiritual growth.

> You are God. . . . You are the total expression of God. . . . Right now you are the total expression of His identity, but you just don't have the awareness of it. And the awareness of it is what makes the difference. That's how we change. We change here. Our spirit stays the same. It's not changeable. We change only by the degree of awareness of what we already are. We are already the total expression of God. . . .

> When you know yourself, then you know God, because the two are one. . . . As you develop the awareness of your self, then you become in tune with your higher self, or the God force. . . .
> You are God. You are unlimited. You are God in limitation only as long as you limit yourself. But you are really unlimited. When you look at yourself with limitations, then you are looking at God with limitations. (Metaphysics II:2/24/75)

Spiritual growth and all its advantages—inner peace, meaningfulness, more positive relationships, prosperity, happiness—derive from an increasing awareness of the existence of the God within. Spiritual growth is a process of accepting the "I am God" metaphor. In the metaphysical groups, "man is God, or more conservatively, becomes ever more like him" (Zaretsky and Leone 1974b:xxvii, point 15).

> Seek first the kingdom of heaven, and all of these things will be added to you. Seek to know yourself, because the kingdom of heaven resides in here. It's not some old man sitting up on some throne with gray whiskers putting little check marks in a book. You are your own judge. You're a spark of that divinity. The word "God" only means deity, it's not some gray-whiskered man. You are God. . . .
> When you know yourself then you know God. Then you truly know him. And you find that there are dominions and principalities beyond the physical plane. And actually they all reside within. (Metaphysics I:11/11/74)

The metaphors "God is my inner self" and "My higher self is God" can be accepted on a conscious, intellectual level. But seeking the kingdom of heaven within should ultimately lead to a state understood by nonrational, or experiential, means: a state in which a sense of identification with God, the universe—with all that lives—is achieved. The state is called "the I am" or "at-one-ment." Jenny described at-one-ment as "lifting the self up, seeking the God consciousness" (Study Group:2/19/75). The state is called at-one-ment because, when it is achieved, the aspirant should feel "at-one" with the universe and all mankind, and experience a sense of "wholeness" within himself. This feeling of

116

wholeness and identity with the "surrounds" is a characteristic of religious experience (Bellah 1970; Greeley and McCready 1974; James 1958; Wuthnow 1978).

"Wholeness" is of great concern to Spiritual Frontiers Fellowship. Lectures and workshops presented at national functions had titles such as "Paths toward Wholeness," "Healing and Wholeness," and "Wholeness: Personality Integration through Communion with God." The formation of a new study group in the Metro Area was advertised with the following: "Participants will study energies, vibrations, healing, etc., with a strong emphasis on wholeness and balance" (SFF 1976g). Lectures given at the Metro Area retreats were titled "From Fragmentation toward Integration," "Prayer and Meditation for Wholeness," and "Loving Yourself to Wholeness." One of these lectures equated wholeness with salvation, and suggested that wholeness was not a state to be attained once and for all, but was, rather, "elusive."

> Wholeness means living at one with God, in harmony. . . .You know when you are living in harmony, within yourself. And that is of course where God dwells. Wholeness is biblically referred to as salvation. Whenever you see the word salvation, you know they are talking about wholeness.
> However, I think that wholeness is an elusive, not whimsical, but elusive, quality or state of being. . . . Each of us is continually seeking this harmony. Now I stated that the power, God, is within. Our task, then, is to find wholeness by finding God or harmony and power within. . . . We each have to find the way back to harmony, to wholeness (Bonacci 1976b).

Meaning that identifies depends on the obliteration of distinctions (Rappaport 1977). The metaphors of spiritual growth, "God is my inner self," "I am God," and "I am," entail an increasing reduction of distinctions and "information" that can be understood on a conscious level. The understanding of "God is my inner self" depends somewhat on distinctions. For Joe, "God is within" meant that God is *not* "some old man sitting up on some throne with gray whiskers putting little check marks in a book." Under-

117

standing that "God is my inner self" can be achieved on a conscious level, and may entail deciding that God is "like" some things and "not-like" others. The metaphor "I am God" begins to reduce distinctions and to "take the person into the subject" (Klapp 1969:22). But "I am" obliterates all distinctions. "I am" no longer depends on distinctions understood by conscious reason. The experience of "I am" is a numinous one. It yields the identifying sense of union with something beyond oneself. In this state the metaphysical student achieves "harmony" and "wholeness."

THE MEANS TO SPIRITUAL GROWTH:
PRAYER AND MEDITATION

One "finds the way back to harmony" through prayer and meditation. Enhanced communication with God, or the divine inner self, is the key to gaining self-realization in a spiritual idiom.

> As men come into what they believe to be valid personal relationships with the spiritual world, they discover a firmer basis for understanding the great questions of life and faith, and for facing the human problems of suffering, injustice, and death. (SFF 1974:Part 2, point 5)

"Valid personal relationships with the spiritual world" are realized in prayer and meditation. Prayer is "talking to God." Meditation is "listening to God."

The essential elements of prayer, as practiced in SFF, are "Ask and ye shall receive" and believe that, as you are praying, God has already answered the prayer. *Principles, Purposes, and Program* (SFF 1974:Part 1, point 1; cf. Bonacci 1976b) says: "Life can be transformed and situations changed when prayer is seen not as 'overcoming God's reluctance but as laying hold on God's willingness.' " The metaphysicians often quote the passage from the Bible that says, "All things whatsoever ye pray and ask for, believe that ye *have* received them, and ye *shall* receive them (Mark 11:24, Holy Bible, Revised Version, emphasis mine). They interpret this as "we are to *ask* God for something we do not have by *affirming* that we have it, *believing* and *accepting* it as so" (Judah 1967:215, emphasis his). This is exemplified in the speech Jenny made at the end of the healing circle described in chapter 2, when she addressed God, saying: "And so we know before we even ask, that Thou has already taken care of that which must be done." This is "affirmative acceptance," which means "accepting the reality of the state one desires concomitantly with its affirmation" (Judah 1967:214). The concept of "affirmative acceptance" gives rise to the use of "affirmations" in which a desired state is simultaneously verbalized and accepted.

The desired state of "wholeness," "at-one-ment," or "Christ Consciousness" is expressed in affirmations such as "I am one with the Creative force—the source of all life. I am thankful. I accept my good" (Parker 1976a). Some of the subjects for meditation used in the study group were metaphoric "affirmations" such as "I rest myself in the sea of universal energy—I am one with it— I am part of it—I am it" (Hayes 1971:79).

Prayer as used in SFF is "affirmative," then, rather than the "petitionary" form traditional in Christian churches (Judah 1967:305-6). Verbalizing and accepting the desired realization of the divine inner self in affirmative prayer is believed to aid in the achievement of that realization.

Meditation is "listening to God," and it is in meditation that direct contact with the divine inner self is achieved.

> Meditation helps us to . . . establish a living relationship with our soul, and of course with the God within. (Bonacci 1976b)
> Meditation reorients us with our source. (Study Group:2/12/75)

Communicating with the divine inner self entails reaching beyond the mundane self, beyond the body and the mind: "Above all we become aware through meditation of our true self which is beyond mind and intellect, ego and biological propulsions" (Parampanthi 1963; see also Hayes 1971). In meditation the relationship with God and the universe can be realized, and thus

119

"improved": "Each time we will an interchange with God [in meditation] we are improving our soul's relationship with God" (Nahl 1975:13; see also Hayes 1971).

The "I am" feeling of wholeness and identification with the universe characteristic of religious experiences may be achieved in meditation. Bellah (1970:210) described a religious experience that transcended the separations of ordinary conscious reason as being "at the still center of the turning wheel." Jenny described the feeling of wholeness that can be achieved in meditation as "being in the stillness in the eye of the hurricane." A member of one of Jenny's study groups who had this experience felt "she was one with everything; totally knowing God. She was Him. . . . She was the whole of humanity and God itself" (Study Group: 1/28/76; see also Wise 1971).

This is the meditative state Jenny encouraged everyone in the study group to attain. As recorded in chapter 2, Dan reported during his meditation experience: "I felt like I was only in my head. The rest of my body didn't matter. I didn't want to come back." Jenny told him, "You'll soon go beyond that and be out of your body entirely. Then you just are." John once said that he had not quite reached the state in meditation he wanted to achieve. Jenny advised, "You should relax and just be. And in time, that being will go beyond the point where you are right now. You'll go beyond a void." Jenny told Sara, "You may get to the void, a state of being, where you just are."

The experience of meditation, as practiced in SFF, can be described as a series of stages:

1. Becoming comfortable and relaxed. Doing whatever is needed to assure that the meditator will be undisturbed; darkening and quieting the room if necessary, and assuming a meditative position. The meditation posture varies from simply lying back in a chair to sitting on the floor in the lotus position, with spine absolutely straight. A common element, however, is the palms-up position for the hands, signifying receptivity to God's love and energy coming into and flowing through one. Some

metaphysical students achieve a relaxed meditative state by simply being still and breathing slowly and deeply. Others use a precise system of rhythmic breathing.

2. Quieting the mind, achieving concentration, and becoming receptive. "A meditation subject" (Metaphysics I: 9/23/74) is generally used to aid concentration. During the meeting described in chapter 2, the study group meditated on the phrase "I am one with the universe." Other meditative subjects used in the class were "There is no way to peace, for peace is the way"; "Be still and know that I am God"; "What a man desires is already within him, but he still wanders here and there in search of it"; and "To know yourself is to know your potentials" (Hayes 1971:24). The meditative subject provides a conduit to the "soul" by blocking out other thoughts.

> Then one has to deal with the restless mind; when the waves of the mind subside the spirit of the soul comes to the surface. The technique is to lead the mind from many thoughts to a few leading thoughts, then to one thought; and to complete thoughtlessness. Concentrate gradually but persistently on one thought. Hold your mind to that thought to the exclusion of other thoughts. (Parampanthi 1963)

The meditation subject provides inspiration for insight, and creates a link between the unconscious and the conscious mind. Metaphysical teacher Bonacci (1976b) explained that, in meditation, we implant symbols (words) *into* the subconscious. Insight and illumination come from the symbols that we put in. "We create a transaction between the conscious and the unconscious. We become our own analyst."

3. Achieving the state of "being" associated with the sense of oneness with the universe. At this stage an insight, an answer to a question, or a solution for a problem may also be obtained. "Quietly, calmly, thoughtfully dwell in the 'still-point' and the doors of perception will open for you" (Bach 1968:80).

4. Coming back. In the study group Jenny called the medita-

tors back with words such as "Begin to come back down now. Very slowly begin to feel your body. Now open your eyes" (cf. Nahl 1975). This is followed by a period of sitting quietly and "coming-to."

5. Contemplating the experience. Thinking about and interpreting "what you got"; if in a group, describing the experience to the other group members. The message received in meditation may be simple, an action statement, such as the answer "Let it be as is" that Louise received to her question. Or the message may be more abstruse, requiring interpretation. The message may, for example, have been received in terms of symbols. David saw blue lights during meditation in the study group, and did not know what they signified. Jenny interpreted this symbol as "more and more healing coming in." (The color blue is associated with healing. Since David is a healer, it can be assumed that this means his healing powers will be increased.) During meditation Grace saw the church, no longer in existence, that she attended as a girl. Jenny suggested that this might signify a warning to Grace not to become too comfortable with the past. "It might mean that you're clinging to the past. We've got to get you going forward now. . . . You've got to expand on that foundation in the past, and get going higher and higher."

I have analyzed spiritual growth as a process of accepting metaphorical relationships, which were expressed as "God is my inner self," "My higher self is God," and "I am God." The analysis has suggested that accepting, on an intellectual level, the concepts that God is within and that the inner self of man is divine is primary to the nonrational *experience* of "I am." But it is also true that the experience of the state of being called "I am," "God consciousness," "at-one-ment," or "wholeness" validates the propositions that God dwells within and that it is possible to communicate with this divine part of oneself.[4] The numinous experience may even precede the belief that such experiences are manifestations of a person's intrinsic divinity.[5]

THE RESULTS OF SPIRITUAL GROWTH

The definitions of spiritual growth and characteristics of a spiritual person discussed above suggest that self-realization in a spiritual idiom serves several functions. The results of spiritual growth may be viewed in terms of the metaphysical students' movement along continua, on which are arranged better and worse positions.

Spiritual, Mental, and Physical Health

Although the metaphysicians do not conceive of the benefits derived from spiritual growth in terms of continua, they do believe that spiritual growth brings with it gains in "spiritual, mental, and physical" health. These gains correspond to the three continua I have labeled "Identity," "Emotional Health," and "Physical Health" (see figure 1). On each of these continua, the negative and positive positions represent the state of a person before and after experiencing spiritual growth.

Identity Continuum. Through spiritual growth the metaphysical student can achieve a more positive position on an identity continuum. The extreme positions along this continuum would be the negative one of an inchoate and fragmented identity, and the positive one of a whole and centered identity.

Spiritual growth satisfies two of the requirements for establishing identity discussed in chapter 1. First, the referent for establishing identity is symbolized by the "God within." The "God within" with which the student identifies is a spiritual symbol, the existence of which can be neither verified nor negated.

> In meditation you went beyond feeling, emotion and thought. And all of a sudden you found yourself empty. You found yourself you don't know what. What am I? I'm not my emotions. I am not my feelings. I am not my thoughts. I am something that is beyond that. What am I?. . .
>
> You are not your physical self. You are not your emotional self. You are not your mental self. You are beyond that. You are ex-

123

Identity continuum

	+
Extreme positions:	Inchoate, fragmented — Whole, centered
Object of comparison:	Self before spiritual growth — Self after spiritual growth

Emotional health continuum

	+
Extreme positions:	Negative attitudes and relationships — Positive attitudes and relationships
Object of comparison:	Self before spiritual growth — Self after spiritual growth

Physical health continuum

	+
Extreme positions:	Unhealthy physical state — Health if physical state
Object of comparison:	Self before spiritual growth — Self after spiritual growth

Fig. 1. Identity, emotional, and physical health continua along which movement can be achieved through spiritual growth

periencing these things to develop the awareness of your total identity. You have a total identity. You are the I am. . .

Not by might, not by power, but by spirit saith the Lord. He says not by might, nor by power, but by my spirit. Now that is your identity. That is your true identity. (Metaphysics II:2/24/75)

Second, spiritual growth is not an intellectual exercise. "Spirituality is not an intellectual concept of truth, love and wisdom or knowledge but an internal actualization of truth, love, wisdom and knowledge" (Hayes 1971:142). The mechanism for spiritual growth is not the activities of reading and thinking, but the experience of meditation, a religious experience that can provide the sense of wholeness that metaphysicians equate with salvation. Although it may take much time and many incarnations to reach the highest levels of spiritual maturity attained by great spiritual teachers like Jesus Christ, Buddha, and Mohammed, a person who is "on the path to spiritual growth" will at least come to feel "more whole."

According to Klapp (1969:39), identity problems can manifest themselves in dissatisfactions with (1) what a person thinks about himself introspectively, (2) his "reputation," how he believes others see him, (3) his feelings (lack of fullness of sentiments), or any combination of these three factors. Spiritual growth can be a means of ameliorating these dissatisfactions. As metaphysical students come to accept the "I am God" metaphor, and thus their own divinity, they can achieve a more satisfying self-image. Examples were provided by study group members.

Sara related that in the past she "spent too much time trying to prove herself to others." She was so dissatisfied with her self-image that she would deny who she was when meeting old acquaintances. After she became involved in metaphysics, she reported that these same people would stop her on the street and say, "you look good, and happy" and she accepted the compliments. "People have said I'm different—people I've known for twenty years."

For John spiritual growth meant that he laid to rest some "con-

125

fusing questions of belief" and obtained "a different concept of God than I had before." With this new concept of God, he came to feel that "you find the answers yourself." He also was "not concerned with what someone else says anymore," and he was "looking at things differently."

Laura came into the group because she "just wanted to know what this world is all about." She reported feeling "changed a little. I have a stronger belief in God. I feel like I know who I am. I don't worry about what others think."

David was "never satisfied with what [he] knew about [his] relationship with the higher power." Specifically, he had not wished to accept the view of God and man espoused by the "fire and brimstone preachers" he had heard as a child. He said, "Through a process of seeking, I have found this a comfortable place. . . . I'm often asked if I am a minister. I have grown through being in this class."

Grace reported that twenty years ago her family had experienced a tragedy that made her "decide there had to be something more to life. I had sort of gotten into just eating, sleeping, and working." After a long search, she felt she had found the "something more" through spiritual growth (Study Group: 7/2/75; 9/10/75).

Emotional Health Continuum. Gaining a more comfortable position on the "identity" continuum enables a more satisfying participation in a second dimension, represented by one's attitudes, feelings, and relationships with others. The polar positions on this continuum are negative and positive attitudes and relationships.

Spiritual growth is not meant to be a vehicle for withdrawing from this earthly life into a saintly and remote existence. Rather, its purpose is to aid in achieving a more comfortable position in this world. In the metaphysical groups, self-realization in a spiritual idiom means "self-improvement" and a happier adjustment to everyday life (see Judah 1967:16, point 11; Zaretsky and Leone 1974b:xxvi, point 13; Zaretsky and Leone 1974c).

126

Metaphysical organizations want to "make spiritual and psychic phenomena practical and related to everyday living" (Johnson 1976b). The content of SFF lectures and workshops show that this principle is put into practice. Workshops have titles such as: "Developing a Prosperity Consciousness"; "Creative Resolution of Conflict in You, Your Family, Your Group"; "Dreams: A Tool for Problem Solving and Spiritual Growth"; and "Integrating the Mystical Experiences of Meditation in Daily Living."[6]

The amount of time spent on personal problems in the study group demonstrates that dealing with problems was a major interest to the participants. The "sharing of psychic and spiritual experiences of the week" portion of the meetings, which was essentially a discussion of personal problems, accounted for about fifty minutes of the three-hour meetings. Group members discussed problems in their relationships with people at work, family, in-laws, neighbors and friends,[7] and difficulties with depression, anxiety, self-doubt, guilt, hostility, irritation, and "negative thoughts." They described worries over family members' troubles, economic problems, and concerns about work that had to be done or decisions that needed to be made.[8]

Psychological and interpersonal problems were often topics of study group lessons. The lesson described in chapter 2 was titled "Hate or Misguided Love" and dealt with negative emotions, how to become more positive, and how to rid oneself of faults. Other lessons had titles such as "Selfishness and Selflessness," "The Art of Relating," "Self-Doubt," and "Depression."

Everyone in the study group attested at some time or another that they were better able to cope with problems than they had been before. "Things" did not "bother" them as they once had. This was partially a consequence of achieving a more comfortable self-image and "not being concerned with what others think," or, as the group conceives it, feeling a "oneness with God." But solutions for problems were also found in meditation and prayer. Meditation and prayer, the means to spiritual growth, can serve functions that are more prosaic than enhancing one's relationship

127

with the universe: they can be used to improve a person's everyday life.

Meditation can help a person attain the commonplace goals he is striving for:

> In meditation I think of ourselves as molders of life. We mold new forms into our life, through tools; through visualization, through symbols, etc.
> The most important tool we have in meditation is visualization: to be able to visualize what you want in your life, a goal. . . . See yourself the way you want to be. (Bonacci 1976b)
> Meditation always joins inner resources with some felt, larger unity. When we meditate all of our inner resources: memory, the senses, music, art, and sensitivity are strengthened. The results can be seen in deeper awareness of life, fuller response to people, wiser decisions, more balanced living, clearer vision of goals and more success in reaching them. (Hayes 1971:39)

Meditation can be used to attain answers to specific questions, or solutions for problems. One can go into meditation with a particular problem, a question, in mind, and come away with an answer. SFF Study Group Leader Helen Nahl (1975:13) wrote instructions on how to meditate for an answer to a problem:

> If you are wrestling with a difficult problem, quiet your mind to the best of your ability, then see the problem acted out on an imaginary television screen. Mentally take the part of each of the other persons involved in the problem. Erase this mental screen. Now picture the solution screen. What is your first thought? What advice would you give another with this problem? Do you now have new insights that will be helpful? Give thanks that you know God's help is with you.

During the study group meeting described in chapter 2, Louise reported that she needed to meditate for an answer to something when she was visiting her family. She obtained her answer, "Let it be as is," which told her what action to take in the situation that was troubling her.

128

After a period of meditation, "our spiritual discernment is definitely sharpened. What was a problem is no more a problem; that is, the struggle to follow a right course of action is no longer a struggle; we are buoyed up and the right action seems happily inevitable" (Bro 1948). Sara reported that if she had "any kind of problem," she meditated. Jenny said "meditation puts you back in tune with all that's around and about you, without all that heaviness and depression, and anxiety. It seems to just wipe it all out." Sara agreed, saying, "There's no medicine on the market, no doctor, who can do it."

Jenny counseled Beverly to choose "one phase of her life" as a meditation subject. "Think about it for five minutes. Why is it important? Why do I go back to this? What should I learn from this? What was I really like then?" Jenny advised Beverly to do this because she felt Beverly had "some clearing out to do." By meditating on problems from her past, about which she was still bearing guilt, Beverly would be enabled to "clear out" the problems and release the guilt. Louise reported that during the group meditation, she "was thinking, if everyone 'thought healing,' there would be no disease. But first you must go within. Then I got this sharp pain at my heart." Jenny interpreted what had happened to Louise: "There must have been something there—love—still unhealed. You healed it just then. You released it." After John had an unpleasant encounter with his employer, he "meditated, then felt better." One evening Grace told the class that she had had "so much typing to do at work, and was just not in the mood." "I meditated at noon. Usually I can type ten pages an hour at the most. I came back after noon and typed 40 pages in two and one-half hours. Then later that day, in ceramics class, we were carving roses, and I made no mistakes. It was as if someone else was using my hands." (Study Group:6/18/75).

An analysis of the uses study group members made of meditation showed it was used to aid in solving problems ranging from depression, anxiety, and guilt to problematic relationships with family, friends, neighbors, and coworkers.

> The answer to your depression, to your restlessness, to your anxiety, your troubled marriage, your conflict with friends, relatives, with anyone; your unresolved resentment or anger, and even your illness, is, of course, within you. . . . Meditation is the door. (Bonacci 1976b)

Meditating makes a person "feel good." There is nothing somber or heavy in the metaphysical rituals, as there is in some orthodox Christian rituals. Although meditation can be silent and alone, the feeling reported afterward is refreshed and light—like "being on a spiritual high" (see Bro 1948). Sara reported that the feeling she had during meditation was "overwhelming." To her, it felt "something like a vibration all the way through, from the toes right up to the head." After meditating in the morning, Sara "felt good" all day. "My sister. . . couldn't figure out what was the matter with me, why I felt so good. I felt wonderful. I could see the sun, but my sister couldn't. She said, 'What's the matter with you? It's raining out.' I said, 'I feel great.'" Dan felt so good during the group meditation he "didn't want to come back." Meditation is advised as a "pick-me-up" to be used when a person is feeling drained or depressed. "Mini-meditations" of five to ten minutes in length serve this energy-giving function. John meditated at work and "felt better". Louise said she meditated in the employees' lounge at work during breaks to feel refreshed and to gather the energy to do her work. Her coworkers wondered if her meditation was the secret to her ability to serve the public always in a good-natured way.

"Talking to God," in prayer, could also aid movement on the emotional health continuum. The metaphysicians believe "ask and ye shall receive." Joe often said, "Prayer changes things." "Affirmations" in which a desired state is simultaneously verbalized and accepted are a manifestation of the kind of "affirmative prayer" used in metaphysical groups.

Affirmations are also a kind of positive thinking. Ernest Holmes (1947:39), a New Thought leader, explained how affirmations "work": "Whatever you mentally affirm, and at the

130

same time, become inwardly aware of, life will create for you." William Parker (1976b, 1977) echoed this in the newsletter of his New Thought church. "The thoughts we entertain become our realities. . . ." "Our affirmations eventually determine our state of being, our affairs and our relationships. They are the building blocks of our feelings." Affirmations are also a manifestation of the notion of "correspondences": what is true in spirit is reflected in the material world. Jenny said, "Thought is the building material. Everything on this earth came from thought" (Study Group: 9/10/75).

As noted above, some "affirmations" express the desired state of "wholeness." Other affirmations used by metaphysical groups affirm more commonplace goals, such as "I am capable of achieving any goal that I set for myself, for the God Power within me knows no insufficiency" (Parker 1977). Other metaphysical groups, notably New Thought and the Unity School of Christianity, make more use of affirmations than does SFF. Unity publishes a monthly magazine called *Daily Word,* which contains affirmations for each day of the month. Some Unity affirmations to assure prosperity are: "The all-providing mind is my resource, and I am secure in my prosperity," and "Divine love bountifully supplies and increases substance to meet my every need." Some examples of affirmations to be used in various situations are: " 'I go to meet my good'—(to be used when answering the doorbell or on the way to an appointment); 'There is nothing lost in Spirit'—(to be used when something seems to be mislaid); 'Peace'-(to be used when there is a distrubing noise, or when you are afraid); or 'I am Spirit, and Spirit cannot be sick'—(to be used when somebody remarks that you are not looking well)" (Braden 1951:177). The newsletter published by William Parker's (1976b) New Thought church prints affirmations such as "I affirm my Unity and Oneness with God. In God there are no failures. There is only success in my life."

In Jenny's groups the power of thought was given expression more often in "programming" and "visualizing" than in the use of affirmations. It is believed that if you think about something, or visualize it, you will "program" it to happen, because there is energy (power) in a thought. Programming and visualizing "can be used on a person or on a situation" (Study Group:3/26/75). Programming could be used to improve relationships. The student could try to "program" other people to do what he wanted them to, or to be more positive toward him. For example, in the meeting depicted in chapter 2, Jenny told Laura that by thinking she would like to join her husband on a business trip, she "programmed" him to take her along. Programming and visualizing were also used for physiological problems. For example, you could visualize an ill person as well, or program yourself not to feel pain when you went to the dentist or "think yourself thin" if you were overweight (Study Group:1/28/76; 2/26/75). The mechanism for "thinking yourself thin" was:

> Set a goal, pick a weight, and mentally visualize yourself as you should look at that weight. By doing that you will be destroying the bad fat cells. And you will eat less. You'll activate energy which will burn up fat. (Study Group:2/26/75).

The use of language in "affirmations" in which a desired state is simultaneously verbalized and accepted is similar to J. L. Austin's (1970:235) "performative utterances" or "performatives," in which "in saying what I do, I actually perform that action." He gives an example: "When I say 'I name this ship *Queen Elizabeth*' I do not describe the christening ceremony, I actually perform the christening." This "doing by saying" Austin calls the "illocutionary force" of a performative. Illocutionary force can only be used to achieve conventional states, i.e., states that are achieved through publicly recognized conventions, like becoming the ship *Queen Elizabeth*, becoming a king, becoming married, and so on. Performatives have another type of force, called "perlocutionary" force because "saying something will often, or even normally, produce certain consequential effects upon the feelings, thoughts, or actions of the audience, of the speaker, or the other persons: and it may be done with the design, intention, or purpose of producing them" (Austin 1962:101). Perlocutionary force is the power words have to convince or persuade. Perlocutionary performative acts can be used to achieve other than conventional states.

The states achieved by "affirmations" are states that are internal to the individual. They are states like "being one with the Creative foce" (Parker 1976a), being "the purity God desires" (Metaphysics I), being (or acquiring) "truth", "honesty," (Hayes 1971:128), "love," "patience," or "self-control" (Setzer 1974), or being "capable of achieving any goal that I set for myself" (Parker 1977). These speech acts, though they cannot be said to partake of illocutionary force since they do not deal with conventional states, do have the "perlocutionary" force of a performative. Affirmations, in which the speaker expresses and accepts desirable inner states, may have the force of convincing or persuading him to aspire toward and achieve these states. Saying "Oh God make me love. Oh God I sense love within me. Oh God I am love" (Setzer 1974) may persuade the speaker to be more loving. In "affirmations"then, the metaphysical groups recognize and make use of the persuasive power of words.

"Visualizing" and "programming" are a somewhat different matter. This use of "the power of thought" is not manifested in utterances. Here the desired goal is not put into words. Visualizing and programming can be used to attain desirable states, just as affirmations can. You can visualize yourself healthy, program yourself not to feel pain or not to contract an illness, or think yourself thin. As long as the reference is to the states of the visualizer, visualizing can be said to possess the same perlocutionary force as performative utterances do. But visualizing and programming that are directed outside oneself, such as visualizing a new school in order to assure the passage of a school millage tax proposal, programming a storm away, programming a change in someone else's attitude, or visualizing an ill person well (unbeknownst to the object of the visualization), go beyond the force that words and thoughts are ordinarily thought to have. Although these uses of thought cannot be said to have illocutionary or perlocutionary force, they would seem to have the ability to impart to the thinker a sense of power. If a person tries to "think a storm away" and the storm in fact does not come (for whatever reason), his sense of power over the situation is enhanced.

By means of the enhanced self-image that spiritual growth entails, and through the practical use of meditation and prayer, the metaphysical student can achieve a better position on an "emotional health" continuum. He can move from drained to refreshed, irritated to calm, unhappy to happy, troubled to at peace, guilty to innocent, unforgiving and unforgiven to forgiving and forgiven, powerless to powerful.[9]

That real changes in self-concept and attitude can be wrought by "spiritual growth" is supported by studies of the beneficial psychological and interpersonal effects of participation in spiritual groups (Johnson 1963), application of a religious philosophy in everyday life (Maddock and Kenny 1972), and intense religious experience (Greeley and McCready 1974; Hood 1974; McCready 1976; Maslow 1964; Wuthnow 1978).[10]

Physical Health Continuum. A third dimension in which it is believed improvement can be made by spiritual growth is physical health. The "wholeness" desired by metaphysical students includes a "whole" or healthy body. Spiritual healing is one of SFF's main concerns. Workshops at SFF functions had titles such as "Four Keys to Vigorous Good Health," "Healing through Awareness of Self," "Meditation and Self-Healing," "Opening to the Healing Consciousness" and "Directing the Flow of Healing Energies."

Study group members lamented (and reportedly cured) their own headaches, back problems, ulcers, hypertension, fatigue, and excesses of smoking and drinking, as well as more serious illnesses and injuries of family and friends. One-fourth of all the problems discussed in the study group concerned physical ailments.

John reported that when he began Joe's metaphysics class he "had a bleeding ulcer, and high blood pressure," his "back was bothering him all the time," and that he "used to hide in the bottle." Influenced by the classes and metaphysical study he had undertaken on his own, John quit smoking and drinking. "And I had no withdrawal (symptoms) from smoking this time. My blood pressure doesn't bother me. I can control it. My ulcer hasn't bothered me. In fact, as far as I'm concerned, it's gone." Sara reported doctors had told her she had high blood pressure. On the way to a follow-up visit to the doctor, she "was very anxious, and talked to God." At this visit the doctors told her she no longer had symptoms of hypertension. "They said, 'Whatever you're doing, you're curing yourself.' "

It was not unusual for Jenny and David to direct healing activity toward a study group member's illness or fatigue, as they did with Grace's cold during the meeting described in chapter 2. The healing circle directed intercessory healing prayers and protective powers to the listed loved ones, as well as to oneself.

The ailments most often discussed in the group (migraine headaches, back problems, ulcers, hypertension, smoking, drinking, and fatigue) are stress-related. Judah (1967:18) discusses Hans Selye's (1956) discoveries of the effects of stress in the etiology of disease, and says, "If stress is a factor leading to the onset of many diseases, there should be some practical benefits in techniques that relieve stress, such as those used by the healing sects. Peace of mind and faith are beneficial to health." He notes that an approach to healing that "increases confidence, faith, acceptance, and reassurance" is bound to be "therapeutic and aid the healing process" (Judah 1967:306).

Further evidence that metaphysical "healing" techniques may indeed be efficacious in treating stress-related symptoms is to be found in the fact that techniques such as meditation are being recommended by doctors for patients with stress-related illnesses on the basis of the relaxation they provide, regardless of whether they are joined with a religious philosophy (see, for example, *TM:*

Discovering Inner Energy and Overcoming Stress, by Harold Bloomfield, M.D., Michael Peter Cain, and Dennis T. Jaffe, and *The Relaxation Response,* by Herbert Benson, M.D.).

The possibility of achieving more positive positions along these three identity, emotional, and physical health continua suggest that study group members gain a sense of power over their own life situations. By the use of prayer, meditation, and healing, they gain a power that can be used in everyday life.

This is affirmed by the fact that, when personal problems were discussed in the study group, 87 percent of the time individual members either reported what action they had taken in an attempt to solve the problem, or were told (usually by Jenny) what action they could take. The rest of the time, the study group as a whole could undertake a solution for the problem, as for example through intercessory healing prayer.[11]

Spiritual Status

Two more continua on which spiritual growth enhances positions are not so widely recognized by group members as are the first three "spiritual, mental, and physical" health continua. These two continua, which I have labeled "In-Group/Out-Group Status" and "Intra-Group Status," are diagrammed in figure 2. The members of the metaphysical network I studied would deny that they are concerned with status, either within or without the group. Yet some of the metaphysical symbols and concepts are unmistakably hierarchical in nature, and readily lend themselves to striving for ever higher levels, or, in effect, "spiritual status seeking."

In-Group/Out-Group Status Continuum. On this continuum people in the metaphysical network are compared to the rest of humanity. This comparison was of some importance to Joe, who often alluded to it in his metaphysics classes. The extreme positions on the continuum are occupied by the unenlightened "masses of humanity" and the "enlightened" who are experiencing spiritual growth. The "masses" have no knowledge of meta-

In-Group/Out-Group Status Continuum

	−	+
Extreme positions:	Unenlightened	Enlightened
Object of comparison:	Masses of humanity not in metaphysical net-work	Network of metaphysical students

Intra-Group Status Continuum

	−	+
Extreme positions:	Undeveloped psychic ability Low level of spiritual evolution	Developed psychic ability High level of spiritual evolution
Object of comparison:	Persons in the metaphysical network	

Fig. 2. Status continua on which positions can be enhanced by spiritual growth.

137

physics. The "enlightened" are involved "in this work." The differentiation can be viewed as a continuum, rather than as a dichotomy, because some of the "masses" are believed to be more "ready" than others to embark on the path to spiritual growth. Joe is influenced in his knowledge of these matters by the lessons he receives (by mail) from Astara.

According to Joe, the enlightened and unenlightened have different experiences at death. A dying person must experience several stages of consciousness. The length of time in any stage depends on the relative degree of enlightenment of the individual. At one stage of death, the dying person encounters the "clear light of the void." Joe said, "If you can melt in with this clear light of the void, other stages of consciousness are bypassed. The light leads to bliss. And you have broken the wheel of karma. You don't have to reincarnate anymore." Joe implied that a person who has seen the clear light of the void before—in meditation, for example (i. e., a spiritually enlightened person)—is more likely to be able to "melt into it" than the unenlightened person (Metaphysics II:2/3/75).

Life after death also holds differential rewards for the enlightened and for the masses. Joe described life "on the other side" in his Metaphysics of Death class. After death less spiritually evolved souls go to the "Borderlands"; those more evolved to the "Highlands." The clothing worn "on the other side" depends on the degree of spirituality attained in this world. "You weave your clothes out of your spiritual bank account. The more you put into your spiritual growth, the more luminescence you will have in your clothing." Those in the Borderlands will wear grays, browns, and negative colors. Those in the Highlands will wear clearer colors, and white. And "the housing you will have there will match your spiritual capacity here" (Metaphysics II:4/21/75).

Joe's beliefs had a messianic flavor, for he believed that the masses and enlightened would experience differential rewards in an Aquarian Age dispensation. He felt that with the New Age would come a division between the enlightened, and the unenlightened (those souls who were "not ready for it"). The enlightened would be allowed to reincarnate on earth, and the unenlightened would not. In 52,000 years the division would be dissolved and the unenlightened race would meet the enlightened one (Metaphysics II:4/7/75).

In the study group, this continuum representing a status differential between metaphysical students and the rest of the world was not stressed. But David and Jenny did occasionally express the conviction that those who had already embarked on their paths to spiritual growth would come to lead others, and to serve as examples for others, as the turmoil concomitant with the change from the Piscean to the Aquarian Age reached its peak.

Whether a concept of one's enlightened status with regard to much of the rest of society is imbued with great specificity, as in Joe's case, or whether it is more general, as in the study group, it could serve to move the metaphysical student to a more positive position along a status continuum.

Intra-Group Status Continuum. The "Intra-Group Status continuum" corresponds to a status gradient among the persons in the metaphysical network. One dimension of this continuum is relative ability to perform psychic phenomena. A status gradient of psychic abilities was apparent in the Metaphysics I class. This class of twenty-nine was heterogeneous and included (1) spiritual leaders (Jenny and Joe);[12] (2) veteran members of the metaphysics classes and study groups; (3) beginners who would become more involved in metaphysics by taking more classes, or by studying on their own; (4) beginners who would "pass through," not becoming further involved in metaphysics, or remaining involved at merely the "play" level. The leaders and veterans displayed more psychic abilities and more familiarity with the style and language used to describe psychic experiences. Beginners expressed feelings of being "outclassed" by these people who already knew what to do.

A status gradient of this sort did not take shape in the smaller

139

study group. Everyone in this group had had some introduction to the concepts and language of metaphysics. All the members of the study group were considered to be on the path to spiritual growth. Only two members were recognized as having more psychic ability and knowledge than the rest of the members. These were Jenny, the "moderator," and David, who was recognized as a spiritual healer who had been "in this work" longer than other members (and was, incidentally, the oldest member of the group). The group often mentioned the "rapport" the members felt and the fact that "we all help each other." Rapport, indeed, describes the feeling tone of the group better than concern for internal status. The respect and attention accorded each member did not correlate with relative psychic abilities (although everyone was expected to *try* to perform psychic experiments). There did not seem to be jealousy of one another's psychic abilities.

The metaphysical leaders are probably more concerned with their place on this continuum than the followers. Becoming a spiritual leader leads to a kind of notoriety within a specialized network of people. Being perceived as endowed with extrasensory powers enlarges and enhances the reputation of such a person. A leader who becomes known for his psychic abilities is constantly confided in and sought out for counsel. He may acquire a retinue of clients who depend on him to various degrees. He will be cornered, questioned, and consulted whenever he enters a roomful of people who are in the "enlightened" network.

Another element that lends itself to concern for internal status is the concept of spiritual growth as soul evolution. According to Joe soul evolution proceeds through awarenesses of seven planes that are arranged hierarchically. In Joe's view, humanity is arranged on the hierarchical levels like a pyramid, with most people at the bottom levels, and only a few highly evolved persons at the highest levels.

"Where one is" in his process of soul evolution is not an easy thing to discern. The manifestations of spiritual growth (a more positive self-image, more positive attitudes and relationships, and a healthier body) do not tell a person exactly where he is along the

140

path—how far he has come and how far he has to go. These things are also not likely to be perceived by persons other than the student himself and those closest to him, which makes comparison of one's own position with that of others difficult. The observable manifestations of spiritual growth are few—a glow in the eyes, an "innerness," perhaps quietness. Facility with psychic abilities is not a good way to judge spiritual attainment, since psychic ability may be achieved without concomitant gains in spirituality.

Metaphysical students are not supposed to be concerned about "where they are" in the spiritual growth hierarchy. Yet, during a meeting of the study group, Jenny implied that she knew where each of us was in our soul's growth, and the cry went up, "Tell us, tell us." But Jenny would not. Although it is considered unbecomingly egocentric to be concerned about one's place on the spiritual growth continuum, if a person is concerned, the intensely personal quality of spiritual growth leaves him free to decide if his position on this continuum has improved over his former position, and if his position is a good one with respect to others.

Although it was not explicitly discussed in class, informal after-class conversations suggested that Jenny and Joe believed they were "old souls" who had lived many lives on earth, on the "other side," and even on other planets and such places as the lost continent of Atlantis. There were times when their conversations made it seem as if they believed they had already "broken the wheel of karma" and reincarnated again on earth of their own volition, in order to teach others what they knew of "the spiritual side of life."[13]

In summary, in modern fragmented society, meaning is found in the individual to a larger extent than was true in premodern societies, where meaning was "located" in the community. Discovering meaning within oneself is "self-realization." Self-realization in Spiritual Frontiers Fellowship is set in a spiritual idiom, and labeled "spiritual growth." Spiritual growth is the increased awareness of one's divine inner self. Enhanced awareness of, and communication with, the divine inner self is achieved through prayer and meditation. The "meaning" found within oneself, though "individual" and not dependent on communal ritual practice, is not totally "private." An SFF member accepts an interpretation, shared by other metaphysical students, that his inner experiences emanate from the spark of divinity he shares with all humanity, and all that lives.

Spiritual growth is a good means of establishing identity because the "God within" with which one identifies is a spiritual symbol, not subject to falsification. The "I am God" metaphor, which symbolizes this identification, serves as a means of predicating an "inchoate subject." Spiritual growth is not an intellectual exercise. It depends on experience—the ritual of meditation. Meditation is a religious experience that can provide a sense of wholeness. This identification with God and the universe, which SFF labels "at-one-ment," is the ultimate goal of the metaphysical aspirant.

Spiritual growth, or identifying with the divine inner self, can enable movement to more positive positions along several continua. The metaphysical student can move:

1. from an inchoate and fragmented position to a whole and harmonious position along an identity continuum;
2. from negative to positive attitudes and relationships in the continuum of everyday life experiences;
3. from a less to a more healthy physical state;
4. from an unenlightened position alongside the "masses of humanity" to an enlightened position among the metaphysically aware. Relative position along this continuum is believed by some to have repercussions in the way one experiences death, in life after death, and in the rewards of the Aquarian Age;
5. from a lower to a higher level of "soul evolvement" and psychic ability. This continuum allows the metaphysical student to weigh, in his own mind, his own growth, and his relative position alongside others in the metaphysical network.

142

Self-Realization in Spiritual Growth

The preceding chapters have analyzed what I take to be the heart of Spiritual Frontiers Fellowship's response to societal fragmentation. Its emphases on individual exegesis and self-realization set in a spiritual idiom are expressions and legitimations of the autonomy that societal fragmentation produces. It would be wrong, however, to assume that SFF makes no attempt to mitigate a second concomitant of social differentiation—the sense of separation from other persons. The next chapter describes these attempts.

1. Spiritual growth thus provides a rationale for the individual differences among group members. Each person may be in a different place on his path to spiritual maturity. For example, the fact that all group members are not equally successful at performing various psychic phenomena can be accounted for by differences in their spiritual development. That everyone does not believe the same things may also be rationalized by the differences in personal growth experiences. For those who believe in reincarnation, this is reinforced by the theory that each person is "working out a different karma."

2. That God is within oneself does not preclude his being "in" other people's "selves" and in all that lives, because "everything comes from one divine Mind" (SFF 1974:Part 2, point 1). In the metaphysical movement groups, "God is regarded as being all and in-all" (Judah 1967:14, point 7).

3. People may be attracted to SFF or to a study group initially because they are interested in the psychic, but their interest usually shifts to spiritual growth. Jenny said occasionally people join her groups who are interested only in "the phenomena," i. e., developing the psychic faculties. But she says they soon lose interest, or find that they don't "fit in" with the rest of the group, and drop out (Study Group:1/15/77).

4. "The validity of [a nondiscursive or numinous] experience seems to be sufficiently demonstrated by its mere occurrence. It happens, it is felt, and it carries with it a subjective validity which can, as Otto (1958) and James (1958) and many others have testified, be extremely persuasive. Since the experience is taken by the communicant to be a response to an expression of an ultimate sacred proposition[in this case, "God is within"], that proposition partakes of the same sense of validity. This is to say that the subjective, affective validity of the experience is likely to be transformed in ritual into the rational . . . truth of the proposition" (Rappaport 1976a:17–18).

5. It is not uncommon for people to join metaphysics groups because they have had psychic experiences (sometimes frightening experiences) for which they are seeking interpretation.

6. A content analysis of the titles of 308 lectures and workshops presented at national and Metro Area activities in 1975 and 1976 (six national retreats, two national conferences, two area retreats, 18 monthly area meetings) showed that about one-third obviously dealt with improvement in interpersonal relationships or emotional or physical health. This analysis of titles probably underestimates the pragmatism of these activities because esoteric titles sometimes hid a pragmatic orientation that came to light when further description was available. For example, the description of a workshop entitled "The Fourth Dimension" said: "Inspiration as to how you can use your full range of consciousness to accomplish your goals and purposes—stimulation of self-confidence through recognition of who you are and why you are here."

7. From a total of 470 problems discussed in the year-long course of the study group, 24% concerned interpersonal relationships.

8. These miscellaneous psychological, social, and environmental problems accounted for 31% of all the problems discussed in the group. Physical ailments and injuries accounted for another 24%. The remaining 21% were problems raised by psychic experiences, such as frightening dreams or out-of-body experiences.

9. Movement on the emotional health continuum was also aided by the use of spiritual formulas and "spiritual laws" learned in the study group. These spiritual solutions for quotidian problems are discussed in chapter 7.

10. The counterargument is that intense religious experiences are regressions into infantile ego states (cf. Prince and Savage 1972, for example), which could imply that persons with relatively *weak* ego strength are more likely to be susceptible to ecstatic experiences.

11. Even if the problem was intrinsic to someone else (a friend's illness, for example) over three-fourths of the time the study group member or the study group as a whole could undertake a solution for it. For example, Louise put the "White Light" around her father before he underwent surgery. And she, along with her aunt, could pray for her troublesome cousin's avoidance of jail. David could help Grace's friend who had cancer by laying-on-of-hands healing, if only to allay some of her anxiety. (In the remaining one-fourth of the cases involving someone else's problem, it was thought necessary that the troubled person himself take action to solve his own problem.)

12. Joe taught the class. Jenny also attended it, and was frequently consulted.

13. Recollections of colorful and spiritually meaningful past lives can enhance one's spiritual status in this life. Some members of the metaphysical network feel they were alive in early Christian times and some feel they were "close to Christ." Most past lives recounted occurred in a metaphysically relevant realm. For example, Joe recalls lives as a Buddhist lama in Tibet, and as an American Indian medicine man. Past lives may be a reflection of status desires, but if so, it is spiritual status. No lives reflecting socioeconomic status, such as a millionaire living on a yacht, were ever reported.

144

6

Spiritual Frontiers Fellowship's
Response to Separation: Fellowship

A feeling of separation from other persons was described in chapter 1 as one aspect of societal fragmentation. The core of values held in common in American society is shrinking (Gruen 1966). Because relationships are specialized, they are increasingly one-dimensional and impersonal. Spiritual Frontiers Fellowship does not build a permanent community where one is sheltered from industrialized society's specialized, nonemotional, and fragmenting roles, but it does try to alleviate separation from others by providing opportunities for "fellowship" (SFF 1974).

> SFF is a *fellowship* of these who, having accepted the validity of one or more of the (nonphysical) phenomena, would encourage each other and ultimately the whole Church to seek for further light and greater reality in the spiritual life. (SFF 1974)

> For its own members, SFF seeks to provide an assurance that they are not alone, but are part of a larger company of people who desire to seek further exploration of truth. . . . It seeks to provide a comfortable climate for sharing and discussing experiences of nonphysical reality. (SFF 1974:Part 3, point 4)

The "comfortable climate for sharing and discussing experiences" is implemented at area meetings, at retreats, and in study groups.

145

The area meetings provide at least a modicum of "fellowship." The Metro Area meetings, held one evening each month, consisted of a healing service, a short meditation, a lecture, and a "coffee hour."

The healing service was performed as a group ritual. The setting was a darkened chapel in the large and sumptuous Methodist church where area functions were held. About twenty people quietly entered the chapel and sat in rows of chairs facing the front.

Jenny and Joe were standing in the front of the chapel, facing the assembled group, when the healing service began at 7:00 P.M. Jenny began the service by instructing the group to "sit in a relaxed manner with feet flat on the floor and hands resting in your lap or on your knees with the palms up" (SFF 1976h). The palms-up position of the hands was perceived as a symbol that the supplicant was "fully receptive." Only in this way could the person "take full advantage of the healing energy" by "letting God's energy flow into and through him." Jenny explained that the healers are actually "letting God use their hands," and invited others to try "to work" at healing if they wished (but no one came forward). At the suggestion of a Metro Area leader, we recited the Lord's Prayer in unison, "to get ourselves centered."

Then, one by one, in random fashion, two volunteers from the "audience" went to the front of the chapel and sat in chairs with their backs to Jenny and Joe. The healers performed "laying-on-of-hands healing" on these volunteers. Jenny touched the supplicants and actively manipulated their heads or arms. Joe, less animated in his healing style, solemnly closed his eyes and held his hands on the head or back of the person to be healed. Often he held one hand in the air, in a gesture reminiscent of a blessing.

The persons seeking healing sat in relaxed positions, most with eyes closed. As the short healing session progressed, the volunteers seemed to grow more relaxed: heads slumped over; bodies

146

slid farther down into the chairs. No one looked frightened or un-aware of how to behave; these were people who had watched "healings" performed many times before. Each volunteer sat for five to ten minutes, and then, prodded by the healers, relinquished his chair to another member of the group and quietly returned to his seat in the audience.

Although not everyone in the audience was touched by the healers, it was felt that everyone in the room shared the energy transmitted. Everyone both "received" and "transmitted" the healing energy, and it is thought that "as this spiritual energy is shared, each individual cell in our bodies begins to reawaken and function more properly" (SFF 1976h).

At a few minutes before 8:00, Jenny asked an area leader to sing the Doxology. As she led, in a clear and loud soprano voice, the group intoned:

> Praise God, from whom all blessings flow,
> Praise Him, all creatures here below,
> Praise Him above, ye heavenly host,
> Praise Father, Son, and Holy Ghost.
> Amen.
>
> (Bishop Thomas Ken)

At 8:00 P.M. the healing service ended, and the group moved into the nave, where they were joined by thirty to sixty more peo-ple. An area leader led the group in meditation. Though it is a highly personal ritual, meditation need not be exclusively indi-vidualistic. It can be performed in conjunction with others, and thus provide a shared experience. The meetings began with a meditation in order to promote "oneness" (harmony) and to "raise the vibrations" (essentially, to help lay aside the cares of the day). This evening the meditation subject was "God and I are one" (SFF Area Meeting:3/20/75).

After a one-hour lecture, there was time for informal talk dur-ing a "coffee hour." The area leadership always went to a restaurant after the meetings for further informal conversation. These gatherings sometimes lasted until midnight. A member of the area steering committee expressed the importance of the "fellowship" aspect of the meetings: "These people! And it's getting so I know them all. It doesn't matter what the lecture is; I come to be with the people."

"Fellowship" is also a primary reason for attending retreats. Retreats are held in secluded settings, such as conference centers or college campuses. At retreats, for three to seven days, a group of people eat, sleep, meditate, sing, hear lectures, and participate in workshops, "rap sessions," and séances together. For these few days, the outside world falls away. A woman at the 1975 Metro Area retreat said, "I hate for this to end. It's nice to get away from people 'out there.' I wouldn't care if they didn't have lectures and workshops." Participants in these gatherings report a sort of "culture shock" when they reenter their workaday world. The "retreat," therefore, is well-named.

SFF members are also joined by a "mail-order fellowship." Each month they receive a newsletter from the national office, and perhaps from their area organization as well. The national newsletter has columns written by the president and the executive director. It contains news of events in areas around the country, and occasionally reports news of individual members. Metaphysical groups that have mail correspondence as their bread-and-butter, such as Astara, publish a more informal and "familial" newsletter than SFF's organ. Astara's newsletter, *The Voice*, makes "all members feel part of the Astara family" (Judah 1967:143–44) through such vehicles as pictures of founders Earlyne and Robert Chaney and their daughter Sita (captioned "Earlyne," "Robert," etc.), pictures of staff members in the midst of their daily activities, and a column called "A Visit with Robert."

SFF's area meetings and retreats, then, provide opportunities for "fellowship" where group rituals, in the form of healing services and meditation, may be performed. The "mail-order fellowship" fostered by correspondence from SFF's national organization may serve to alleviate a feeling of "separateness" by confirming that there are others around the country who share the reader's metaphysical interests. But the "fellowship" attained at area meetings and through the *Newsletter* is sporadic, short-lived, and casual. The fellowship at the retreats is more intense, but also short-lived. It is the study groups that provide the best opportunity for developing fellowship and alleviating the sense of separation from other people.

FELLOWSHIP IN THE STUDY GROUP

Toffler (1970) predicted that high rates of mobility, which cause identity-giving reference points to change rapidly, would create a need for strategies for developing (and terminating) close but short-term relationships. Fair (1974:43–44) writes that because of our lack of closeness to others "we have been obliged to create a new profession, or rather to modernize and vastly expand an old one—that of the listener-helper."

The study group is an example of close but short-term relationships, and the leader, Jenny, is an example of a new form of listener-helper. Jenny often repeated the sentiment that in the old days neighbors were friends who talked over the back fence and ironed out their problems. Today, neighbors are not close, and this back-fence problem-solving is no longer viable. "Today people can go to psychiatrists, but they are expensive, so people come to groups like this, and to me."

The study group is not an attempt to build a life-enfolding, on-going community. Some study groups do continue for as long as the members wish to meet, but most follow the pattern of Jenny's study group, meeting weekly over one year. On the basis of the instrumental/expressive typology of roles, study group membership is more "instrumental" than "expressive." Characteristically, instrumental roles are (1) functionally specific, (2) performance or achievement oriented, (3) means to ends, and (4) unemotional or affectively neutral. Expressive roles, on the other hand, are (1)

149

diffuse, spilling over into many different sectors of the person's life (2) ends in themselves, and (3) emotional or affective (Parsons 1937).

The study group members' relationships did not "spill over into many different sectors" of their lives. The members were close within the confines of the group, yet most did not see each other from one meeting to the next. Their homes were dispersed over a wide area.[1] Only Louise and Sara lived in close proximity to one another. The other members were not likely to see each other in their daily round of activities. The study group member role was also more a means to an end (the goal of achieving individual spiritual growth) than an end in itself. The "listener-helper" role of the study group leader is also largely instrumental in character. The members listen to one another, and offer advice and encouragement, but other kinds of resources (monetary or physical) are neither expected nor offered.

Unlike the "ideal type" instrumental role, the role of study group member did lead to affective relationships. There was much talk in the group of "rapport" and "harmony." The members often said, "we all help each other." Actually, the leader, Jenny, was the center of the group's relationships, and it was she who did the majority of the helping.

Jenny's Leadership

That Jenny was the focal point of the group was demonstrated by the manner of recruitment into the study group. The members joined the class because they either knew Jenny or knew about her from others. They knew her through her work in Spiritualist churches or through her participation in Joe's metaphysics classes. The members of Jenny's study group were all acquainted with her reputation as a psychic, a healer, and a highly spiritual person. Some manifestations of her greater knowledge and powers were that she was a psychic counselor to a retinue of clients; she conducted the healing service at the Metro Area SFF meetings; she gave workshops on healing at area and national SFF functions;

150

she preached sermons and gave messages in Spiritualist churches; and she was acquainted with many of the best-known workers in the psychic field. In addition, she had been a member of two study groups and had led one, and was leading three simultaneously when our study group met. The group did not call itself an SFF study group. It was labeled "Know Yourself class," after the book we used, or "Jenny's class," after our leader. We met in Jenny's home, surrounded by the signs of her devotion to the "spiritual side of life," and the diverse philosophies she had drawn upon to fashion her personal meaning system.

That the group revolved around Jenny was also manifested in the dynamics of the group meetings. Because Jenny was charismatic in the etymological sense of the word—that is, she had more highly developed charismata, or gifts of the spirit, than the rest of us—she had greater insight and ability to interpret, and thus it was Jenny who was most likely to interpret messages received through ESP or in meditation. As recorded in chapter 2, she interpreted the symbols in the vision Dan saw when he concentrated on Laura in the ESP experiment. Jenny also interpreted the meditation experiences of Louise, Dan, David, and Grace; and she told us what she had received for each of us in her own meditation.

Jenny was also most likely to suggest solutions for member's problems, although everyone did actively listen to everyone else's problems. If a successful resolution of a problem was reported, there were usually exclamations of "Oh, that's wonderful," "That's really great," from fellow class members. In the meeting described in chapter 2, John, Dan and Sara, as well as Jenny, gave Beverly suggestions on how to meditate. John and David sympathized with Louise when she felt she was too critical of others. But it was Jenny who was most likely to actually offer solutions for problems. As reported in chapter 2, she told Laura and me not to get too involved in other people's lives. She gave John the book that enabled him to find a more comfortable identity. She suggested that John should put the Light around his troublesome boss, and I around my rattling car door. Grace was counseled not to "claim" her cold, and Jenny and David tried to cure the cold by laying-on-of-hands healing. A quantitative analysis of 316 solutions suggested for problems raised by group members[2] in the year-long course of the study group showed that one-third of the time Jenny suggested what should be done about a problem. In only 21 cases (7 percent) did group members suggest solutions for each other's problems, and in 8 of these Jenny also provided some input. In the remaining 60 percent of the cases, group members proposed their own solutions for their own problems, or recounted what they had already done about them. In 17 of these 173 cases, Jenny also commented on the solution the troubled person had proposed.

Jenny did endeavor to follow the "democratic" and anti-authoritarian policy set down by SFF for the leadership of study groups. She labeled her role "moderator" (as suggested in *Know Yourself*) and said her function was to guide us, but "you're going to be doing a whale of a lot of it all by yourself" (Study Group: 1/8/75). Throughout the study group meetings, everyone had free rein to express their own opinions and relate their experiences. The discussion of lessons and the reporting of experiences always proceeded in an "around the room" fashion that gave each member his chance to talk. Only occasionally did Jenny say, "That brings us to the lesson" (whether it did or not) when the hour was late and the lesson in the book had not been completed.

Since one of the functions of study groups is to produce more study group leaders, Jenny sometimes tried to involve the members by asking them to bring something to read for the inspirational reading at the beginning of the class, to do research pertaining to a particular lesson, or to lead the healing circle. But no one assumed these duties very readily. At the last meeting of the study group, the members were told that they were now ready to lead their own groups.

With the close of this meeting, you will have ended a stage of growth in your development. You are about to enter the second and very necessary stage of your development. You are now ready to share what you have learned and experienced with those who are just beginning their quest. This group will come to a close in hopes of all the members becoming moderators or assistant moderators, forming their own groups. You are ready for this. (Hayes 1974:184–85)

In our group this precipitated laughter and incredulity. Jenny persisted in encouraging members to begin their own groups, but no one expressed readiness. To the admonition from Jenny "You have the book" (*Know Yourself*), Sara replied, "But you taught me things which weren't in that book."[3]

The manner of recruitment into "Jenny's class," the acknowledgment of her greater knowledge and power, and the dynamics of the group (i.e., the magnitude of Jenny's input in interpreting experiences and suggesting solutions for problems) attest to her leadership. Contact with other study group leaders at area and national functions provided evidence that they, too, were frequently the focal points of their groups. Because of the "listener-helper" role of the study group leader, it seems likely that strong leadership would arise in study groups, despite SFF's efforts to avoid it.[4] Jenny's influential leadership did not, however, lessen the "harmony" and "rapport" the members felt, nor the "sharing" that took place in the group.

Study Group "Sharing": Quotidian Problems, Rituals, Meditations, and Past Lives

In the study group meetings, there was much "sharing." Each person shared his experiences of the week: the problems he had encountered in his "larger world" outside the "small world" of the study group (Hayes, 1971:84). (It was possible, however, for group members to share their problems without really saying much about them. The references might be vague, and understandable only to Jenny, who had been told of the problem outside class. An example from chapter 2 is Louise's statement, "I needed to meditate for an answer to something." She reports meditation produced the answer "Let it be as is," but never tells us what the problem was.) The "sharing of psychic and spiritual experiences" portion of the meeting was essentially a discussion of personal problems. Any sort of therapy or mutual help group could have provided this kind of sharing.[5] But the study group was joined in ways other groups could not have been—through rituals, psychic means of maintaining contact, and a mythos that joined members together in past reincarnations.

Group rituals served as a basis for shared experiences. The rituals of prayer and meditation were performed together. Intercessory healing prayers were said in the healing circle at the end of each meeting. Such prayers could, of course, be said on an individual basis, but it was felt that performing them in the context of the group gave them added force. God could take the energy emanated by the entire goup and use it where it was needed. According to the beliefs of the group, the energy created in the circle emanated through everyone in common, and was used in the healing of all the listed loved ones in common. In the healing circle described in chapter 2, Jenny said, "Take that Light [energy] and split it in half and feel it flowing down your arms to the person on either side of you, and going down through their bodies, healing, cleansing, and making them whole." Sometimes in the healing circle, energy was passed from you to the person on your right, and from the person on your left to you. Eventually, everyone's energy had passed through everyone else. This sharing of energy might be seen as functionally somewhat akin to sharing the same food, as in a sacramental meal. It might also be somewhat similar to exchanging blood in order to become "blood brothers."[6]

Meditation served as the basis for another shared experience. Time was always set aside in the meetings for a group meditation. We all meditated on the same subject, and the experiences and insights gained in meditation were shared with the group. Members were drawn closer together if they had similar experiences during

154

meditation. Jenny said if she "tuned in on it," she could "go with" a person in meditation, and see what they were seeing, or be where they were (Study Group:8/16/75).

Instances of similar meditation experiences occurred, especially in the latter half of the year. By this time we had been joined by Nell and Anita, who joined our study group after others ended. Nell, sixty, was married to an executive, and was a friend of David and Jenny. The rest of us were acquainted with her from the after-class get-togethers at the restaurant. Anita was twenty-seven and had two small daughters. Her husband was an automotive technician, whose job was a demanding one. He attended Alcoholics Anonymous to gain relief from a drinking problem. Anita was a friend of Jenny and Nell. Laura and I knew her because she had attended Metaphysics I.

One evening, meditating on the phrase "I am in tune with the creative force of all," Nell and I both reported receiving the word "Love." Jenny brought the similarity to our attention, and Nell said, "Yes, when Melinda is here we often get the same word, or come up with the same idea in different words. There's something there. I don't know what it is" (Study Group:9/10/75). Another time Sara reported that during meditation "I felt a tickle in my throat, and I felt a person standing beside me." Anita indicated that it was she who was standing beside Sara. "I shared this Light with everybody. Then I put my hands on your [Sara's] shoulders, and said if there's anything that needs to be worked out of your system—for it to be done." At the last class meeting, Anita said her meditation was "weird. I kept hearing somebody talking." Jenny reported in turn that "a song kept going through my mind—'Love is nothing 'til you give it away'." Then Jenny and Anita decided Anita must have been hearing Jenny's meditation—hearing her song (Study Group:1/28/76).

Meditation was also a means of maintaining a degree of "contact" with other group members when separated from them. Study group members were expected to meditate daily, and part of this meditation was to be the visualization of each other mem-

155

ber of the group: "Mentally visualize the face of each member and send them a good thought or a prayer. This enables the group to get in 'tune' and helps develop rapport" (Hayes 1971:24). Sometimes the results of the visualization—how the meditator "saw" the person, what he was doing, and so on—were reported in the group meetings. In the early meetings, this was a way of becoming acquainted, of discovering what the other members did during the day. For example, Louise "saw" me at a desk and "saw" Laura running back and forth. I explained that I did work at a desk, and Laura said she spent a lot of time running after her young son.

Members could "visit" in each other's homes by means of "astral travel" (leaving the body). In chapter 2 Sara is reported as saying that, although Louise was away in a distant city, Sara felt her presence in the car driving to the study group meeting. Sara was also able to "see" Louise and her mother in her mother's home. These experiences of "contact" were interpreted as instances of astral travel.[7]

Another means of enhancing cohesion between group members was through the concept of reincarnation and past lives. A series of reincarnation accounts were woven that joined group members together in prior lives, because "you don't come together in a group as close as this unless you have been together before" (Study Group:1/21/76).[8]

Who was joined with whom in the accounts of prior reincarnations suggests that past lives were more or less representations of present relationships. Jenny was the central hub of these past lives, just as she was the focal point of the present relationships. The identifying myth was created during the last third of the study group's year together. By this time the configuration of the group had changed from that described in chapter 2. *Know Yourself* is divided into two sections: Beginning (January 1975–June 1975) and Advanced (June 1975–January 1976). During or prior to the Advanced section, Louise, Dan and John all left our study group and joined other groups and classes that Jenny led. Beverly also stopped coming to the meetings regularly. People who came to the latter half of the meetings regularly were David, Laura, Grace,

Sara, Melinda, Nell, and Anita. (Nell attended from July to November, and Anita from September to January.)

The mechanics of past-life development was that the seed was always planted by someone's feeling that "there is something between us." This was followed-up by meditating on the relationship, or by asking Jenny how she "saw" the relationship. Thus, the discovery of the specific nature of the past lives, when members had "been together before," actually took place outside class, during solitary meditations or private psychic consultations with Jenny. They were discussed, however, at a meeting in October. Jenny, Grace, Sara, Anita, and I were present. While we were doing an experiment on "mediumship" during which each person gave a "message" to each other person, informal conversations were carried on in the background:

Anita to We were in France as nuns you know. We were discussing
Jenny: that the other day. I got the willies—the feeling I get when I'm really into something. We were very, very close friends. We had household duties that we did together. I can't picture you looking any other way than very similar to the way you look now. There's a fluffy nice cloud around you. And a rainbow—green. Green is understanding.

Jenny: Rainbows symbolize God's love.

Sara (to You had said all my lives were perfect. In my thing, I saw
Jenny):   myself as very small. I felt I was a love child.

Jenny: Well, many nuns had——. But it seems I raised you from a baby, rather than was your mother. Once Laura was here at my house, and asked what her relationship was with David. She and I were can-can dancers in a cabaret in France. And it turns out David was the owner!

                               (Study Group:10/29/75)

Nell believed that David was her father in a prior life. She often called him "Father" or "Daddy," and told him, "When you were my father, you sort of pampered me." To which David replied, "I am paying for that!" (Study Group:9/10/75).

Nell, Anita, Sara, and Laura seem to have actively sought to discover the basis for present relationships in past lives. David was a somewhat passive participant in these relationships. He acquiesced to Nell's belief that he had been her father, and sometimes played the role. He was not present on the evening when his status as owner of the cabaret where Jenny and Laura had worked was revealed. Grace believed in reincarnation, but there is no evidence that she sought to discover past relationships with the group members. The group members who were joined by past lives were also close in this life.[9]

Thus, past lives represented present relationships. The conviction that, as Jenny expressed it, "we have all been together before," also explained how group members could become close so quickly. The past lives sanctified the study group relationships, making of them something different from the ordinary relationships encountered in the workaday world. Reincarnation gave the study group a note of perpetuity it otherwise would not have had. The members had been together before; perhaps they would be again.

A feeling of closeness explained and enhanced by past life relationships was not unique to our study group; it occurred in Jenny's other groups. But Jenny reported that only "once in a while" did she have a study group that had the degree of "rapport" experienced by our group. In Jenny's other groups, there was often a core of people who were "drawn close together" and some "outsiders," who maintained their "reserve." They might remain "almost total stangers—like ships passing in the night." These "outsiders" did not feel they had prior life relationships with other members (Field Notes:7/5/77).

Jenny believed in a "group karma" of "people who have been together. There's a bond there. The same bond brings you back together. At times you touch again." In Jenny's life in the convent, she had known Sara and Anita, as well as members of three or four other study groups. Members of several different groups had likewise been together in the cabaret. "When[these people from various study groups who had "been together before"] meet,

[they experience] the same draw. It's like a family, or clan group-
ing" (Field Notes:7/5/77). Thus Jenny is the center of a clan
based not on kin ties but on past lives together and present relationships with her.

ATTENUATION OF FELLOWSHIP

In-Group Fellowship, Out-Group Alienation

The study group created an "in-group" from of fellowship, supported by sharing everyday problems and ritual experiences. The
members were joined in past lives as well as by their present relationships. Yet the very aspects of this group that enable it to join
people together in extraordinary ways—healing circles, meditation, astral travel, and reincarnation—can increase alienation
from those outside the metaphysical network.

On the highest ideological level, there is to be no rift among
men.The concept of a God within provides the basis for a
"brotherhood of man." The spark of divinity that all men share
theoretically gives humankind a common basis for identity. As
Jenny said, "I can always say 'I love the God within that person'.
. . . I can love the God within him, because that's a part of me,
too."

In practice, however the "brotherhood" and the "love" may not
extend to one's own kin and neighbors. Involvement in the study
group may increase alienation from spouse, coworkers, relatives,
and friends who are not sympathetic with metaphysics. Louise
found her beliefs were "hard for her mother and aunt to understand." Sara complained that her husband had "had his own experiences, but wouldn't open up to it. She said he would not listen to her when she talked of her experiences, but just "shut her
off". Sara assumed her neighbors would not appreciate her interest in the metaphysical. Jenny once proposed that if a person felt
drained, touching something of nature would restore energy. "Go
out and hug a tree" she recommended. Said Sara, "That's all my
neighbors need to see, is me hugging a tree." Jenny advised her to

"pull down a branch and hold it, look at it as if you're looking for bugs." Sara's sister also looked askance at Sara's interest in the psychic. "My sister calls me a jinx" (Study Group:7/2/75). Yet when the sister herself had a dream about their ailing mother, she came to Sara for interpretation, and began to take what Sara believed more seriously. David's wife did not share his interest in metaphysics. Jenny had a sister who objected to her role as a spiritual leader.

Laura's husband, Bob, came to an early study group meeting and told Laura that in his opinion it was "good therapy" and would not hurt anyone; but he did not continue to come to the meetings. Later in the year, Laura was able to convince Bob to accompany her to a yoga class, which she said would enable him to learn to relax and shed the frustrations of his job. Laura reported that Bob's acquaintance with John and Beverly convinced him that people with middle-class jobs and life-styles, much like his own, were interested in the psychic.[10] "Bob always thought this was weird. But he sees John and Beverly, and thinks they're normal—so it can't be all weird" (Study Group:7/2/75).

Anita said, "When I started these classes, my husband thought I had really flipped out" (Study Group:10/15/75). He had accompanied Anita to some of Joe's Metaphysics I classes, but then lost interest. Anita's sister dubbed the first half of the study group lessons "Beginning Weird," the second half "Advanced Weird," and the class Jenny held for veteran study group members "Graduate Weird." Although these labels were meant as criticism, the group took them on, and often described itself as "weird."[11]

Some group members dealt with the disapproval of the "outside world" by keeping their participation in metaphysics confidential. Sara said, "I don't tell everybody what I tell you people" (Study Group:10/1/75). In a discussion of what to do about depression, Sara said, "But if you need to talk to someone, don't call upon someone who doesn't believe as you do. Be careful who you choose. You may scare people away, and be very lonely, until you realize that God is there, and always with you. People will say you're crazy." Jenny replied, "If people say I'm crazy, I tell them I am!" (Study Group:2/19/75). But Jenny was secure in the spiritual role. The "straight" world, in fact, came to Jenny for help. She told of a stockbroker who asked her for tips. Her doctor said he "wished he had more like her," because her healing activities had helped people. The local police consulted Joe and Jenny on baffling cases, and Jenny offered to teach them psychometry. Sara said, "I don't push myself on anybody. It just gets pushed back to you." David tried to comfort her: "I've had that happen to me. But then I say, what have I done wrong here—nothing" (Study Group:8/6/75).[12] David is perhaps more secure than Sara, but not as bold as Jenny.

Another means of dealing with alienation from nonbelieving friends and neighbors is to take comfort in membership in a sort of ideological elite discussed by some leaders. Joe drew a distinction between the "enlightened" and the "masses of humanity." Persons who are involved in metaphysical "work" are "enlightened." The rest of the world, those who have no knowledge of metaphysics, are the "masses." Joe believed that the masses and the enlightened would have different experiences at death, and in life after death. He also believed that the two groups would experience differential rewards in an Aquarian Age[13] dispensation. The enlightened would come to lead others, and to serve as examples for others, as the turmoil concomitant with the change from the Piscean to the Aquarian Age reached its peak. In the dawning of the Age of Aquarius, "numerous changes are to transpire in the minds of men, there will be a slow swing toward mysticism, and a gradual awakening of consciousness as humanity en masse begins to turn from darkness to light" (Chaney 1974:347).[14]

Study group members did not always experience increased alienation from friends and relatives. Often the nonbelievers eventually joined the metaphysical student. Recruitment into Jenny's classes, and into SFF in general, is largely a process of members bringing in their friends (SFF 1975c). Many of the study

161

group members had themselves been recruited in this way. John brought Beverly into the group, David brought Grace, Louise and Dan brought Sara.

Several group members were able to interest their friends or relatives in metaphysics and in Jenny's classes.[15] Grace and John were particularly successful in sharing their interest in metaphysics. Grace's coworkers became interested in such numbers that Jenny began a study group just for them. John owned several copies of the book that had meant so much to him, William Parker's *Prayer Can Change Your Life*, and he distributed them among his colleagues when they came to him with their problems. John also reported demonstrating the efficacy of healing to coworkers.

It is of interest that Nell, Sara, David, and Laura all had non-believing spouses, and all were thought to be joined with other group members, or Jenny, in prior lives. Grace, who had no reported difficulty with the "outside world," was not included in a past life relationship, nor did she seek to be included.[16]

Short-Term Fellowship

The study group, as harmonious as it was, shared experiences and prayed and meditated together for just one year. Despite the protests of group members, Jenny was not willing to continue the group beyond that time. When we finished the last lesson in *Know Yourself*, we "graduated" and the group terminated. The group members were invited to join other classes taught by Jenny, and some of them did. Thus, Jenny continued to be the focal point of relationships among study group members.

The study group was close and affectionate, but short-lived, providing an example of the kind of relationships Toffler (1970) posits will become the norm in modern society. This type of relationship is made necessary by the pervasiveness of specialized, fragmented roles, and by mobility. These conditions render neighbors, friends, and coworkers useless as continuing reference points for establishing identity. The study group offered an "ingroup" of people with similar interests and shared experiences. A

162

group identity was formed through rituals, out-of-body contacts, and by reference to relationships in past lives. Although providing arenas for "fellowship" is a concern for SFF, fostering group identity and building community is not its ultimate goal. The study group "community" was a once-a-week affair that required its members to share only "spiritual" resources. "Fellowship" thus is secondary to the encouragement of individual spiritual growth, or self-realization, described earlier. The next chapter discusses the kind of alternative SFF offers to an overly rational system of symbols in our culture, or, as SFF leaders see it, a "world grown too material."

1. Aside from Louise and Sara, the nearest neighbors were Beverly and John and Laura, who lived ten miles apart. The most dispersed were Beverly and John and Louise and Dan, who lived almost 50 miles apart. Nell drove 67 miles from her home twice every week for three years to attend Joe's classes and Barbara's study group.

2. This excludes 115 problems that were raised by Jenny herself, and for which she gave the solutions. Forty-one percent of the problems she raised were "hypothetical, " that is, they were not being experienced by anyone at the moment, but were potential problems. For example, Jenny might say, "If any of you ever encounter an energy sapper, you should close yourself off to keep from being drained," thus raising a potential problem and giving a solution for it.

3. As far as I was able to ascertain, this spin-off of leaders from study groups has actually occurred only once in the history of the Carroll County study groups. The original study group in the county, in 1972, had ten members and a revolving leadership. Of these members, four became spiritual leaders of one type or another. Joe began teaching metaphysics in the county's adult education program, which generated further interest in study groups. Barbara and Jenny became study group leaders. Another member became a Spiritualist minister. The remaining six members continued their roles as group members by joining a study group taught by Barbara or healing classes taught by Jenny.

4. This would, of course, depend on local circumstances. For example, in the early study groups in the Metro Area, there were no strong leaders, and the first study group in Carroll County had a revolving leadership. But Jenny and Joe, who were members of the original study group, subsequently arose as the metaphysical leaders in the county. Joe concentrated more on explanation and a class-oriented group structure. Jenny, with closer ties to the SFF area and national organizations, preferred to lead the more experiential study groups.

163

5. Although the *sharing* function may be similar to other therapy groups, the *solutions* offered are not. In the study group, *spiritual* solutions are counseled for everyday problems. These solutions are discussed in chapter 7.

6. "Giving out energy" to others was common. Jenny once told me she had taken energy from me (unbeknownst to me) during a group meeting and given it to a fellow member who needed it.

7. Members of all of Jenny's study groups were to visualize each other during their meditations. But this means of getting "in tune" and "developing rapport" (Hayes 1971:42) was more successful in groups where the members felt close to one another. In some of Jenny's study groups, there were members who were "outsiders." These people had difficulty visualizing members. In some groups these people eventually drop out. If the number of "outsiders" in a group prevents development of "rapport," Jenny may disband the group (Field Notes:7/5/77).

8. This was a manifestation of the belief that if persons are drawn to one another, or repulsed by one another, they "must have been together before." Jenny frequently gave this as an explanation for problems in interpersonal relations.

9. The current relationships among members, and their corresponding past life relationships, were as follows: David and Nell, father and daughter in a past life, had been friends for several years. Jenny and Anita were friends in a prior life at a convent. The present relationship between Jenny and Anita was a friendship that existed before Anita joined the study group. Jenny and Sara were also joined in a convent, where Jenny was a mother figure, but *not* a mother per se, to Sara. Sara had not known Jenny before the study group, and in fact had not liked her when the classes first began. After a time Sara felt she had been helped by Jenny, and came to like her, in the same way all the other group members did. The Jenny, Laura, David triad in the cabaret is the only past life described in such secular terms. Laura met Jenny in Metaphysics I, and sometimes visited her outside the confines of the study group. David had been acquainted with Jenny prior to the class because of her work in his Spiritualist church. Laura and David had no ties outside the group, other than occasionally meeting together for lunch (along with Beverly and me) in the town where David lived, but they were close within the group. When Laura brought her baby to class in September, David and the baby got along well. Jenny explained this by saying, "Well, when you get two monks together—." This implied that David and Laura's baby had both been monks in prior lives; thus, they would have a lot in common, a lot to "talk about." (Jenny also said Anita's baby girl was a monk in a prior life). Thus, past lives represented present relationships. But some current relationships among the people who were attending the study group at the time the prior lives were discussed were not represented in past lives. For example, Grace was not included in the past lives discussed in the group meeting in October. Grace's closest relationship with another group member was with David, who brought her into the class and drove her to each meeting. Neither Grace nor David were active participants in discovering past lives. This may be the reason for Grace's absence

164

in the prior lives discussed in October. In July 1977 I asked Jenny about Grace's relationship, and she said, "I haven't been able to figure her out. She was sort of in and sort of out. I see her as a mother type—maybe a housemother, looking out for others. She plays that role well now." I also was not included in the past life relationships. This was probably due to the mechanics of past life formation. When the possibility of past life relationships that included me were mentioned, I did not follow them up, and so was not ultimately included in them.

10. The friendship between John and Beverly and Laura and Bob was a consequence of Laura and John's meeting in Joe's metaphysics class.

11. "Weird" was a term used with humor and affection in the class. Jenny reported being introduced at school functions as "my weird little mom" by her children. In the reporting of psychic experiences, a person might say, "I haven't had anything psychic." Another would ask, "Have you had anything weird?" Laura once asked Jenny, "When did you begin this weird stuff?"

12. Jenny advised, "Just give them books to read, rather than advice; then it can't come back on you" (Study Group:8/6/75). When members complained about their disbelieving spouses, Jenny said, "Usually, the less said the better" (Study Group:2/19/75). She also counseled against trying to "prove" psychic phenomena by displaying abilities to the spouse. Sara reported that her husband kept asking her to "do something," so she agreed to try to find an object he had hidden, and was successful. That upset her husband. "It scares him. He wonders, 'What else does she know I'm doing?'" Jenny said, "You shouldn't play games with it. You don't need to" (Study Group:1/28/76). Active proselytization is prohibited by the principle of individual exegesis. David said, "Don't try to force it on others"; and Sara agreed: "Let them learn. Our own experience is best anyway" (Study Group:2/19/75). Each person will begin his search for truth "when he is ready." The "readiness" might be encouraged by prayers, however. Jenny said, "The spark is from outside often. . . . Doors open in many ways. A prayer from outside may help" (Study Group:3/19/75). "Put it in the Light. Pray, ask for enlightenment" (Study Group:12/17/75). "Just keep radioing him love. It'll get through eventually. The block of ice will melt" (Study Group:1/28/76). But Joe thought it wrong that Nell constantly prayed for her husband to experience what she had experienced (Metaphysics II:5/5/75). He thought it better to pray for "whatever is best for that soul's growth" (Metaphysics II:4/28/75). If a person does express interest, it is suggested that he be given a book to read, such as *The Sleeping Prophet*, by Jess Stearn, *There is a River*, by Thomas Sugrue, both about Edgar Cayce; or Kahlil Gibran's *The Prophet*; or William Parker's *Prayer Can Change Your Life*.

13. In astrology the heavens are divided into 12 signs of the zodiac. The signs are fixed, but the constellations for which they are named move. This sets up cycles. Each one of the 12 constellations lines up with its corresponding sign for about 2,150 years. It takes 25,800 years for the entire cycle to be completed. For about 2,000 years the Piscean sign and constellation have coincided, and this era has been designated the Piscean Age. The next coincidence will be between the sign and constellation of Aquarius. Precisely when the Aquarian Age will begin

165

(some astrologers believe it has already begun) is open to interpretation because there is controvery regarding when the Piscean Age began. Times of "crossover" from one age to another are thought to be turbulent.

14. This quote is from the founder of Astara, whose lessons are the source of Joe's messianic belief. "Such views are also held in slightly differing forms by Theosophy, the Arcane School, Christian Science, the Unity School of Christianity, and other New Thought derivatives" (Judah 1967:144).

15. Most of the members of David's Spiritualist church joined Jenny's study groups or healing classes. Louise's sister, daughter, and son-in-law joined a study group. John brought his wife, Beverly, into the study group. Their two teenage daughters subsequently became interested in the psychic. Several of Beverly and John's friends asked to have their names put into the healing circle.

16. Others who had little difficulty with nonbelievers were the two couples, Louise and Dan and Beverly and John. They also were not included in past lives. Since they were not attending class when the past life relationships were discussed, however, it cannot be said with certainty that they would not have been included in them.

7

Spiritual Frontiers Fellowship's
Response to "Rational" Culture:
Spiritual Science

Chapter 1 identified two trends in modern American society that
exacerbate individual meaninglessness. One trend was social
fragmentation. Chapters 3 through 6 have analyzed Spiritual
Frontiers Fellowship's response to the concomitants of fragmentation. The other trend noted in chapter 1 was an overemphasis on the rationally understood aspects of life. It was theorized
that discursive messages and modes of communication—information in the technical sense, facts, and logical, rational ways
of knowing—were not well suited to the process of establishing
identity. Information and facts change rapidly, and can be falsified. Conscious, rational means of understanding do not provide
the sense of union that can enhance individual identity.

Spiritual Frontiers Fellowship's response to the overemphasis
on rational symbols and means of understanding is twofold. On
the one hand, one of SFF's purposes is to encourage interest in the
spiritual side of life, and it favors intuitive, experiential modes of
communication. On the other hand, SFF and the other metaphysical groups consider metaphysics a *scientific* religious philosophy

167

(Judah 1967:11). SFF is both a spiritual reaction against a culture it considers too "material" and an expression of the need to be "scientific" in today's world.

THE SPIRITUAL OVER THE MATERIAL

SFF recognizes a distinction between the spiritual and the material that is much like the nonrational/rational dichotomy discussed in chapter 1. "Spiritual" refers to nonphysical and nonmaterial "phenomena which relate to God, the human spirit, and the future life" (SFF 1974; cf. Ford 1967). "Material" refers to the physical phenomena that can be observed with the five senses. Jenny and Joe spoke of "the body, the mind, and that which is beyond the body and the mind, the soul," and the "physical, mental, and spiritual worlds."

Of course, among metaphysicians the "spiritual" is more highly valued than the "physical" or "mental" aspects of life. One of SFF's purposes is to "open the eyes of a materialistic and skeptical generation to man's intrinsic spiritual nature" (SFF 1974:Part 3, point 2; cf. SFF 1969, 1971). SFF's founders felt that society had put too much emphasis on the material, or physical, aspects of life, and that the churches had become too "rationalistic." SFF accuses the orthodox churches of disavowing, and being suspicious of, emotion and mysticism (Althouse 1974; Higgins 1966).

Thus, SFF recognizes an imbalance between material and spiritual concerns, and endeavors to correct it by emphasizing the spiritual.

> SFF knows as does every sincere religious movement, that unless man's exploration and achievement in science are matched by an equally effective exploration and achievement in man's spiritual life, our culture will be in an imbalance. . . . Hardly anyone doubts that our culture is strained by the imbalance of the materialistic over the spiritual. But now Spiritual Frontiers seeks to bring into balance the scale of science and religion. (Rauscher 1970)

168

Spiritual Explanations and Solutions

The potpourri of ideas presented by SFF includes ways of viewing the mysteries of "life and faith," and spiritual means for "facing the human problems of suffering, injustice and death" (SFF 1974:Part 2, point 5). One of SFF's "main areas of concern" is "personal immortality and the eternal life of the spirit" (SFF 1974:Part 1, point 3). Joe's view of life after death is not a vague belief in immortality. As we have seen, he has knowledge of the appurtenances and activities of "life on the other side." He is familiar with the clothes, housing, food, entertainment, and education experienced by the spirit after death. He knows what the experience of death itself entails.[1]

Spiritual explanations were also offered for the more commonplace problems and situations discussed in the study group. The concepts of reincarnation, astrology, and the power behind a thought provided explanations for most problems. Past reincarnations were often used to explain present interpersonal relationships; past life relationships could explain either animosities or loving feelings. Karma, or the force generated by a person's past actions (in this and prior lives), could explain current life situations. Astrology, which studies the influence of the relative positions of the moon, sun, and stars on human affairs, was used to explain the state of the world, and individual psychological characteristics. "The power of thought" explained some personal problems because a person's own thoughts could cause things to happen to him. For example, a person could "program" himself to become ill or to remain so.

More conventional explanations for problems were also not ignored by the study group. A person's problems might be due to alcoholism or guilt, rather than to a past life or an astrological birth sign. An accident could be caused by carelessness. A physical disability could be hereditary. But a quantitative analysis showed that when explanations for problems were discussed,[2] 52 percent of the time they were spiritual in nature. Present life situations were usually explained by reference to reincarnation, karma, astrology, or the power of thought.

Belief in reincarnation, karma, and astrology implies a teleological, or patterned, view of life, and may produce a sense of "destiny." Grace reported that a friend had not been hired for a job she wanted, and Jenny replied, "Well, if it's not meant to be. She probably has something to work out there yet" (Study Group:7/2/75). David suggested that perhaps the boss John did not get along with was "there for John to learn a lesson." "He's there so you'll learn to cope with it" (Study Group:4/16/75). When John discussed his guilt over his past actions, Jenny said, "Forgive yourself. This is the way you should be for this life. This is what you're supposed to do" (Study Group:4/30/75).

But any idea of "karma" or destiny was tempered by the power of thought, prayer, and Light to "change things." Sara asked what a person should do if he sees that another needs help, but feels "they may need to go through that." Jenny said, "You only program love and the White Light" (Study Group:1/28/76). If you see that a person needs healing, "don't be afraid you're going to ruin their karmic pattern. God doesn't mean for us to be sick. We build these things ourselves. Begin to let the healing Light come through. It will manifest itself in many ways. Don't be afraid" (Study Group:2/26/75).

Thus, the explanations *and* the solutions for the everyday problems discussed in the study group were spiritual in nature. It is the spiritual solution that can undo the patterns of karma and astrology and the webs we build by negative thinking. Spiritual solutions were applied to a wide range of physiological, environmental, psychological, and interpersonal problems. Spiritual means of solving problems included meditation, prayer, positive thinking, spiritual formulas, and the correct use of spiritual laws.

Solving problems through meditation, prayer, and "affirmations," which utilize the power of words and thoughts, was discussed in chapter 5. Another way of changing things is to use spiritual formulas,[3] such as "Giving it to God," or simply saying

"God" or "God bless you." These spiritual formulas were used for a variety of problems. In the meeting described in chapter 2, Dan reported that by saying the word "God" he could preempt the anger he felt when driving in traffic. "Saying 'God' breaks negative thoughts" (Study Group:1/15/75). Grace said she could say "God, you do it" to ease the pressures of concentration required in her job. If Laura found herself becoming too emotionally involved in other people's problems, she was to say, "God help this person." In the same vein is advice that if a person is overtaken by anxiety when he hears a siren wailing, he should simply say "Bless them—God be with it" (Study Group:8/6/75).

A ubiquitous spiritual formula in SFF was "putting it in the White Light." The White Light can be put around people, objects, and situations. It can both improve and protect. Using the White Light is a simple matter. To put the Light around yourself, it is necessary only to "bring it up around you like a cocoon, or visualize it coming from you, and surrounding you like a fog" (Study Group:2/19/75). All that is necessary to putting the White Light around someone else or around an object is to think and believe that you have done it. This can be an act of visualization too, but it can be "visualized" completely in the mind. That is, the person or the object does not have to be in view in order to be put in the Light.

Relationships with others could be improved by the White Light. "It *is* possible to change people. Prayer and Light can" (Study Group:3/19/75). John was counseled to "put his boss in the Light," as well as to "put him in the proper perspective."

Objects, as well as people and situations, could be changed by the White Light. When I complained that my car door rattled, Jenny said, "You should put it in the Light and ask God to remove the rattle."

The White Light also provides a means of protection. It can provide protection from other people, accidents, natural phenomena such as storms, or from negative spiritual forces. Putting yourself in the White Light is also called "putting your protection

171

up" (Study Group:5/7/75). Sara sometimes "put her shield up around her" when her sister called, to protect herself from her sister's negativity (Study Group:1/21/76).

The Light can also protect property. Putting the Light around a car or a house protects it from theft and natural disaster. Jenny does not lock her doors because she believes the White Light sets up a positive force field that will not allow negative forces to enter (Study Group:1/28/76). Putting yourself and your car in the Light prevents accidents. As indicated in chapter 2, if Jenny had put her son "in the Light" and thought, "Don't touch anything," she could have saved her refrigerator from harm. It is not necessary that the protection of property have a human link. That is, the *driver* of the car or the *defroster* of the refrigerator need not be in the Light. Putting the car or the refrigerator themselves in the Light would protect them.

Abiding by the "spiritual laws" is still another spiritual means of improving life. The spiritual "Law of Cause and Effect," on which karma is based, was the one most often discussed in the group. During the meeting described in chapter 2, Dan was abiding by a manifestation of this law—"If you give love, you receive love"—when he said, "If you're happy, this will mirror back at you. If you snarl, you'll end up surrounded by a snarling bunch of people." The same law, conceived as "You have to give to receive," assured that Laura would not have to worry about having enough money as long as she herself was generous.

Another spiritual law, the "Law of Grace," mitigated the "As ye sow, so shall ye reap" aspect of the Law of Cause and Effect (Hayes 1971:123). This law, which was also called the "Law of Complete Forgiveness and Release," helped alleviate guilt. Several of the study group members harbored guilt over actions in their pasts. Jenny constantly reiterated that they should "forgive themselves and release the guilt." She said if a person truly forgives himself for guilts built up from past actions, these will be released, and he will no longer be troubled by them. It is not a question of needing forgiveness from God: "God wipes the slate clean every night." But "you must forgive yourself, and release it."

172

These spiritual solutions do have psychological components. Forgiving yourself for past wrongdoing is psychologically good for the soul, whether or not one believes he is following a spiritual law in so doing. Meditation has been shown by several researchers to lead to a feeling of psychological well-being (e. g., Greeley and McCready 1974; Hood 1974; McCready 1976; Maslow 1964; Wuthnow 1978).

The efficacy of the "power of thought" can be explained by positive thinking and the persuasive force of words. Using the spiritual formulas probably has the effect of terminating worry over things about which little can otherwise be done. Jenny said "to *dispel* problems 'put it in the Light' " (Study Group:3/19/75, emphasis mine). By the use of the formulas, the person feels he *has* done something, and worry and anxiety are alleviated. In some situations the formulas also have an effect like "counting to 10." Jenny said, "Saying 'God' raises a negative emotion to a mental state that says 'wait a minute.' " When John was breaking his smoking habit, if he reached for a cigarette he would say, "God, you take care of it," and leave the cigarette in its package.

More traditional sorts of solutions for problems were sometimes discussed by group members. For example, the lesson recorded in chapter 2 asked the study group members to report on the sources of their negative feelings and what they did to alleviate these feelings. While many of the ameliorative acts were spiritual, such as "giving it to God" and "putting it in the Light," some were not. For example, Louise said if she had interpersonal problems, she asked for "God to change me and the other person"; but she also said, "Sewing calms me." Grace found relaxation in her ceramics class. Dan was helped by "writing his problems down." Jenny told John to put his troublesome boss "in the Light," but she also counseled him to "put him in the proper perspective." And Jenny and Dan advised, "When things bother you, ask yourself, will it make a difference five years from now, or one month from now?" In cases of serious illness, spiritual healing was not substituted for the usual medical methods but joined with them.

173

In sum, although mundane methods of solving problems were sometimes used, a quantitative analysis of the solutions proffered for problems discussed in the study group (N = 436 solutions) showed that most frequently spiritual means were proposed to ameliorate the problems of everyday life. Three-fifths (62 percent) of the solutions offered were spiritual in nature—meditation, prayer, affirmative thought, spiritual formulas, and following spiritual laws. In another 13 percent of the cases, a conventional solution was joined with a spiritual one. For example, a person would go to a doctor or chiropractor and also undergo a laying-on-of-hands healing. Or a person would confront a hostile coworker, as well as put him in the Light.

In response to what they view as an overly "material" society, SFF's proponents emphasize the spiritual, the "nonphysical phenomena which relate to God, the human spirit, and the future life" (SFF 1974). The ideas and concepts discussed at SFF functions provide a way of thinking about death and life after death. In the study group, the explanations for more commonplace situations and the methods of solving everyday problems are, by and large, spiritual in nature. SFF deemphasizes the "material" and emphasizes a spiritual, "nonrational" view of the world.

Experiential Epistemology

SFF favors intuitive, experiential ways of knowing over modes of communication based on the intellect. Meditation, SFF's major ritual property, is taken to be a religious experience capable of providing the sense of union that identifies and the feeling of wholeness that metaphysicians equate with salvation (Bonacci 1976b; Braden 1951:139; Judah 1967:293). Personal experience is the recognized criterion for truth, and is preferred over other methods of learning, such as reading or listening to a lecture. Joe drew a distinction between "knowledge" and "wisdom." "Knowledge is gained by reading. Wisdom is gained by meditating and letting God show you" (Metaphysics II:5/12/75).

SFF carries this principle of the value of experience into its program planning. The study groups, conferences, and retreats are to

174

have an experiential component (Perkins 1976a:7). The *Procedures Guide* recommends involvement as the watchword in conducting study groups: "Always bear in mind that the underlying purpose is not *study about* but *involvement in* the subject at hand. Learning through doing should be the methodology" (SFF 1976e:6–7).

The metaphysical students' desire for experience and participation was substantiated by questionnaires distributed by an area chairperson, which showed that people preferred workshops ("where they become involved") to lectures (SFF 1975c). This was confirmed in my own field work. Joe's method of teaching the metaphysics classes was to teach the philosophy of spiritual and psychic awareness ("what you are doing and why") before actually experimenting with it, although most of his class sessions did have an experiential element (meditation or an ESP experiment). If Joe slighted this portion of the class, at the next class meeting there would be complaints: "Let's *do* something." "I hope we *do* something tonight." Joe regularly lost some of his followers to Jenny, who was the more experiential and pragmatic leader.

METAPHYSICS: THE SCIENTIFIC RELIGIOUS PHILOSOPHY

SFF, then, emphasizes spiritual explanations, and experiential methods of learning. Yet SFF, and the other metaphysical groups, consider metaphysics a *scientific* religious philosophy (Judah, 1967:13, point 3; Marty 1970; Zaretsky and Leone 1974b:xxx, point 26). SFF's desire to be aligned with science is explicit in *Principles, Purposes, and Program:*

> SFF takes the *scientific* attitude that all human experiences, including extrasensory perception (telepathy, clairvoyance, precognition and related phenomena) are to be studied without prejudice for better understanding of the invisible world, and the nature of man and the universe. . . .
> SFF seeks to share with *science* the implications of its own method, which is the examination of all available evidence as the basis of understanding and progress. (SFF 1974:Part 2, point 4; Part 3, point 2)

175

Further evidence of the desire to be scientific is SFF's Research Committee, "which encourages investigation in the principle fields of the paranormal" (SFF 1974:Part 4, point 6). SFF's late research director, Robert H. Ashby, authored *A Guidebook to the Study of Psychical Research* (1972), which has been used by both academic and nonacademic students of the psychic. Studies in parapsychology and research on life after death are reported on at conferences and in the scholarly appearing *Spiritual Frontiers* journal. The 1975 national conference included a lecture on "Psychiatry and Biofeedback," which concerned research at the Menninger Clinic into the use of biofeedback (the process of obtaining feedback about out-of-awareness physiological states by the use of machines) in curing psychosomatic illness. Research on life on other planets was reported on at the 1975 Metro Area retreat by John W. White, an associate of astronaut Edgar Mitchell, who performed ESP experiments while traveling in outer space.

Certain aspects of the philosophy, social organization, and rhetoric of the metaphysical groups savor of science. The metaphysical participants are called *students*, and the groups are *classes*. It is not beliefs that are discussed in the *classes*, but *theories*, *concepts*, or *ideas* (the *theory* of reincarnation, for example [Hayes 1971:76]). When the *classes* end, the students *graduate*. Joe said metaphysics was concerned not with the "supernatural," which is forever scientifically inexplicable, but with the "supernormal," which is amenable to eventual scientific explanation, though it is not yet fully understood by science. In his classes Joe taught that there are physiological and neurological (and thus scientific) explanations for psychic phenomena. A good example of joining science and religion was a meditation given at the 1975 leadership conference based on the "Laser Beam of God's Love":

> The laser beam is a concentration of light. . . . Concentrated it has added power. Laser means Love Activated Spiritual Energy Ray. Take love, activate it, and put it into a spiritual force. Make one concentrated ray out of it and it can become a healing process. It's the

power of the mind and the power of God, coupled together. Once you combine these forces you can create a laser beam of prayer . . . a creative force. (SFF 1975c)

Part of the metaphysical philosophy basic to the idea that metaphysics is a *scientific* religious philosophy is the concept of spiritual laws. According to Joe, nothing God does, and nothing Jesus did while he lived on earth, is supernatural. Their works proceed by the rules of spiritual laws, not all of which have been discovered by man (Judah 1967). Thus, for the metaphysicians, the "spiritual laws" are another set of natural laws that have not yet been discovered by science. In the metaphysical "scientific religion," salvation and improved life situations are attained not by propitiation of unpredictable supernatural forces but by learning about, and working within, constant spiritual laws.

But more fundamental to the definition of metaphysics as a "scientific religious philosophy" than these scientifically oriented beliefs is the metaphysical epistemology. The metaphysical methodology for finding truth is equated with scientific thought. It is the process of relying on personal experience as the authority for truth that metaphysicians identify with science. That is, metaphysical students withhold faith until the facts of their own personal experience are in. Withholding faith until an evidential experience manifests itself is considered akin to the scientific method (see Zaretsky and Leone 1974b:xxx, point 26).

The metaphysical student is expected to "test" what he reads and hears and to be "skeptical" about any concept until it is proved in his own experience. This process of "sorting, surveying, analyzing and abstracting" (Whitehead 1974:560), described by Jenny as "deciding what to keep and what to throw out" (Study Group:9/10/75) and by John as "picking and choosing for yourself" and "filing away" what is not now understood or accepted (Study Group:6/11/75), "constitutes an intellectual style to which the [metaphysician] is often deeply committed. What this resembles, and not by coincidence, is the intellectual democracy of the scientific or academic community" (Whitehead 1974:560).

177

The "free market place of ideas" (SFF 1975c) is seen as similar to the intellectual freedom of science.

There are, of course, some very real differences between the way scientists and metaphysicians use "experience" to verify their propositions. First, the propositions to be verified are different in nature. One of the defining characteristics of a "spiritual" proposition, such as "God is within," is that it cannot be tested by observing with the senses, as can, for example, the second law of thermodynamics (a manifestation of which is that heat will transfer from a warmer to a cooler body until the two are in equilibrium).

Second, in science the observations that validate propositions can be made by anyone, given the same experimental conditions. One of the necessities of a scientific experiment is that it can be replicated by other researchers. The results are "objective." They are derived from sense perception, and are publicly verifiable. The essence of the nonrational religious experiences by which metaphysicians validate spiritual propositions, on the other hand, is that they are *personal* (and "ineffable"). This is not to deny that they do happen, or that they are "real." They do, in fact, have some external manifestations. Recently, machines that monitor brain activity have demonstrated differences in ordinary waking states and meditative states.[4] But one person's extrasensory "experience" is not another's. Researchers can watch the signs of changes in brain activity, but they cannot feel what the meditator is feeling, or, if you will, "observe" what he is "observing." They cannot be convinced, as he is, that in his meditative state he has discovered "truth." The results of this type of experience are "subjective." The "subjective, affective validity" this kind of experience carries with it can be "extremely persuasive" (Rappaport 1976a:17–18; cf. James 1958 and Otto 1958). Yet these "results" exist, however validly, in the mind of one observer.

As noted in chapter 3, other kinds of personal experiences are taken to be proofs of metaphysical claims. For example, feeling better after "having a healing" is proof of the efficacy of healing. Buying things you want at bargain prices after tithing is proof of the Law of Cause and Effect ("You have to give to receive"). Although not as "internal" as a meditative state (i. e., "healings" can be verified medically, and whether something is a bargain is a substantive question), these are no better than "correlations." The scientist would not accept them as proofs because he could not trace the causal links.

We can say, then, that SFF's response to the rationality of modern American culture is largely to provide an emphasis on the "spiritual" as opposed to the "material." The "God within" through which metaphysical students achieve self-realization, and thereby establish their identity, is a spiritual symbol, the existence of which cannot be verified by logical or empirical procedures. It can be "verified" only by personal religious experience of the sort invoked in meditation. Intuitive ways of knowing—meditation and personal experience—are preferred to logical, rational modes of understanding, such as reading and listening to a lecture. Reincarnation, karma, astrology, spiritual laws, and the power of thought provide spiritual perspectives for explaining death, life after death, and the mundane problems encountered in life on this earth. Solutions for ordinary problems are cast in a spiritual idiom, and consist of using spiritual formulas and psychic abilities and following the spiritual laws.

But at the same time, SFF considers itself to be a scientific religious philosophy. The variety of ideas presented to metaphysical students includes scientific studies of, and explanations for, psychic phenomena. The metaphysical epistemology, based on personal experience as the criterion for truth, is viewed as scientific. Metaphysical students are to maintain their "skepticism" and to "test," by their own experience, the metaphysical ideas.

Thus, by "joining science and religion" the metaphysical groups provide an emphasis on nonrational symbols and ways of knowing that are underemphasized in American culture, and simultaneously express the concern with science that imbues modern technological society.

1. Metaphysicians can "know" these things because they may believe that (1) they themselves have been "on the other side" previous to their present incarnation, and have memories of it; (2) they can communicate with discarnate spirits who are on the other side; and (3) they can receive revelations of these things from God through meditation.

2. Explanations were not given for 60% of the 470 problems discussed in the group. One reason for this is that the group members seemed to be less interested in explanations and philosophy than in how-to-do-it solutions. It may also be that ordinary causes could often have been assumed and not mentioned. For example, if the cause of an ailment such as a cold was not given, it was probably assumed to have been caused by the things most of us think of as causing colds, i.e., contact with viruses or germs. However, if a member felt a person had "programmed himself" to catch a cold, he would state this cause. Only specifically stated explanations for problems were recorded for the purposes of the quantitative analysis.

3. The group does not refer to these words as "formulas." I have labeled them this to convey that they are a set of words in a fixed form, spoken (or simply thought) in order to achieve some end.

4. "Alpha waves, produced by electrical activity in the brain and generally associated with a feeling of relaxation, become denser and more widespread in the brain during meditation" (*Time* 1975:74).

8

Conclusion

People in modern industrialized societies are particularly troubled by meaninglessness, or lack of identity. Lives and "meanings" are not structured as they were in primitive society, where life was a "one possibility thing" (Bellah 1970:40). Two trends in contemporary American society dissolve meaning: social fragmentation and an overemphasis on rational messages and modes of communication. Societal fragmentation makes finding meaning difficult because it promotes a sense of individual autonomy and leads to a feeling of separation among people. In modern industrialized society, life is an "infinite possibility thing" (Bellah 1970:40), and meaning is a matter for the "private sphere" (Luckmann 1967:97). There are, in fact, so many life-styles and meaning-giving groups and principles to choose from that we may suffer from "overchoice"--"the point at which the advantages of diversification and individualization are cancelled by the complexity of the consumer's decision-making process" (Toffler 1970:239). Yet, it seems that "as the number of potential reference points [for establishing identity] has multiplied, the ability to refer oneself to these points has declined" (Klapp 1969:21). This difficulty is magnified by the fact that the potential reference points are largely rational in nature. The rational--dependence upon information, facts, and logical, rational means of communication—is not well suited to the process of establishing identity. Facts and information are empirical, and can change rapidly. Conscious, rational modes of understanding do not provide an identifying sense of union with the universe.

The alleviation of individual meaninglessness is a primary function of Spiritual Frontiers Fellowship and groups like it. This discussion has proposed that SFF's response to meaninglessness serves to support current social values, yet provides individuals with the means to establish personal identity. Judah (1967:21–49) describes the metaphysical movements as a "mirror of American culture" (see also Zaretsky and Leone 1974b:xxvi, point 14), a view supported by this study. SFF expresses and legitimates individual autonomy through its philosophy of individual exegesis and the internalization of authority. Individual exegesis is permitted and encouraged by SFF's democratic and decentralized structure, and its antiauthoritarian leadership style. A belief in a "God within" is the rationale for the ability to be your own theologian and arbiter of truth. SFF thus expresses the mainstream American values of individualism and democracy. It does not build a small "countercultural" community where life is structured and meaning emanates from an authority external to the individual; instead, the individual is the authority for truth, and meaning is found within oneself.

The means for establishing identity provided by SFF is a form of self-realization called "spiritual growth." The central belief that God dwells within the souls of men is the basis for spiritual growth. Spiritual growth is the process of developing awareness of the divinity of one's own self, and of learning to communicate with this God within. Spiritual growth is an effective way of finding meaning because the God within is a spiritual concept and so is not subject to falsification. The mechanisms for spiritual growth—prayer and meditation—are experiential ways of knowing. These are the modes of understanding that provide the sense of "just being," in which distinctions are obliterated and identification with all that lives emerges.

182

The state that all metaphysical students should aspire to attain is "at-one-ment," or wholeness. At-one-ment is manifested in an enhanced self-image, a healthier physical state, and more positive attitudes and relationships with others. These pragmatic aspects of the group support Zaretsky and Leone's (1974b:xx) conclusion that "the popular revival [of religious movements] is . . . an interest people have in improving themselves and their lives." "It is a variation of 'how to win friends and influence people,' how to bring up your child, and how to do a thousand other necessary human tasks."

This pragmatism, coupled with metaphysics' optimism, ameliorates the sense of powerlessness that can accompany alienation. A "pessimistic" concept of sin and an awesome, angry god are far from the metaphysical construction of reality. Rather, anyone who follows the spiritual laws will achieve salvation, or "at-one-ment" with the divine inner self. There is no wrongdoing that cannot be forgiven (by mortal and supernatural alike). Most unpleasant situations encountered by humans can be "changed" through prayer, meditation, use of spiritual formulas, or positive thinking. But even if "things" cannot be changed, the burdens of anxiety and guilt can still be lifted by "giving them to God," or by accepting that "this is the way it's supposed to be for this life." The spiritual nature of all these remedies puts them beyond the reach of empirical proof (or falsification); their efficacy can be judged only in personal experience. Thus, their applicability to a myriad of situations, and their "no-fail" character, is assured.

That SFF is largely a "mirror of American culture," reflecting individualism and pragmatism, makes it attractive to people who want to improve themselves––who want to fill the void left by the feeling that "there must be something more to life"––but who do not want to make major changes in their life-styles. SFF does not reject the values that the "middle American" brings into the group with him. It does not require that he remove himself from the mainstream of American society. Indeed, his acquired spiritual power and enhanced sense of self are meant to help him improve his position in that society. Although metaphysical students report major changes in identity and sense of being, life-rending changes in lifestyle and physical comforts need not be made. Vegetarianism, celibacy, refutation of material goods, are not required. A spiritually mature person is not a saint; he is a success at his job, and on good terms with his neighbors. This spiritual "community" also does not burden its followers with demands for their money or their time. The only support fellow travelers on the path to spiritual growth require is spiritual support.

Thus, the metaphysical groups, unlike the new "youthful" religious forms that have received the lion's share of scholarly and media attention, are, for the most part, not countercultural. SFF can be said to be "countercultural" only insofar as it tries to correct what it sees as the overly rational nature of American culture by emphasizing spiritual concerns and experiential modes of learning. (Even here, the controversion is mitigated by the attempt to join science and religion.) Social scientists and group leaders alike interpret the existence of contemporary religious groups as a reaction to society's emphasis on the material aspects of life. The churches are accused of being too concerned with social ethics and rational understandings of liturgy, and of devaluating personal religious experience.

But recently some observers have expressed the fear that the perceived imbalance has been corrected, and that the ideological pendulum is in danger of swinging too far away from social concerns. It has plummeted headlong, they fear, toward emphasis on the self. Author and avante-garde educator Peter Marin (1975) labels the trend toward development of the self "the new narcissism." Social critic Tom Wolfe calls the 1970s the "Me decade" (see also Lasch 1978; Schur 1976). Herbert Hendin, a psychoanalyst, says that the seeking after material things prevalent in earlier generations has been transformed into "a very egocentric greed for experience" (*Time* 1976a:63).

Marin (1975:45) sees an overemphasis on the self in the ther-

184

apies and groups that make up the "human potential movement" (such as *est,* Arica, Esalen Institute, Scientology, the spiritual growth groups, etc.). He says "the trend in therapy [is] toward a deification of the isolated self." SFF would deny that its form of self-realization is the "deification of the isolated self." Spiritual growth is seeking to become aware of a God force that is within oneself and all other men. This god is all, and is in-all (Judah 1967:13, point 4). The spark of divinity that all men share implies a brotherhood of man. Yet, perhaps there is the danger, voiced by Charles Hampden-Turner (1976), that "you seek to become one with the universe, but instead, you isolate yourself."

In fact, it does seem that SFF is not as successful at ameliorating the sense of separation from others as it is with individual meaninglessness. A form of "fellowship," buttressed by references to past lives and psychic means of maintaining contact, can be achieved in the small study groups; but these groups occupy a compartmentalized portion of the member's life, and are short-lived. Certain metaphysical interests—psychic development, spiritual healing, spirit communication, and reincarnation—may alienate SFF participants from nonbelieving family and friends.

The joining of religion and pragmatism in metaphysics would perhaps cause Bellah (1976) to criticize it as a form that corrupts what he sees as the strongly social and collective "biblical tradition" in the United States, by joining this tradition with "utilitarian individualism". Then, says Bellah, religion itself becomes an instrument for maximizing self-interest.

But American metaphysics can be viewed in a different, more positive light. It is a synthesis of strains in the American culture; it is philosophical yet practical, spiritual yet scientific, and above all individualistic and flexible. I take it to be adaptive for the middle-class seeker after identity in our time. Adaptability must always be judged in the context of a particular time and place. The successful survivor of today and tomorrow may well be the "protean person," who takes his name from the Greek god, Proteus. Proteus had the ability to change his form at will. Thus, a

"Protean person" changes identities and life-styles easily (cf. Ellwood 1973, 1979; Gerlach and Hine 1973; Lifton 1970; Orr and Nichelson 1970; and Pfeiffer 1978, all of whom have evaluated "Protean man" positively; only Fair 1974 dissents).

In order to see how the style of Protean man is adaptive for our time, let us again compare the primitive and modern worlds. In primitive cultures, success depended on learning well traditions, skills, and beliefs that will be the same when passed to grand-children as when imparted from grandparents. Social scientists who ask inhabitants of premodern societies what they desire for their children have forgotten the underlying assumption that the children's lives will re-create the parents' own. In today's quickly changing world, on the other hand, survival requires flexibility. The capacity for *modifying* knowledge and beliefs may well be vital to our future survival (Pfeiffer 1978).

The religious experimenters of today could be said to be Protean in style, since they change congregations with alacrity. Many of the metaphysical students described here have sampled a variety of religious forms.

Yet Spiritual Frontiers Fellowship is not simply another stop on the Protean person's subway line of identities. It is itself a *Protean philosophy*. Metaphysics institutionalizes "flexibility" in the religious realm. John wanted to "try something and move on." Within six months of entering the metaphysical milieu, he had been "out-of-his-body" twice, had obtained a psychic "reading" from a Spiritualist medium, had learned to meditate, tapped some psychic abilities, and was experimenting with healing himself and others of physical ailments. His list of things yet to do included a visit to a séance, witnessing a "materialization," and trying a pyramid hat. All this, and more, he could find *within* SFF.

John had also found ways of answering the great philosophical questions of life and death; he had come to feel that "you find the answers within yourself." Metaphysics provides techniques that an individual uses to find the "truth which makes sense to him."

186

The expectation is that this truth may well change as the individual "grows spiritually."

Metaphysics, then, is a working-out, in the religious sphere, of the autonomy that imbues every other aspect of American life. SFF's emphasis on individualism and self-realization make it an example of the religious form Bellah (1970) and Luckmann (1967) theorized would emerge in modern society. This form of religion is both a reaction to, and an accommodation of, the increased freedom of the individual in the modern world. SFF is an ultimately modern adaptation to society's fragmentation. Rather than turning back toward a small and structured community, reminiscent of *Gemeinschaft*, SFF carries *Gesellschaft*'s freedom into the religious realm. The metaphysical groups recognize the new freedom and give modern man his anchor from within. "Overchoice" is assuaged because the metaphysician is given the means to look within himself and discover which of the barrage of principles and ideas "make sense to him," and which will help him integrate his life. In the context of a supportive but noncommunal and nonenduring fellowship, the individual seeks his own path to a spiritual "truth" that will enable him to ponder the mysteries of life and death. No matter if the student, caught up in the mobility of complex society, must leave the group behind. No matter if the group is not enduring, for the meaning the student finds within himself goes with him.

Appendix A: Field Work Methodology

Evans-Pritchard described "what the anthropologist does" as follows:

> He goes to live for some months or years among a people. He lives among them as intimately as he can, and he learns to speak their language, to think in their concepts and to feel in their values. He then lives the experiences over again critically and interpretatively in the conceptual categories and values of his own culture and in terms of the general body of knowledge in his discipline. In other words, he translates from one culture into another. (Evans-Pritchard 1962:148)

An ethnographic description presents the concepts that make up one culture in terms meaningful to readers in another (Spradley and McCurdy 1972). In order to write an ethnographic description, the anthropologist must first acquire understanding of these "concepts that make up the culture" himself. "The meaning system is presumed to have been acquired when the investigator can participate in the symbolism, ritual, and patterned interactions of the culture in a way that is deemed acceptable or 'correct' by its members" (Anthony and Robbins 1974: 481–82). My own understanding of, and ability to participate in, the metaphysical milieu seemed to progress in stages that might be labeled (1) gaining entrée, (2) experiencing culture shock, (3) establishing rapport, and finally, (4) an ever-increasing understanding of the culture. Other anthropologists have noted a similar progression of stages, whether their field work has taken them to primitive or urban societies. My own participant-observation research will be discussed below under headings that delineate these stages, followed by subheadings that indicate the major activities of the field work.

When I began field work, I had determined that I wanted to study an occult group of some sort. I had written a paper that studied divination cross-culturally (Bollar 1970), and had studied a modern American psychic who divined for clients. Knowing that many occultists believed that everyone possesses latent psychic abilities, I wanted to study a group in which people developed these abilities.

GAINING ENTREE

The anthropologist must somehow become acquainted with the group he wishes to study. In the summer of 1974, I began work on an inventory of the nonmainstream religious groups in a two-county area in the Midwest. I narrowed my scope by excluding groups that were mainly student-oriented, since these groups had received considerable academic attention already. Most of the groups then left on the list were metaphysical groups. My study of these groups began in Spiritualist churches.

Spiritualist Churches: June–August 1974

My entrée into the Spiritualist churches was arranged by two older part-time university students who were Spiritualists. During the summer I attended Sunday services of two Spiritualist churches, a message circle, and a trumpet séance (a séance in which a piece of paraphernalia shaped like a trumpet is used in the attempt to communicate with spirits).

190

This experience in Spiritualist churches provided a good background for the field work to follow, since some of the people in Jenny's study group had ties to these churches.

Metaphysics I: September–December 1974

In September 1974 I enrolled in the weekly metaphysics class taught by Joe at the high school in Carroll County, under the auspices of the adult education program. Joining this class was a way of discovering whether I wanted to study a group of this type. Eventually, this class became my entrée into the local manifestations of the metaphysical network, and into Spiritual Frontiers Fellowship.

Throughout the field work, I tried to maintain the holistic approach traditional in anthropology. I tried to determine what the essential qualities and elements of the group were. I tried to see what the group was doing, what it was offering to its members, and how. I was more interested in how the group worked in the lives of individuals than in the effect it had with respect to other social institutions. In the metaphysics class, I took notes on "everything". The only limitations were my own perceptual filter and my physical ability to write what was being said or done. Other class members also took notes, so my note-taking activity was not unusual, except for the quantity. Some class members brought tape recorders to class. In October I also began taping the class sessions. Even with the tape recorder, I continued to take notes, making an outline of the recording, noting who was talking, and recording things the machine could not pick up, such as facial expressions, body movements, and seating arrangements.

CULTURE SHOCK

The ethnographer—the student of culture—is by no means insulated from culture shock. When field work is undertaken in a subculture of one's own society, the culture shock should not be as broad, nor last as long, as it would in a totally "foreign" culture. Yet the vocabulary used in the metaphysics class was nearly a new language to me (see Zaretsky 1969, 1972), and I was puzzled.

My ability to understand the concepts presented in the class was very slight from September through November. From earlier readings of occult literature (Bollar 1970), I surmised that the ideas Joe was teaching were not idiosyncratic or new but had been proposed before, in Theosophy, for example. An astrology class I attended weekly from October 1974 through January 1975 in neighboring Allen County confirmed my thoughts on this.[1] Depite differences in style arising from the differences in the teachers and their students, the subject matter was very much the same. Still, I had no feeling of how widespread these concepts were, nor an idea of interconnections among various groups.

In December a professor who knew of my interest in religious groups introduced me to a student who was a member of the Association for Research and Enlightenment. Her research paper on ARE (Pastor 1974) made it clear that the ideas taught by ARE and by Joe were very similar. I accompanied her to an ARE meeting where I met people who had been labeled local experts by Joe, and found that they in turn labeled him an expert in the metaphysical field. At this meeting I learned that many of the ARE members were also members of SFF. I was aware that Joe and some of the advanced students in the metaphysics class belonged to SFF, and I began to see the outlines of the local network of metaphysical groups.

Probably the most valuable resource discovered in a search of the literature on spiritual groups was J. Stillson Judah's excellent book *History and Philosophy of the Metaphysical Movements in America* (1967). This book clarified the common characteristics of the various groups in the metaphysical network (the same characteristics I had observed), and labeled the groups "American metaphysical movements." By the end of Metaphysics I, I had learned that the emphasis in these groups is meant to be spiritual growth, not psychic development.

ESTABLISHING RAPPORT

The anthropologist "breaks out" of culture shock and can begin to understand the meaning system of a culture when he has established rapport with people in the group. This occurrence does not necessarily follow from his own efforts; it is a give-and-take between the anthropologist and his informants. At this point the anthropologist and the group, in a joint effort, clarify the anthropologist's role.

In December I began to attend after-class get-togethers of a subset of the metaphysics class at a local restaurant. I did not tape-record these sessions, since it seemed inappropriate. At the after-class meetings, I became much better acquainted with Joe. During one of these sessions, I explained to him that I would like to write a paper about metaphysics. In this way my status as a student *of* the group, and not just *in* the group, became known to members of the metaphysical network. Several times thereafter, when the opportunity arose, I would reiterate my reason for being there and try to clarify what I was studying. Most of these opportunities were during after-class discussions with Jenny and Joe. For example, in March I explained to Joe and Jenny, "I'm trying to be able to describe it [metaphysics] to people who haven't had any experience with it." Joe at first thought my paper would prove that the metaphysical philosophy was true, but I explained, "It's not my place to do that. . . . Perhaps if I were a parapsychologist I would be testing your psychic abilities—hooking you up to machines. . . . But they [the readers of the book] are interested in how it works for you." Jenny said, "I understand. You are writing a book and they are interested in how it works in our lives" (Field notes:3/31/75). Jenny eventually became an apologist for me, and several times during the field work would explain what I was doing ("She's writing a book. She's all right.") to people who were wondering why I was taking notes.

UNDERSTANDING THE CULTURE

Once rapport is established (and it is a fragile thing, which waxes and wanes), the anthropologist can begin to understand the culture and to participate in it with greater and greater ease.

After December I began to be able to use the vocabulary, and to

193

think metaphysically, with increasing facility. In March, for example, I could discuss a suicide that had occurred in the metaphysical network with a professor in terms of the social science explanation I would normally ascribe to the situation, and also explain it to her in terms of the metaphysical idiom. In May I wrote in my field work diary, "I don't notice the things that used to seem so strange to me anymore. I take note of them, of course, but they don't make a big impression on me the way they used to. I think this may be a certain plateau of field work, when you are no longer surprised by the things the people do, if they are consistent with what you've learned to expect." It is very much like learning a language. As long as one remains in the group, ability to use their concepts grows. As one moves away, facility with use of the idiom lessens.

Metaphysics II: February–May 1975

I attended the winter term adult education metaphysics class, taught by Joe, from February through May 1975. This class was concerned with the metaphysics of death.

A subset of the Metaphysics II class always went to the restaurant after class for informal discussions and often met Jenny's Monday night study group there. I went along on all these excursions, and usually stayed until the last person went home. Much was learned in these informal sessions, since it was here that the metaphysical idiom was used in discussions of other people, their problems, and why they had these problems.

SFF Study Group: January 1975–January 1976

In January 1975 I joined the SFF study group led by Jenny which met in her home every week for one year. I entered the study group by the same means as most of its other members: by being acquainted with Jenny. I met Jenny in Metaphysics I, and the formation of the study group was announced there.

Jenny and the other group members were aware that I was studying their group. Sara and I brought tape recorders to the first two group meetings, but Jenny asked us not to bring them again, since in her experience things of a sensitive and personal nature were often discussed in group meetings. From this time I took notes by hand. There was no sanction against my doing this. My note-taking was not particularly disruptive, since I was a member of the group from beginning to end, five of the group members already knew me from Metaphysics I, and the rest of the members quickly became used to me.

In the study group, I again tried to take notes on "everything." Exceptions to this were I could not take notes during meditation because it would not have been appropriate, and I could not take notes very effectively during the sharing of meditation experiences because the lights were still dimmed. Nor could I take notes during the healing circle. If I felt that it was inappropriate to take notes at a particular time, it seemed quite possible that others were feeling this too, since we did share most cultural norms, so I would stop writing and try to fill in later.

I attended the informal after-class restaurant get-togethers of the study group. During the winter of 1975, I attended the metaphysics class on Monday nights and the study group on Wednesday nights. These sessions, including the after-class restaurant sessions, sometimes lasted until 2:00 A.M.

SFF Metro Area Retreat: February 1975

In February 1975 I attended the Metro Area's annual three-day winter retreat, in which Joe and Jenny played a large part. Joe and his wife, Barbara, with whom I had by now become very close, provided me with transportation to the retreat and introduced me to area and national leaders. All the activities of the retreat, including eating and sleeping, took place under one roof. There was therefore ample opportunity to meet a wide variety of SFF participants, through the small group workshops, at communal meals in the dining hall, and in free-time informal discussions.

Many participants at this retreat had tape recorders, but my own tape recorder and clipboard were the most visible. I taped all of the formal sessions of the retreat, and some of the informal ones.

SFF Metro Area Meetings: March–June 1975

In the spring and summer of 1975, I attended monthly Metro Area meetings, including the annual business meeting, riding to and from them with Joe and Barbara and Jenny. These meetings provided further opportunity to meet SFF participants and to discover the kinds of cultural stimuli to which they were exposed. Since I accompanied area leaders, I was able to attend post-meeting informal gatherings of the area leadership at local restaurants.

Because of my ties with the area leaders of Carroll County, I was also invited to a "message circle" at a Metro Area leader's home. I went to this message circle with Jenny, Joe, Barbara, and the two Spiritualist mediums (also SFF members) who conducted the circle. I was also invited to accompany Joe and Barbara to a party at which Joe was the entertainment: he took Kirlian photographs of fingerprints (which show the "aura" or energy force around the fingers) and practiced hypnosis. I attended two parties given by Joe and Barbara for their study group graduates, and visited two Spiritualist churches in which Jenny often spoke.

There was no difficulty in attending the activities of the metaphysical groups; people would call me and say, "Melinda, you should go to this." Although the Carroll County leaders graciously provided me with entrée and transportation to many activities, once there I acted as a "free agent," so as not to meet only the people they knew, or to take on their particular biases, and such. Because of the "sharing" nature of the group and the sensitive, aware, and introspective nature of most of the people, the atmosphere at any activity was open and friendly. I came to feel very close to Joe and Barbara and Jenny. I easily could have developed closer relationships with some of the study group members than I did, but refrained from doing so because of my participant-observer role.

SFF Membership: April 1975–July 1977

In April 1975 I joined SFF. With membership I received the monthly newsletters of both the national and Metro Area organizations and all announcements of SFF activities. Subsequently I acquired a collection of SFF *Gate Way* and *Spiritual Frontiers* journals, dating from 1956 to 1977, and all the literature SFF publishes on its organization and governance.

I also collected the newsletters and announcements of some other groups that had ties to SFF, such as the Community Church by the Bay, a New Thought church in California headed by Dr. William Parker, who was a frequent SFF speaker and former SFF Executive Council member; and the Spiritual Advisory Council (SAC), which was formed in 1975 by SFF leaders for the purpose of promoting advanced spiritual and psychic study.

SFF National Conference: May 1975

In May 1975 I attended the SFF National Leadership Conference and the National Annual Conference, including the annual business meeting. Jenny and several other Metro Area leaders with whom I was acquainted attended these conferences, and I was part of their contingent. They introduced me to national leaders, and I roomed with one of their friends who was a leader in another SFF area. I tape-recorded all sessions of these conferences.

By this time patterns were beginning to emerge. The individualism valued by the group and the emphasis on the self, self-development, and self-realization were brought into sharp focus at the Metro Area retreat and at the national conference. The problem-solving aspects of the group were clear from the time spent on personal problems in the study group, and the ubiquitous seeking out of psychics by persons with problems at area meetings and message circles.

It became increasingly clear that the theories that had been used to explain revitalization movements did not fit these metaphysical groups. Neither did the goals and rituals of the group fit the traditional anthropological analysis of religion. The rituals of these groups did not seem to establish and inculcate the social order. They were instead a means for discovering and developing one's "self." Zaretsky and Leone's fine compilation of research in *Religious Movements in Contemporary America* (1974) made it clear that other researchers had recently reached similar conclusions.

During the course of the field work, I was fully a participant-observer. The SFF activities I attended were attended by about 900 other participants (SFF had about 8,000 members in 1975). I came into contact with about 250 people (by sharing a meal, a small group workshop experience, or a room), and became acquainted with about 65 people. I was exposed to the same kind of SFF cultural stimuli, to the same experiences and presentations of philosophy, to which an SFF national member, a Metro Area participant, and a member of Jenny's study group was exposed. I collected about 2,000 pages of handwritten field notes and 110 hours of tape recordings. I did not ask many "anthropological questions." The modus operandi that worked best for me was to attend group meetings, listen, and take notes.

There was nothing expected of me in the group's activities that I felt I should not do for ethical or moral reasons. In the study group meetings, each person was asked in turn whether they had any psychic or spiritual experiences to share. I sometimes reported on problems at my place of work during this time. The problems I discussed were similar to those reported by other group members. We were also asked to share meditation experiences following the group meditation. At first I reported on my mind's imaginings during the quiet meditation times. However, I did not feel comfortable with the "budding psychic" role that seemed to come with this, and I remembered Festinger, Riecken, and Schacter's (1956) report that a metaphysically relevant statement can assume much importance in these groups that believe in the legitimacy of individual personal experience and personal revelation. A more likely occurrence in the study group was that Jenny would gain clues to a person's character by the "messages" he received in meditation. Thus, by reporting on meditation experiences, it was possible to give inadvertent clues to my character that might change my relationship with the group. I therefore determined to maintain a lower profile, and was all-in-all considered to be a mediocre student of the psychic. During one class meeting, we attempted an ESP experiment of guessing the shapes and colors of hidden forms. I answered so many wrong (not purposely) that Jenny said that fact must have some significance. The group was so lively and fun-loving, however, that I often could not maintain my "mouse in the corner" stance and found myself easily entering into the bantering and joking that went on.

During the field work, I recorded my own feelings toward the group and the people in it in a diary. This was a record of feelings, my own cultural and personal values matching or mismatching theirs. Keeping a diary helped make my methodology clear to me, and writing it was a cathartic experience. The diary shows several shifts from negative to positive feelings. As an example, at times I felt some negativity toward the self-righteousness I thought some group members showed, and the self-centeredness of others. At other times the group appealed to me more than any other peer group I had, and I felt they were the most positive and optimistic people I knew. These shifts were probably necessary to maintaining the overall balance needed in the participant-observer role.

The only problem I had during field work did not affect the collection of data, but rather was of an ethical nature. In my field work, it was clear to me that there was a difference in my own conception of my role and the group's conception of it. To me I was a member of the group *because* I was studying it. To the group I was a member who was *also* studying it. Although the group leaders and most of the members knew I was a student of the group, they insisted from time to time that I was undergoing spiritual growth, just as they were. If I did not protest, I would be uncomfortable. If I protested too much, it would make the group uncomfortable, which would in turn make me uncomfortable.

199

This is the epitome of the anthropological double-bind. The field worker wishes not to disturb or influence the people he is studying, yet wants them to know he is studying them. The problem is magnified when working within one's own culture.

It seems that the major difference in doing participant-observation field work in one's own culture and an alien culture must be that when one crosses cultural boundaries one must constantly struggle to "get close," to get in as far as he can, and to see as much as he can. He will never be all the way in because he is obviously foreign in some way. He is of a different color, taller or shorter, has a different native tongue, or at least a different background. Unlike anthroplogists who do field work in foreign lands and foreign languages, I had nothing to separate me from my informants. I was not different in age, sex, or background from many of my informants. Even the fact that I did not share the beliefs that some of the group members held did not set me apart because each person can believe just as his own common sense and experience tell him to believe. When we were asked, in an around-the-room fashion, whether we believed in reincarnation, for example, I answered that to me it was a theory of the after-life as good as any other, but a theory. Jenny said, "There's been nothing in your life to make you believe in it." I said that was correct, and was not by these remarks set off from the group at all. When all the obvious cultural differences are obliterated, one must struggle to stay somewhat "out" of the group, to remember to observe and not just participate.

The only constant reminder of my "different" status in the group was my note-taking. The paraphernalia of clipboard and tape recorder became most obvious during the area retreat and the national conference. This was highlighted by the comments of participants. Waiting for a lecture to begin in an auditorium at the area retreat, Jenny turned round in the seat in front of me and said, "I knew that was you back there from the scratching of the pen." John, who was also attending the retreat, would say to me, "Be sure you spell my name right," and teased me about my attempts to make head counts. At the national conference, Jenny introduced me to a former executive director of SFF by saying, "She only joined us so she could write her book."

I enjoyed my field work, and I think the people I studied were not upset by my presence, judging from their willingness to have me attend all activities. They were not "my people." Rather, I was "their anthropologist." I believe that I was aware of the effect I might have on the group, and that this was minimal. At the same time, I was also sensitive to the ethical necessity of keeping my informants apprised of my activities, and did not compromise this issue too much.

1. Data from the astrology class are not used in the thesis, since the teacher and students had no connection with SFF.

Appendix B: Spiritual Frontiers Fellowship's
Principles, Purposes, and Program, 1974

Spiritual Frontiers Fellowship (SFF) was incorporated in Illinois in 1956 by about twenty-five religious leaders and writers from all sections of the United States, to encourage and interpret to the Churches, and receive interpretation from the Churches of the rising tide of interest in mystical, psychical and paranormal experience.

SFF is *spiritual* in that it is concerned with nonphysical phenomena which relate to God, the human spirit, and the future life. It is *frontier* because it explores matters beyond the usual range of church worship and activity, the para-normal. It is a *fellowship* of those who, having accepted the validity of one or more of these phenomena, would encourage each other and ultimately the whole Church to seek for further light and greater reality in the spiritual life.

203

I

Among various manifestations of man's psychic and spiritual nature there are three main areas of concern which SFF would emphasize at this present time.

1.   Most important is the development of creative and mystical *Prayer* in order to meet the need for a greater reality in prayer. God meets us in prayer. Life can be transformed and situations changed when prayer is seen not as "overcoming God's reluctance but as laying hold on God's willingness."

2.   *Spiritual healing*, which is a frequent outgrowth of intercessory prayer. Well-attested success in healing has led to a larger recognition of the place of faith as a factor in mental and physical health, and there is increasing cooperation between the medical profession and religious leadership.

3.   *Personal immortality* and the eternal life of the spirit. If, as the Scriptures would indicate, the spiritual world is another dimension, near us and not to be measured in light years or distance, may there not be some glimpses within the veil, as Peter and Paul and John experienced? Scripture testimony indicates that "The Communion of Saints" means far more than fellowship of believers on earth. How much more? To sift and weigh the evidence of the survival of the soul after death, as it is presented through psychical research, is a most serious concern. With open minds, and seeking to develop spiritual sensitivity, we believe in the reality of a future life and that spiritual guidance and personal communion with our beloved dead are possible.

Certain other practices and beliefs of the New Testament Church are now being accepted by growing numbers of people. These include recognition of the presence and ministry of angels, the reality of demon possession as far more than mere mental illness, and of deliverance by exorcism, guidance through dreams and visions, manifestation of the gifts of the Spirit described in First Corinthians as prophecy, interpretation, and discerning of spirits; and, more widespread than other phenomena, 'glossolalia' or speaking in tongues. Likewise, some of the insights of modern depth psychology are proving for many to be roads to self understanding and spiritual reality.

More important than even these special concerns which may change from time to time, is a pioneer spirit which always looks forward to further steps in understanding and experience. SFF recognizes that no individual or institution can both stand still and follow truth.

II

Certain philosophical principles and viewpoints lie back of the special interest of SFF, although they may not necessarily be accepted by all its members:

1.   Its basic *world view*, like that of the New Testament and many of the greatest philosophers, is that there is a physical world subject to the laws of physics and biology, and a nonphysical, or psychic world, which is just as real, yet entirely different. Since everything comes from one divine Mind, both are under the moral law of God with freedom, responsibility, and purpose. This implies the distinction of good from evil, and the concepts of heaven and hell.

2.   *Man* is a creature of both worlds, and in spiritual experience becomes aware of his true heritage as a child of God with unlimited capacity for growth. Any effective religion must include acceptance of, experience with, and obedient response to the laws of the spiritual world.

3.   The *Bible*, and more specifically the New Testament, is a reliable report of the experience of men and women in their dealings with Jesus Christ and the spiritual world. Thus, while SFF accepts the fruits of modern technology and the insights of critical Bible study as gifts of God, it is close to the fundamentals of New Testament Christianity.

4.   SFF takes the *scientific* attitude that all human experiences, including extrasensory perception (telepathy, clairvoyance, precognition and related phenomena) are to be studied without prejudice for better understanding of the invisible world,

and the nature of man and the universe. SFF acknowledges the part that the sciences, including psychology, parapsychology, physics and biophysics, physics, have played in directing the attention of many lay people and ministers to the non-material nature of the world.

5.   As men come into what they believe to be valid personal relationship with the spiritual world, they discover a firmer basis for understanding *the great questions of life and faith,* and for facing the human problems of suffering, injustice, and death.

6.   SFF holds that the doors of *revelation* are never closed; God is still speaking, and by the disciplines of study, prayer, and healing our generation may learn more of those truths which Christ said his disciples were "not yet able to bear."

III

On the basis of these general principles, SFF has certain specific purposes:

1.   It seeks to enlarge the churches' interpretation of their Old and New Testament heritage; it endeavors to recapture the faith and experience of the First Century in order to speak with conviction to contemporary Man.

2.   SFF seeks to share with *science* the implications of its own method, which is the examination of all available evidence as the basis of understanding and progress, and to urge that it be just as open-minded in dealing with parapsychology as it is with physics and biology.

3.   It would open the eyes of a materialistic and skeptical generation to man's intrinsic spiritual nature.

4.   For its own members, SFF seeks to provide an assurance that they are not alone, but are part of a larger company of people who desire to seek further exploration of truth and avenues for more effective service to God and Man. It seeks to provide a comfortable climate for sharing and discussing experiences of nonphysical reality.

206

SFF implements these purposes by means of a national office and officers, a book service and lending library, publications, research, seminars and conferences, area organizations, pray-study groups, spiritual and psychical study groups for spiritual development and healing.

IV

In line with its spiritual philosophy and church-centered purposes, there are certain matters of strategy and practice which should be kept in mind by officers and committees within the Fellowship, and by those outside in evaluating it. These are guidelines rather than rigid rules, but they represent the general attitude of both the organizers and the present national directors.

1. While SFF stresses the validity of spiritual and psychic gifts, its purpose is to bring them back into life of the church, so that there would be no reason for SFF to perpetuate itself indefinitely as an organization.

2. In a broad sense, SFF was church-conceived, born and bred. Therefore, it chooses its leadership from among church members, and, as far as is practicable, it holds its public meetings in church buildings.

3. While it appreciates the contributions of the numerous movements which have sought to satisfy specific spiritual needs not otherwise met, it seeks to recall those who have broken away from the redemptive fellowship of the church.

4. SFF seeks to cooperate with like-minded individuals and groups within and outside the churches. It invites the support of all spiritual pioneers and specifically seeks sponsorship by courageous and forward looking ecclesiastical leaders. It therefore welcomes cooperation with such groups as the Churches' Fellowship for Psychical and Spiritual Studies in Great Britain, and Imago Mundi, the Catholic oriented international study group in border areas of science.

5. SFF prefers to avoid public demonstrations of mystical

and psychic phenomena which may attract curiosity seekers rather than the spiritually hungry. It makes a distinction between the mystical and the psychical in terms of their source and use. SFF investigates the psychical and encourages the mystical life.

6. While the Fellowship is not primarily a research group, it has created an active Research Committee which encourages investigation in the principal fields of the paranormal without being dogmatic about their validity or their interpretation. It welcomes the help and interest of all, regardless of religious background.

7. SFF recognizes that the frontier is always fraught with the dangers of extremism, individualism and self-deception. Both scripture and common sense require that we "try the spirits to see whether they be of God" (1 John 4:1) and give some ground rules for doing so. But it also remembers that the growing edge is always on the frontier.

8. The Fellowship seeks to be democratic in its committees and official actions, and so seeks the participation of its members in the making of policy and program. For this reason also, it avoids "official endorsements" of specific persons and points of view.

9. The spiritual can never be put into a rigid mold, so there will always be diversities of emphasis, practice and theology. Therefore, SFF holds that the only essentials are loyalty to the truth as one perceives it, and willingness to venture out in obedience to it.

This is the Spiritual Frontiers Fellowship, we believe, called by God for such a time as this.

If the Spirit bears witness with your spirit that this is so, you are invited to bear witness also by your membership, your active participation and your public support.

When people ask about. . .
Spiritual Frontiers Fellowship

. . . it is explained that SFF is an inter-faith, non-profit fellowship incorporated in Illinois in 1956 "to sponsor, explore, and interpret the growing interest in psychic phenomena and mystical experience to the traditional churches and others, and relate these experiences to effective prayer, spiritual healing, personal survival and spiritual fulfillment."

As a spiritual fellowship, SFF does not seek to change or replace the basic experience recorded in the Bible, but to apply them to our present day experiences. Through discussion, reading, research and other forms of personal and group development, SFF is dedicated to the expansion of consciousness toward the realization of Man's intrinsic spiritual nature.

SFF MEMBERSHIP PROVIDES

1. SFF provides members with a progressive reading list and study lesson materials.

2. SFF offers a free lending library by mail that covers psychical, mystical and allied research materials, SFF also operates a bookstore for members to purchase books, pamphlets and cassettes, etc. by mail.

3. SFF maintains a library of tape recordings of lectures and addresses which are loaned to members for a 50¢ handling fee.

4. SFF publishes the Quarterly Journal of Spiritual Frontiers Fellowship which is included in membership dues. (Non-members may subscribe at $5.00 per year.)

5. SFF publishes a monthly Newsletter of events of interest to members. ($1.00 of your dues covers subscription cost.)

6. SFF conducts a research program to collect data about psychical and mystical experiences for further study and provides

guidelines for psychical research experiments by individuals and groups.

7. SFF encourages members and friends to attend regional seminars and Area Chapter programs where organized.

8. SFF extends voting privileges to members at SFF's Annual Conference each spring.

9. SFF encourages spiritual growth through study groups in prayer, in spiritual healing, and in psychic development.

SPIRITUAL FRONTIERS FELLOWSHIP

Bibliography

Ahlstrom, Sydney E. 1978. From Sinai to the Golden Gate: The Liberation of religion in the Occident. In *Understanding the new religions*, ed. Jacob Needleman and George Baker, pp. 3–22. New York: Seabury Press.

Albanese, Catherine L. 1977. *Corresponding motion: Transcendental religion and the new America*. Philadelphia: Temple University Press.

Aldrich, C. Knight, and Ethel Mendkoff. 1963. Relocation of the aged and disabled: A mortality study. *Journal of the American Geriatric Society* 11:185–94.

Althouse, Lawrence W. 1974. The Spiritual Frontiers Fellowship and its critics. President's address at SFF Annual National Conference, 24 May. Evanston, Ill: Spiritual Frontiers Fellowship.

———. 1976a. Letter to SFF members from president of SFF. March.

———. 1976b. Letter to SFF members from president of SFF, accompanying ballot for SFF officers, 26 March.

211

Bibliography

————. 1976c. The president's corner: Swansong from a lame duck? *Newsletter* of Spiritual Frontiers Fellowship 10 (5):1.

————. 1976d. SFF—who needs it? *Newsletter* of Spiritual Frontiers Fellowship 10(2):1,6.

Anthony, Dick, and Thomas Robbins. 1974. The Meher Baba movement: Its effect on post-adolescent social alienation. In *Religious movements in contemporary America*, ed. Irving I. Zaretsky and Mark P. Leone, pp. 479–511. Princeton, N.J.: Princeton University Press.

Ashby, Robert H. 1974. The findings of the SFF Survival Research Questionnaire. *Spiritual Frontiers, Journal of Spiritual Frontiers Fellowship* 6(3):131–56.

Austin, J. L. 1962. *How to do things with words*. London: Oxford University Press.

————. 1970 Performative utterances. In *Philosophical papers*. Second ed. London: Oxford University Press (first ed. 1961).

Bach, Marcus. 1946. *They have found a faith*. Indianapolis: Bobbs-Merrill.

————. 1968. Spiritual understanding through meditation. In *Spiritual Frontiers Fellowship Procedures Guide*. Evanston, Ill.: Spiritual Frontiers Fellowship.

Balch, Robert W. 1980. Looking behind the scenes in a religious cult: Implications for the study of conversion. *Sociological Analysis* 41(2): 137–43.

Balch, Robert W., and David Taylor. 1977. Seekers and saucers: The role of the cultic milieu in joining a UFO cult. *American Behavioral Scientist* 20(6):839–60.

Bateson, Gregory. 1972a. Conscious purpose versus nature. In *Steps to an ecology of mind*, pp. 426–39. New York: Ballantine.

————. 1972b. Effects of conscious purpose on human adaptation. In *Steps to an ecology of mind*, pp. 440–47. New York: Ballantine.

Bateson, Mary Catherine. 1974. Ritualization: A study in texture and texture change. In *Religious movements in contemporary America*, ed. Irving I. Zaretsky and Mark P. Leone, pp. 150–65. Princeton, N.J.: Princeton University Press.

Baum, Gregory. 1970. Does the world remain disenchanted? *Social Research* 37(2):153–202.

212

Bellah, Robert N. 1970. *Beyond belief.* New York: Harper & Row.

_____. 1976. New religious consciousness and the crisis in modernity. In *The New Religious Consciousness,* ed. Charles Y. Glock and Robert N. Bellah, pp. 333-52. Berkeley: University of California Press.

Benson, Peter, and Bernard Spilka. 1973. God image as a function of self-esteem and locus of control. *Journal for the Scientific Study of Religion* 12(3):297-310.

Berger, Peter, and Thomas Luckmann. 1969. Sociology of religion and sociology of knowledge. In *Sociology and religion: A book of readings,* ed. Norman Birnbaum and Gertrud Lenzer, pp. 410-18. Englewood Cliffs, N.J.: Prentice-Hall.

Bollar, Melinda. 1970. Divination. B.A. honors thesis, Sociology Department, Purdue University.

Bonacci, James. 1976a. Loving yourself to wholeness. Lecture at SFF Metro Area Winter Retreat, 29 February. (Text by William R. Parker.)

_____. 1976b. Prayer and meditation for wholeness. Lecture at SFF Metro Area Winter Retreat, 27 February. (Text by William R. Parker.)

Braden, Charles Samuel. 1951. *These also believe: A study of modern American cults and minority religious movements.* New York: Macmillan.

Bro, Margueritte Harmon. 1948. *More than we are.* New York: Harper & Brothers.

Buckner, H. Taylor. 1968. The Flying Saucerians: An open door cult. In *Sociology and Everyday Life,* ed. Marcello Truzzi, Englewood Cliffs, N.J.: Prentice-Hall.

Campbell, Joseph. 1949. *The hero with a thousand faces.* New York: Bollingen Foundation.

_____. 1968. *The masks of god: Creative mythology.* New York: Viking Press.

Chaney, Earlyne. 1974. *Remembering: The autobiography of a mystic.* Los Angeles: Astara, Inc.

Cobb, Sidney. 1974. Physiological changes in men whose jobs were abolished. *Journal of Psychosomatic Research* 18(4):245ff.

Bibliography

Cooley, Charles H. 1909. *Social organization.* New York: C. Scribner's Sons.

Cooper, John Charles. 1972. *A new kind of man.* Philadelphia: Westminster Press.

Cox, Harvey. 1965. *The secular city: Secularization and urbanization in theological perspective.* New York: Macmillan.

Daily Word. 1975. *Daily Word.* November 1975. Unity Village, Mo.

Dohrman, H. T. 1958. *California cult: The story of "Mankind United."* Boston: Beacon Press.

Durkheim, Emile. 1933. *The division of labor in society.* George Simpson, trans. New York: Free Press. (Original:1893).

Eliade, Mircea. 1976. *Occultism, witchcraft, and cultural fashions.* Chicago: University of Chicago Press.

Ellwood, Robert S., Jr. 1973. *Religious and spiritual groups in modern America.* Englewood Cliffs, N.J.: Prentice-Hall.

———. 1979. *Alternative altars: Unconventional and Eastern spirituality in America.* Chicago: University of Chicago Press.

Ethics and Religion, Office of, University of Michigan. 1974. *Spiritual and religious resources.* Ann Arbor: Office of Ethics and Religion, University of Michigan.

Evans-Pritchard, E. E. 1962. *Social anthropology and other essays.* New York: Free Press.

Fair, Charles. 1974. *The new nonsense: The end of the rational consensus.* New York: Simon & Schuster.

Fenske, Paul. 1975. Personal communication, 1 March.

Fernandez, James. 1974. The mission of metaphor in expressive culture. *Current Anthropology* 15:119–45.

Festinger, Leon, Henry W. Riecken, and Stanley Schacter. 1956. *When prophecy fails.* Minneapolis: University of Minnesota Press.

Fischler, Claude. 1974. Astrology and French society: The dialectic of archaism and modernity. In *On the margin of the visible*, ed. E. Tiryakian, pp. 281–93. New York: Wiley.

Ford, Arthur. 1967. A force or a farce. Lecture at SFF Annual National Conference 13 May. Evanston, Ill.: Spiritual Frontiers Fellowship.

Galbreath, Robert. 1971. Introduction: The occult today. *Journal of Popular Culture* 5(3):629–34.

214

Geertz, Clifford. 1966. Religion as a cultural system. In *Anthropological approaches to the study of religion*, ed. Michael Banton, London: Tavistock Publications.

Gerlach, Luther P., and Virginia H. Hine. 1973. *Lifeway leap: The dynamics of change in America*. Minneapolis: University of Minnesota Press.

Glock, Charles Y., and Robert N. Bellah. 1976. *The new religious consciousness*. Berkeley: University of California Press.

Gruen, Walter. 1966. Composition and some correlates of the American core culture. *Psychological Reports* 18:483–86.

Goldfarb, Russell M. 1971. Madame Blavatsky. *Journal of Popular Culture* 5(3):660–72.

Greeley, Andrew M. 1974. Implications for the sociology of religion of occult behavior in the youth culture. In *On the margin of the visible*, ed. E. Tiryakian, pp. 295–302. New York: Wiley.

Greeley, Andrew M., and William C. McCready. 1974. Some notes on the sociological study of mysticism. In *On the margin of the visible*, ed. E. Tiryakian, pp. 303–22. New York: Wiley.

Hall, Edward T. 1959. *The silent language*, Greenwich, Conn.: Fawcett.

Hampden-Turner, Charles. 1976. When is egoism, egotism? Paper presented in symposium, Is modern therapy and the human potential movement narcissistic?, at the 84th annual convention of the American Psychological Association, 3–7 September. Washington, D.C.

Hayes, Patricia. 1971. *Know yourself.* Miami, Fla.: Patricia Hayes.

Heenan, Edward F. (ed.). 1973. *Mystery, magic, and miracle: Religion in a post-Aquarian age*. Englewood Cliffs, N.J.: Prentice-Hall.

Heron, Laurence T. 1967. The Pike declaration stirs public interest in survival evidence. *Gate Way, Journal of the Spiritual Frontiers Fellowship* 12(9):197–200.

Higgins, Paul Lambourne. 1966. Spiritual Frontiers Fellowship—history of its first ten years. *Gate Way, Journal of the Spiritual Frontiers Fellowship* 11 (7): 161–68.

Hine, Virginia H. 1974. The deprivation and disorganization theories of social movements. In *Religious movements in contemporary America*, ed. Irving I. Zaretsky and Mark P. Leone, pp. 646–64. Princeton, N.J.: Princeton University Press.

215

Holmes, Ernest. 1947. *This thing called life.* New York: Dodd, Mead & Co.

Hood, Ralph W., Jr. 1974. Psychological strength and the report of intense religious experience. *Journal for the Scientific Study of Religion* 13(1):65–71.

James, William. 1958. *The varieties of religious experience.* New York: Mentor (First ed. 1903).

Johnson, Kenneth. 1963. Personal religious growth through small group participation: A psychological study of personality changes and shifts in religious attitudes which result from participation in a spiritual growth group. Ph.D. diss. Pacific School of Religion.

Johnson, Paul V. 1976a. Healers haven't soothed skeptics. *Spiritual Advisory Council Newsletter* 1(3):3.

———. 1976b. *Spiritual Advisory Council Newsletter* 1 (3):2.

Judah, J. Stillson. 1967. *The history and philosophy of the metaphysical movements in America.* Philadelphia: Westminster.

———. 1974. The Hare Krishna movement. In *Religious movements in contemporary America,* ed. Irving I. Zaretsky and Mark P. Leone, pp. 463–78. Princeton, N.J.: Princeton Unviersity Press.

Klapp, Orrin E. 1969. *Collective search for identity.* New York: Holt, Rinehart & Winston.

Kluckhohn, Clyde, and Dorothea Leighton. 1946. *The Navajo.* Cambridge, Mass.: Harvard University Press.

Kortzfleisch, Siegfried von. 1970. Religious Olympism. *Social Research* 37(2):231–36.

Langer, Susanne K. 1942. *Philosophy in a new key: A study in the symbolism of reason, rite, and art.* Cambridge, Mass.: Harvard University Press.

Lasch, Christopher. 1978. *The culture of narcissism: American life in an age of diminishing expectations.* New York: Norton.

Leighton, Alexander H., and Dorothea Leighton. 1944. *The Navajo door: An introduction to Navajo life.* Cambridge, Mass.: Harvard University Press.

Leone, Mark P. 1974. The economic basis for the evolution of Mormon religion. In *Religious movements in contemporary America,* ed. Irving I. Zaretsky and Mark P. Leone, pp. 722–66. Princeton, N.J.: Princeton University Press.

Lewis, Jeanne Gerlach. 1973. Freedom, authority, and control in a Catholic Pentecostal community, Ph.D. preliminary examination paper, Anthropology Department, University of Michigan.

———. 1977. Personal communication, 9 August.

Lifton, Robert Jay. 1970. Protean man. In R. J. Lifton, *History and human survival.* New York: Random House.

Lindsey, Robert. 1976. "Psychics" are flourishing in southern California, gaining social acceptance among middle class. *New York Times,* 15 December.

Luckmann, Thomas. 1967. *The invisible religion: The problem of religion in modern society.* New York: Macmillan.

McCready, William C., with Andrew M. Greeley. 1976. *The ultimate values of the American population.* Beverly Hills: Sage Publications.

Macklin, June. 1974. Belief, ritual and healing: New England Spiritualism and Mexican-American spiritism compared. In *Religious movements in contemporary America,* ed. Irving I. Zaretsky and Mark P. Leone, pp. 383–417. Princeton, N.J.: Princeton University Press.

Maddock, Richard C., and Charles T. Kenny. 1972. Philosophies of human nature and personal religious orientation. *Journal for the Scientific Study of Religion* 11(3):277–81.

Mandic, Oleg. 1970. A Marxist perspective on contemporary religious revivals. *Social Research* 37(2):237–58.

Marin, Peter. 1975. The new narcissism. *Harper's,* October, pp. 45–56.

Marty, Martin. 1970. The occult establishment. *Social Research* 37(2): 212–30.

Maslow, Abraham H. 1964. *Religion, values, and peak experiences.* Columbus: Ohio State University Press.

Melton, J. Gordon. 1976. The Chicago psychic/metaphysical/occult/ New Age community: A directory and guide. In *Psychic City Chicago,* ed. Brad Steiger, pp. 161–86. Garden City, N.Y.: Doubleday.

———. 1977. *A directory of religious bodies in the United States.* New York: Garland.

217

Metaphysics I. 1974. Metaphysics I Adult Education Class, September–December. Field notes and tape recordings.

Metaphysics II. 1975. Metaphysics II Adult Education Class, February–May. Field notes and tape recordings.

Naegele, Kaspar D. 1961. The institutionalization of action. In *Theories of society*, ed. Talcott Parsons et al., pp. 183–90. New York: Free Press.

Nahl, Helen. 1975. How to increase joy—God still enables: a group leader's experience with study suggestions for individuals and groups. Evanston, Ill.: Spiritual Frontiers Fellowship.

Needleman, Jacob. 1977. *The new religions*. New York: E. P. Dutton.

Needleman, Jacob, and George Baker. 1978. *Understanding the new religions*. New York: Seabury Press.

Nelson, Geoffrey K. 1969. *Spiritualism and society*. London: Routiedge & Kegan Paul.

Ollman, Bertell. 1971. *Alienation: Marx's conception of man in capitalist society*. London: Cambridge University Press.

Orr, John B., and F. Patrick Nichelson. 1970. *The radical suburb: Soundings in changing American character*. Philadelphia: Westminster Press.

Otto, Rudolph. 1958. *The idea of the holy*. London: Oxford University Press (first ed. 1923).

Parampanthi, Swami. 1963. Meditation and activity sustain each other. *Gate Way, Journal of the Spiritual Frontiers Fellowship* 8(3).

Park, Robert. 1915. The city: Suggestions for the investigation of human behavior in the city environment. *American Journal of Sociology* 20(5):577–612.

Parker, William R. 1976a. Be open to the new. *Science of Life Newsletter*, July/August.

———. 1976b. Spiritual exercises. *Science of Life Newsletter*, February, September.

———. 1977. Spiritual exercises. *Science of Life Newsletter*, February, March.

Parker, William R., and Elaine St. Johns. 1957. *Prayer can change your life: Experiments and techniques in prayer therapy*. New York: Pocket Books.

218

Parsons, Talcott. 1937. *The structure of social action.* New York: Free Press.

Parsons, Talcott, and Edward A. Shils. 1951. *Toward a general theory of action.* Cambridge, Mass.: Harvard University Press.

Pastor, Joni Faye. 1974. The Edgar Cayce records: Their philosophy, their use, and their effect. Anthropology 452 paper, Anthropology Department, University of Michigan.

Perkins, James O. 1976a. A view from the base of the pyramid. *Newsletter* of Spiritual Frontiers Fellowship 10(4):7.

_____. 1976b Personal communication from SFF Executive Council member, 24 September.

Pfeiffer, John E. 1978. *The emergence of man,* Third edition. New York: Harper and Row.

Pilleggi, Nicholas. 1970. The age of the occult. McCalls, March.

Prince, R., and C. Savage. 1972. Mystical states and the concept of regression. In *The highest state of consciousness,* ed. J. White, pp. 114–34. New York: Anchor.

Prince, Raymond H. 1974. Cocoon work: An interpretation of the concern of contemporary youth with the mystical. In *Religious movements in contemporary America,* ed. Irving I. Zaretsky and Mark P. Leone, pp. 255–71. Princeton, N.J.: Princeton University Press.

Rappaport, Roy A. 1971. The sacred in human evolution. *Annual Review of Ecology and Systematics* 2:23–44.

_____. 1974. Obvious aspects of ritual. *Cambridge Anthropology* 2(1).

_____. 1976a. Liturgies and lies. *International Yearbook of Sociology and Religion* 10:75–104.

_____. 1976b. Personal communication, 18 February.

_____. 1977. Ecology, adaptation, and the ills of functionalism. *Michigan Discussions in Anthropology* 2 (Winter): 138–90.

Rauscher, William V. 1970. Spiritual Frontiers Fellowship. *Psychic Magazine,* September/October.

Redfield, Robert. 1947. The folk society. *American Journal of Sociology* 52(4):293–308.

Reiss, Ira L. 1976. *Family systems in America.* Second edition. Hinsdale, Ill.: Dryden Press.

219

Robbins, Thomas. 1969. Eastern mysticism and the resocialization of drug users: The Meher Baba cult. *Journal for the Scientific Study of Religion* 8(2):307–17.

Robbins, Thomas, Dick Anthony, and James Richardson. 1978. Theory and research in today's "new religions." *Sociological Analysis* 39(2):95–122.

Rowland, Kay K. 1977. Environmental events predicting death for the elderly. *Psychological Bulletin* 84(2):349–72.

Rowley, Peter. 1971. *New gods in America: An informal investigation into the new religions of American youth today.* New York: David McKay.

SAC (Spiritual Advisory Council). 1976. Spiritual Advisory Council Spring Festival information. Glenview, Ill.: Spiritual Advisory Council.

SFF (Spiritual Frontiers Fellowship). 1965. *Gate Way, Journal of the Spiritual Frontiers Fellowship* 10(2):copyright page.

———. 1968. *A procedures guide for the formation and conducting of Spiritual Frontiers Fellowship study groups.* Evanston, Ill.: Spiritual Frontiers Fellowship.

———. 1969. Principles, purposes, program of SFF. *Spiritual Frontiers, Journal of Spiritual Frontiers Fellowship* 1(3):191–92.

———. 1971. *Handbook of the Spiritual Frontiers Fellowship: A guidebook on policy and practice for the use of National Council and committee members and of local chairmen, officers, and committees.* Evanston, Ill.: Spiritual Frontiers Fellowship.

———. 1973a. *Constitution and by-laws of the Spiritual Frontiers Fellowship.* Evanston, Ill.: Spiritual Frontiers Fellowship.

———. 1973b. *Spiritual Frontiers Fellowship by-laws (local organizations).* Evanston, Ill.: Spiritual Frontiers Fellowship.

———. 1974. *Spiritual Frontiers Fellowship: Its principles, purposes, and program.* Evanston, Ill.: Spiritual Frontiers Fellowship.

———. 1975a. Spiritual Frontiers Fellowship annual national business meeting, 22 May. Field notes and tape recordings.

———. 1975b Spiritual Frontiers Fellowship Annual National Conference, 22–24 May. Field notes and tape recordings.

220

_____. 1975c. Spiritual Frontiers Fellowship Annual Leadership Conference, 21 May. Field notes and tape recordings.

_____. 1975d. *Spiritual Frontiers Fellowship membership report and publications inventory, compiled as of May 15, 1975.* Evanston, Ill.: Spiritual Frontiers Fellowship.

_____. 1975e. Spiritual Frontiers Fellowship Metro Area Winter Retreat, 28 February–2 March. Field notes and tape recordings.

_____. 1975f. Spiritual Frontiers Fellowship study group defined. *Newsletter of Spiritual Frontiers Fellowship* 9(8):4.

_____. 1976a. *By-laws for local chapters of Spiritual Frontiers Fellowship, revised November 1, 1976.* Independence, Mo.: Spiritual Frontiers Fellowship.

_____. 1976b. *Eighth annual national SFF Carleton retreat information.* Minneapolis: Twin Cities Chapter of Spiritual Frontiers Fellowship.

_____. 1976c. *Newsletter* of Spiritual Frontiers Fellowship10(9).

_____. 1976d. Our readers write. *Newsletter* of Spiritual Frontiers Fellowship 10(6):6.

_____. 1976e. *The procedures guide for the formation and conducting of Spiritual Frontiers Fellowship study groups, revised edition.* Independence, Mo.: Spiritual Frontiers Fellowship.

_____. 1976f. Special prayer needs? SFF Metro Area Newsletter, November.

_____. 1976g. Study group forming. SFF Metro Area Newsletter, December.

_____. 1976h. The faith healing. SFF Metro Area Newsletter, October.

_____. 1977a. A brief principles, purposes, and program for SFF. *Newsletter* of Spiritual Frontiers Fellowship 11(1):7.

_____. 1977b. Spiritual Frontiers Fellowship chapter chairpersons, January 1, 1976. *Newsletter* of Spiritual Frontiers Fellowship 11(1):5.

Sahlins, Marshall. 1972. Primitive economics. Anthroplogy 461 lectures, University of Michigan.

Schur, Edwin. 1976. *The awareness trap: Self-absorption instead of social change.* New York: McGraw-Hill.

Bibliography

Scott, Gini. 1976. Social structure and the occult: A sociological analysis and comparison of the social organization, behavior patterns, and beliefs of two occult groups: A spiritual growth group and a witchcraft group. Ph.D. diss., University of California, Berkeley.

Selye, Hans. 1956. *The stress of life.* New York: McGraw-Hill.

Setzer, J. Schoneberg. 1974. Love+ joy + peace and other mudras for the masses: A spiritual development and protection exercise that utilizes hand ritual. Highland Park, Ill.: Clark Publishing Co.

Simmel, Georg. 1950. The metropolis and mental life. In *The sociology of Georg Simmel,* ed. Kurt Wolff, pp. 409–24. Glencoe, Ill.: Free Press.

Spradley, James P., and David W. McCurdy. 1972. *The cultural experience: Ethnography in complex society.* Chicago: Science Research Associates.

Study Group. 1975. Spiritual Frontiers Fellowship study group weekly meetings, January 1975–January 1976. Field notes.

Time, Inc. 1969. Astrology: Fad and phenomenon. *Time,* 21 March.

———. 1974. Boom times on the psychic frontier. *Time,* 4 March, pp. 65–72.

———. 1975. Meditation: The answer to all your problems? *Time,* 13 October, pp. 70–74.

———. 1976a. Narcissus Redivivus. *Time,* 20 September, p. 63.

———. 1976b. Soap operas: Sex and suffering in the afternoon. *Time,* 12 January, pp. 46–53.

Tönnies, Ferdinand. 1957. *Community and society.* Charles P. Loomis, trans. East Lansing: Michigan State University Press. (Original: *Gemeinschaft und Gesellschaft,* Leipzig: Reisland, 1887).

Toffler, Alvin. 1970. *Future shock.* New York: Random House.

Truzzi, Marcello. 1971. Definition and dimensions of the occult: Towards a sociological perspective. *Journal of Popular Culture* 5(3): 635–46.

———. 1972. The occult revival as popular culture: Some random observations on the old and nouveau witch. *Sociological Quarterly* 13: 16–36.

U.S. Bureau of the Census. 1973. *Census of popluation: 1970.* Vol. 1,

Characteristics of the Poplulation. Washington, D.C.: U. S. Government Printing Office.

———. 1975. Current popluation reports, Series P-20, No. 287 *Marital status and living arrangements*: *March 1975*. Washington, D.C.: U.S. Government Printing Office.

van Baal, Jan. 1971. *Symbols for communication: An introduction to the anthropological study of religion*. Assen, the Netherlands: Koninklijke Van Gorcum.

Van Baalen, Jan Karel. 1956. *The chaos of cults: A study in present-day isms*. Grand Rapids, Mich.: Wm. B. Eerdmans.

Wallis, Roy. 1974. Ideology, authority, and the development of cultic movements. *Social Research* 41(2):299–327.

———. 1975. Reflection on when prophecy fails. *The Zetetic: A Newsletter of Academic Research Into Occultisms* 4(1):9–14.

Weber, Max. 1947. *The theory of social and economic organization*. A. M. Henderson and Talcott Parsons, trans. New York: Free Press.

Whitehead, Harriet. 1974. Reasonably fantastic: Some perspectives on Scientology, science fiction, and occultism. In *Religious movements in contemporary America*, ed. Irving I. Zaretsky and Mark P. Leone, pp. 547–87. Princeton, N.J.: Princeton University Press.

Wirth, Louis. 1964. *On cities and social life*. Chicago: University of Chicago Press.

Wise, Charles C., Jr. 1971. A meditation on meditation. *Spiritual Frontiers, Journal of Spiritual Frontiers Fellowship* 3(4):237–53.

Wuthnow, Robert. 1976. *The consciousness reformation*. Berkeley: University of California Press.

———. 1978. *Experimentation in American religion*. Berkeley: University of California Press.

Zaretsky, Irving I. 1969. The message is the medium: An ethnosemantic study of the language of Spiritualist churches. Ph.D. diss., University of California, Berkeley.

———. 1972. The language of Spiritualist churches: A study in cognition and social organization. In *Culture and cognition: Rules, maps, and plans*, ed. James P. Spradley, pp. 355–96. San Francisco: Chandler.

223

Bibliography

————. 1974. In the beginning was the word: The relationship of language to social organization in Spiritualist churches. In *Religious movements in contemporary America*, ed. Irving I. Zaretsky and Mark P. Leone, pp. 166–219. Princeton, N.J.: Princeton University Press.

Zaretsky, Irving I., and Mark P. Leone. 1974a. Conclusion: Perspectives for future research. In *Religious movements in contemporary America*, ed. Irving I. Zaretsky and Mark P. Leone, pp. 767–70. Princeton, N.J.: Princeton University Press.

————. 1974b. Introduction: The common foundation of religious diversity. In *Religious movements in contemporary America*, ed. Irving I. Zaretsky and Mark P. Leone, pp. xvii–xxxvi. Princeton, N.J.: Princeton University Press.

————. 1974c. Psychological dimensions of religious innovation: Introduction. In *Religious movements in contemporary America*, ed. Irving I. Zaretsky and Mark P. Leone, pp. 275–82. Princeton, N.J.: Princeton University Press.

Zygmunt, Joseph F. 1972. Movements and motives: Some unresolved issues in the psychology of social movements. *Human Relations* 25(5):449–67.

Index

Acupuncture, 91
Affirmations (affirmative prayer): analyzed, 132–33; uses of, 119, 130–31, 170, 179
Alienation from nonbelievers, 159–62
Altered states of consciousness. *See* Meditation; Out-of-body experiences
Aquarian Age: dispensation in, 138–39, 142, 161; explanation of, 165–66
Arcane School, 22, 166
Argot: metaphysical and spiritualist, 62, 140, 153–54, 176
Association for Research and Enlightenment: as metaphysical group 4, 14, 95, 106; memberships in, 31, 35, 37, 96, 104, 192
Astara: as metaphysical group, 4, 22, 97, 148, 166; memberships in, 25, 110, 138
Astral travel. *See* Out-of-body experiences
Astrology, 15, 91, 165, 169–70, 192
Auras, 26, 196
Austin, J.L., 132–33

Bellah, Robert N., 12, 13, 80–81, 83, 108, 120, 181, 185, 187
Blavatsky, Madame Helena Petrovna. *See* Theosophy

Chakras, 52, 110–11
Charismatic leadership, 101, 106, 151
Christian Science, 4, 22, 166
Church of Religious Science, 22
Clairaudience, 29, 30
Clairsentience, 30
Clairvoyance, 29, 30
Communitarian religious groups, 17–19
Correspondences: between spiritual and material realms, 5, 131
Countercultural religious groups, 17–19, 184
Creedlessness: of metaphysical groups, 89; of Spiritual Frontiers Fellowship, 89–91, 103
Cultic milieu, 6, 93, 186

225

Index

Divine Light Mission, 19
Divine Science Church, 22
Dream interpretation, 26, 160

Eclecticism: of Spiritual Frontiers Fellowship, 39, 91, 103, 151
Esalen Institute, 185
ESP. *See* Psychic
est, 185
Experience, personal: as validation for truth, 29, 65, 78, 83–88, 94, 116–18, 125, 142, 174–75, 177, 182; equated with science, 177; importance of, in metaphysical groups, 6, 21, 184, 198
Experiential epistemology: Spiritual Frontiers Fellowship's response to rational culture, 174–75, 179
Extrasensory perception. *See* Psychic

Family activities, 95
Field work methodology. *See* Methods
Ford, Arthur, 89, 102, 107, 109, 168. *See also* Spiritual Frontiers Fellowship: founders of
Fragmentation of modern society: effects of, 14, 108, 141, 181; effects of (autonomy), 11–12, 80, 91, 108; effects of (separation), 11, 145; explanations for, 10; Spiritual Frontiers Fellowship's responses to autonomy (individual exegesis), 80–92; Spiritual Frontiers Fellowship's responses to autonomy (self-realization), 108–43; Spiritual Frontiers Fellowship's response to separation (fellowship), 145–66

Gate Way (Journal of Spiritual Frontiers Fellowship), 197
Gemeinschaft/Gesellschaft, 11, 19, 21, 187
God, concept of: benevolent, 115; immanent/transcedent, 88; monistic (God within), 4, 5, 87–88, 109, 113–15, 123, 142–43, 182

Hare Krishna (International Society for Krishna Consciousness), 14, 17–18
Healing: as characteristic of metaphysical groups, 5, 91, 111, 185; epistemology of, 46–47; examples and uses of, 122, 129, 134–36, 162, 173, 186; laying-on-of-hands, 26, 146–47, 152, 174; part of experiential epistemology, 85–86, 179
Healing circle, 26, 66–68, 86, 154
Healing service, 146–47
Health, mental (emotional): improvement of, through spiritual growth, 126–34
Health, physical: improvement of, through spiritual growth, 134–36
Hypnosis, 25, 196; regression, 70, 84; self-, 91
Human potential movement. *See* name of specific group

Identity: gained through spiritual growth, 21, 108–44, 123–26 *See also* Meaning; Self-realization; Spiritual growth
Identity problems: types of, 23, 125; Spiritual Frontiers Fellowship's response to, 109–44
Individual exegesis, 77, 80–92, 103–4, 106, 109, 182
Individualism: emphasis on, in American society, 181–83; emphasis on, in metaphysical groups, 20, 22, 80, 182, 185, 187, 197; emphasis on, in Spiritual Frontiers Fellowship (individual exegesis), 80–92; emphasis on, in Spiritual Frontiers Fellowship (individualistic structure), 93–107; emphasis on, in Spiritual Frontiers Fellowship (self-realization), 108–44
Informants. *See* Methods
Internalization of authority. *See* Experience, personal: as validation for truth
Intuitive. *See* Experiential epistemology
"Invisible religion," 80

Judah, J. Stillson, 4–6, 22, 78, 83–89, 119, 135, 143, 166–68, 174–75, 177, 182, 192

Karma. *See* Reincarnation
Kirlian photography, 196
Klapp, Orrin E., 8, 11, 12, 23, 113, 118, 125, 181

Leaders, spiritual: as entrepeneurs, 32. *See also* Spiritual Frontiers Fellowship: founders; Spiritual Frontiers Fellowship: leadership of

Index

229